D0179636

Rebecca Stone-Miller was born Rebecca Rollins Stone in Manchester, New Hampshire, in 1958, and educated at the universities of Michigan, Ann Arbor and Yale. She received her PhD in History of Art from Yale in 1987 and now holds the post of Assistant Professor of Art History and Curator of Art of the Ancient Americas at Emory University in Atlanta, Georgia. Professor Stone-Miller has conducted extensive research and published articles on Andean art and architecture, particularly textiles and ceramics. She has curated numerous exhibitions on ancient American art of various cultures at Emory's Michael C. Carlos Museum and the Museum of Fine Arts, Boston. One of them resulted in her book, *To Weave for the Sun: Ancient Andean Textiles,* (Museum of Fine Arts, Boston 1992; Thames and Hudson, London 1994).

WORLD OF ART

This famous series
provides the widest available
range of illustrated books on art in all its aspects.
If you would like to receive a complete list
of titles in print please write to:
THAMES AND HUDSON
30 Bloomsbury Street, London, WC1B 3QP
In the United States please write to:
THAMES AND HUDSON INC.
500 Fifth Avenue, New York, New York 10110

Printed in Slovenia

REBECCA STONE-MILLER

ART OF THE ANDES

from Chavín to Inca

183 illustrations, 24 in color

THAMES AND HUDSON

Frontispiece: This tall Chancay Black-and-White-style ceramic female effigy displays elaborate body and facial painting. Originally she wore an actual cotton dress, an imprint of which was left on her torso. Late Intermediate Period.

Any copy of this book issued by the publisher as a paperback is sold subject to the condition that it shall not by way of trade or otherwise be lent, resold, hired out or otherwise circulated without the publisher's prior consent in any form of binding or cover other than that in which it is published and without a similar condition including these words being imposed on a subsequent purchaser.

© 1995 Thames and Hudson Ltd, London

First published in the United States of America in 1996 by Thames and Hudson Inc., 500 Fifth Avenue, New York, New York 10110

Library of Congress Catalog Card Number 95-60285
ISBN 0-500-20286-9

All Rights Reserved. No part of this publication may be reproduced or transmitted in any form or by any means, electronic or mechanical, including photocopy, recording or any other information storage and retrieval system, without prior permission in writing from the publisher.

Printed and bound in Slovenia

Contents

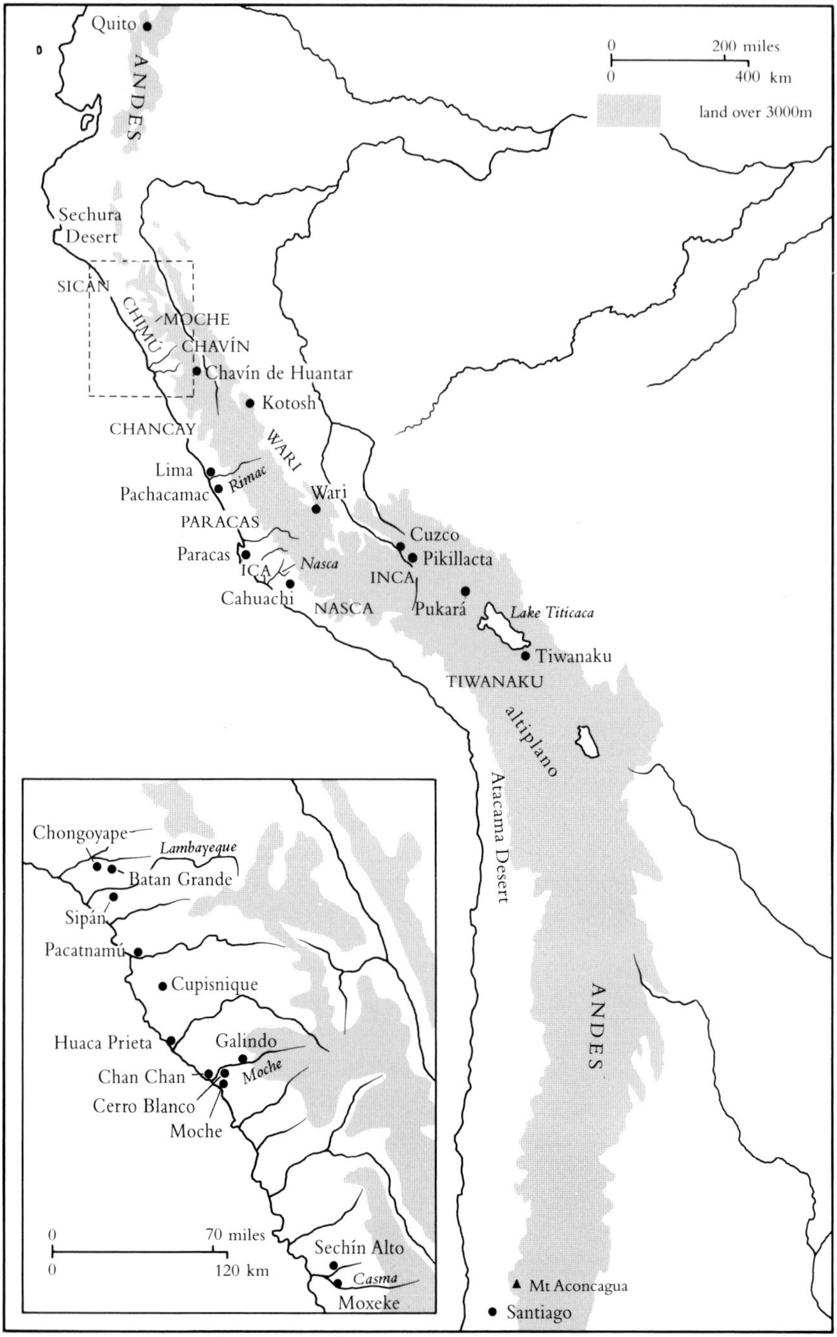

1 Map of the Central Andes, with sites mentioned in the text.

Preface

This book intends to introduce briefly the history of Andean art and architecture to the general reader, whether student or traveler. The aesthetic achievements of this important cradle of civilization have been sadly neglected until recently; this necessarily limited study is offered to begin to redress this lack. Drawing on the research of my colleagues in Art History and Archaeology, I have attempted to highlight the major, representative art styles over a vast stretch of time. Obviously this has meant that some cultures are not considered at all, and others only cursorily. For those whose interest is piqued, further readings are suggested in the Select Bibliography.

The twelve millennia during which the Central Andes have been inhabited are subdivided by specialists into a system of periods whose names are intended to be neutral, although they are not in fact completely so. All the dates are generalized and approximate until the Late Horizon and the Spanish takeover. The earliest and longest period is known as the Lithic (10,000–3000 BC), to cover from the first known remains to the first major geologic stabilization. Next, the Pre-Ceramic (3000–1800 BC), as its name implies, denotes the time before clay was fired. Some scholars would rather the period title emphasized the textile achievements characteristic of this time instead of giving preference to clay, as in Old World schema. However undescriptive, the Pre-Ceramic remains the most widely used name and thus will be employed here as well, with the understanding that clay did not take priority. From 1800 to 1000 BC is known as the Initial Period, setting the stage for the first unifying cult style of the Early Horizon (1000–200 BC). 'Horizons' feature widespread similarities in the art and culture of various areas that can be generally ascribed to the power of a cult, state, or empire. These alternate with 'Intermediate Periods' in which regional diversity is seen as more characteristic. Thus, the Early Horizon, dominated by the Chavín aesthetic message, is followed by the Early Intermediate Period (200 BC–AD 500) in which the Paracas, Nasca, Moche, and other peoples flourished in their respective segments of the coast. The Middle Horizon (AD 500–900) unified to a degree much of the Central Andes under two closely related states, the Wari and Tiwanaku. The Late Intermediate Period (AD

900–1400) then saw several peoples, the Chimú, Chancay, and Ica, among others, gain ascendancy. Finally, the Late Horizon, unequivocally dominated by the mighty Incas until toppled by the Spanish, took up the final century (*c.* 1438–1534). Although scholars have recently called into question the oversimplification of the Horizon scheme – more research revealing the diversity within Horizons and the unities within Intermediate Periods – it remains a useful overall structure for introductory purposes.

I would like to thank Mary Ellen Miller for her encouragement to undertake this and other valuable projects over the years. Rudolf Arnheim and George Kubler deserve credit for imparting to me their quest for a rigorous history of all the world's art. Richard Burger, Colin McEwan, and Izumi Shimada supplied most useful comments; naturally any errors remain my own. I also appreciate the efficient, expert staff of Thames and Hudson who guided this endeavor with alacrity. Emory University generously gave support to this project in the form of Summer Faculty Development awards. For their assistance with the minutiae, I am grateful to Valerie Watkins, Virginia Gardner, Elisa Mandell, and Laura Brannen. My growing family, Doug, Dylan, and Rhiannon, has been a source of constant joy and inspiration. I dedicate this book to my parents, Al and Grace Stone, my models for boundless thinking.

TIME SCALE	PERIODS/ HORIZONS	COASTAL PERU			HIGHLAND PERU			TITICACA REGION		
		North Coast	Central Coast	South Coast	North	Central	South	Moquegua	Arica	Titicaca-Altiplano
1500	LATE HORIZON	INCA	INCA	INCA	INCA	INCA	INCA	INCA	INCA	INCA
1250	LATE INTERMEDIATE PERIOD	CHIMÚ	CHANCAY							
1000		SICÁN		ICA						
750	MIDDLE HORIZON		WARI							
500		MOCHE	Pachacamac			WARI	WARI	TIWANAKU		
250	EARLY INTERMEDIATE PERIOD			NASCA	RECUAY					TIWANAKU
AD BC		GALLINAZO SALINAR				HUARPA				PUKARÁ
500	EARLY HORIZON	CUPISNIQUE		PARACAS	CHAVÍN Kotosh					
1000	INITIAL PERIOD	Caballo Cerro Muerto Sechin	Garagay						CHINCHOROS	
2000	PRE-CERAMIC PERIOD	Huaca Prieta	La Florida El Paraíso		Galgada					
4000										
6000	LITHIC PERIOD									
8000					Guitarrero

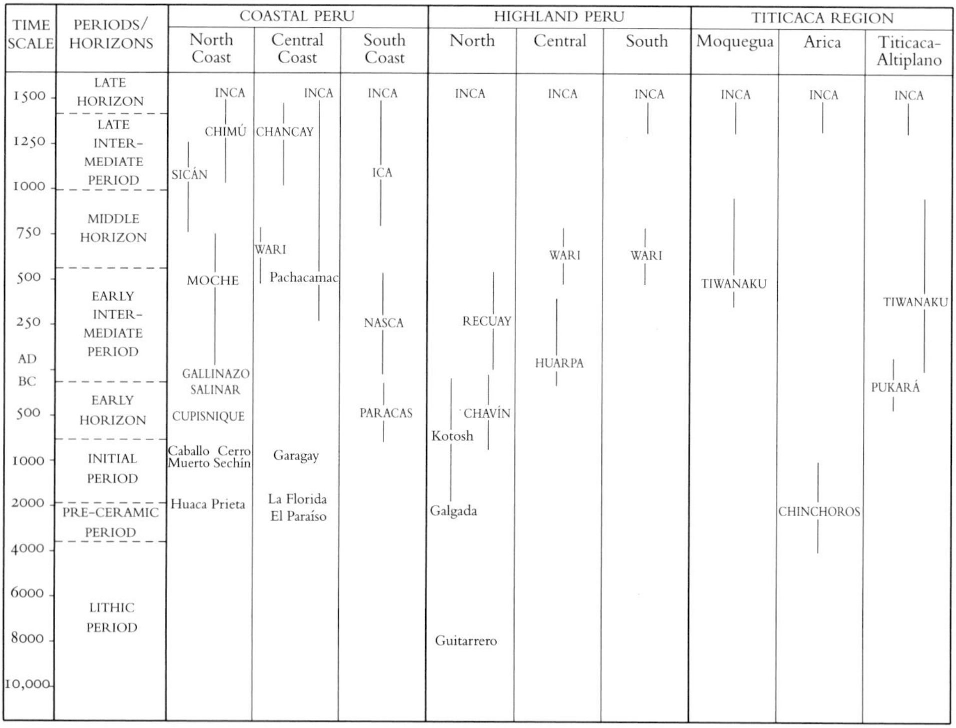

CHAPTER ONE

Introduction

The varied cultures of the South American Andes created some of the most transcendent art the world has ever known. In a formidable and demanding environment, the ancient peoples not only survived and prospered, but spent precious time and energy on aesthetic endeavors, from elaborate rituals to vast cities, from delicate goldwork to sumptuous textiles. Highlights of these many accomplishments will be introduced in this art historical overview of the Central Andes. We will be concerned specifically with the related cultures existing in the area between Quito and Santiago, *1*
the territorial span of roughly 3400 miles (5500 km) ultimately ruled by the Inca empire in the early sixteenth century. Cultural and artistic traditions differ substantially in both the Northern Andes of Ecuador and Colombia and the Southern Andes of Chile. Thus, the modern countries of Peru and Bolivia constitute the main focus here; but our political boundaries rarely correspond to indigenous cultural zones, hence the more neutral 'Central Andes.'

Andean art has been preserved from as early as 8000 BC; however, the earliest sophisticated art forms date from around 2500 BC. Our primary concern here will be the time of large-scale organized aesthetic systems, the three millennia between 1500 BC and AD 1550, encompassing the Chavín through the neo-Inca styles. Brief consideration of the important precursors to the Chavín and post-invasion continuations of the Incas will expand these time boundaries somewhat at either end.

ANDEAN ENVIRONMENTS AND ART

Given the environmental extremes, it is astonishing that humans have lived for so long, much less thrived, in the Central Andes. The western edge of South America contains the world's driest coastal desert, its longest and *2,3*
second-highest mountain chain, and one of its largest and densest tropical jungles. None of these three zones offers a satisfactory balance of water and land for agriculture, hence the indigenous populations have had to develop social organizations in which travel, reciprocity, diversification, and control

2 View of the Andes between Ollantaytambo and Vitcos. The longest mountain chain in the world, the Andes are second only to the Himalayas in altitude. Yet people have survived and thrived in this rugged environment for thousands of years.

are paramount. These concerns naturally are found in the art, since it inherently expresses the fundamental beliefs and practices of its creators. This juxtaposition of environments has had many other important effects on culture and art. The sea abruptly giving way to the desert, which in turn swiftly rises to the Andes, which themselves then become the jungle has provided these traditions with a series of extraordinarily sharp contrasts to resolve. Dualistic, complementary relationships seem to pervade the art, politics, and religion of this area.

3 The desert sand dunes, some of which have never recorded a drop of rain, dramatically plunge into the Pacific Ocean where the Humboldt Current's deep, cold waters harbor the world's richest fishing grounds for anchovies and many other marine species. From the teeming sea to the barren waste-

land of the coast, abundance juxtaposes with paucity; such contrasts can be strongly felt in many Andean styles. Fish, birds, crustaceans, fishing, boats, and waves also play recurrent roles as subject matter. The protein available from the sea made the coastal area vital to mountain peoples and secured the need for trade and even conquest over the centuries. Furthermore, the arid coast acted as the perfect shelter for buried art. Cities, cemeteries, and middens (refuse piles) filled with the most fragile of materials – cotton, camelid fiber, feathers, wood – survive from around 3000 BC onwards when the sea level, and thus the coastline went through a major stabilization (although tectonic upheavals continue to be a recurrent feature). The ancient peoples were aware of the preservative nature of the dry sands; even mountain cultures buried their treasures here so as to send their bodies and their works of art to the afterlife intact. In fact, artificial mummification began in northern Chile centuries before the more famous Egyptians began a similar tradition in the Old World.

The desert coast is segmented by east–west streams, thirty of which link their high Andean glacial sources to the ocean. However, the streams' relatively low water volume does not suffice to irrigate the sands along their shores beyond a few hectares. The ultimate effect of the coastal environment was to isolate and regionalize early coastal cultures into small units. Thus, coastal art styles typically vary widely from one valley to the next. Nevertheless, largely through major hydraulic projects, the Nasca, Moche, and Chimú states managed to unify increasingly large coastal areas. But it was the imperial Incas who helped to integrate the entire Andes so that the complementary environments of coast and highlands together could provide sustenance for all. Yet not even the mighty Incas could prevent the periodic upheaval brought by the so-called El Niño, a massive environmental disaster that still plagues the coast today. Unusually warm water currents bring on torrential rains, producing flooding and erosion that 'rearranges' the coast every generation or so. El Niños are partly responsible for the ruined state of ancient coastal capitals such as Cerro Blanco and Chan Chan. This is one of the many ways in which the Andean environment challenges human existence, its unpredictability lending a sense of anxiety to inhabitants.

With peaks as high as Mt Aconcagua at 22,830 ft (6960 m), the Andes rank second only to the Himalayas in altitude and physical challenge, while surpassing them by three times in length, stretching 4660 miles (7500 km). Although the mountains are the source for the coastal rivers, there is an extremely low water volume in the highland streams. Given the precipitous mountainsides, only proportionately minute areas of arable land can be exploited. The combination of extreme altitude and consequent strength of the sun's ultraviolet rays means searing day heat and as much as fifty-degree temperature drops at night. Few foodstuffs grow, from only dry grasses on the high plains (*altiplano*) up to 15,750 ft (4800 m), to potatoes up to 13,750 ft (4200 m), to maize (corn) up to 11,100 ft (3400 m), and coca – a stimulant and appetite suppressant – up to 4000 ft (1200 m).

Because the highlands consist of a series of agricultural zones according to altitude, the adaptive strategy named by John Murra 'verticality' was developed. In order to obtain all the necessary foods and materials, people from different altitudes physically traverse the resource zones and trade with one another in a system of strict reciprocity, often claiming a kin relation-

3 View of the Andean desert coast, Independence Bay, Paracas Peninsula, showing how the dunes plunge into the sea. Ancient peoples understood the preservative qualities of the world's driest coastal desert and buried people and works of art in the sands for millennia.

ship in order to cement the levels of their inclined world. The highlanders were more reliant on different resource zones for obtaining certain essential foodstuffs and artistic materials than the coastal peoples. Hence it was the mountain peoples who generated the large-scale, unifying religious-political movements across ecological zones. These movements to a limited degree incorporated the images and products of the jungle. Highland art *104*
reflects an understandable preoccupation with survival and embodies the concept of verticality itself. On the practical level, highlanders have always relied on the New World camelids – llamas, alpacas, guanacos, and vicuñas *4, 94, 178*
– for protein, fuel, and all-important fiber. Camelids' silky hair, spun and woven into cloth, provided vital protection from the elements. These animals were crucial to the transportation of objects and people over the rugged terrain, and figure prominently in highland, and even some coastal, iconography. Verticality is also expressed more abstractly, ranging from a strong topographic emphasis in architecture to recurrent stepped patterning in the visual arts.

Although the Amazonian jungle was never formally unified with coast or highlands, it was unquestionably involved at the level of inspiration, symbolism, and trade in 'exotic' materials. The riverine lowlands were often con-

ceived of as an origin place, certainly as a focus of abundance and fertility. Animals such as the fearsome cayman and the agile monkey are found in works of art far removed from jungle habitats. The Amazon functioned as an important source of highly prized and inaccessible aesthetic products,
142 such as feathers, dyes, and plant fibers. However, the rainforest remained too remote for fullscale conquest by the Andeans.

Even the most marginal of environments have their advantages for art and society (such as the dry desert providing optimal preservation). The very harshness and incompatibility of the different zones seem to have challenged the ancient peoples to forge strong social organizations. Such social networks gave artists support and prominence, as well as providing them with diverse materials, images, and ideas. Yet alongside emphases on control, standardization, and collective thinking, Andean cultures also seem to have developed a social climate of artistic virtuosity, perhaps out of the same determined spirit that allowed them to build empires on the edge of the world. The interplay between creativity and constraint is one of the most interesting features of the art and architecture of the Andes.

ANDEAN CULTURE AND WORLDVIEW

Creativity, control, and other patterns of thought all form what is known as a worldview, a set of beliefs and assumptions about the universe and the place of humans therein. Andean worldviews, although by no means the same for 3000 years, seem to have shared many features. We know most about the Incas and often use them to understand earlier peoples. Four of the most important features of the Andean worldview – collectivity, reciprocity, transformation, and essence – help contextualize the diverse arts of the Andes.

Collective, 'corporate,' thinking means that the group takes precedence over the individual, the whole over its parts. The adaptive necessity of favoring 'the common good' in such a difficult environment is quite obvious. However, within the group people are not necessarily equal; in fact, Andean cultures tended to be quite hierarchical and power unevenly distributed. Such societies usually adopt a pyramidal structure in which a small number of elites control large numbers of 'commoners.' Earlier Andean cultures are less hierarchical, later ones more so, the tendency culminating with the Incas, who organized as many as ten million people.

Collectivity manifests itself in art as a general de-emphasis on portraiture, historical detail, and narrative. The particular features, physical location, or

4 Herd of alpacas, one of the four types of New World camelids, whose abundant silky fur is used for warm clothing and aesthetic objects in the Andes. Notice the decorative tassels used to identify individual animals.

actions of a specific person are rarely important (the Moche being the primary exception). Rather, Andean arts tend to focus on a person's role, explore continuous patterning, and feature supernatural imagery. Individual artists are not known, at least by name, although increasingly their particular styles or hands are being distinguished. Anonymity does not mean that all Andean art is somehow generic; styles are distinctive and varied, shapes and colors are manipulated in very dynamic and idiosyncratic ways, and iconography is complex and challenging, revealing the presence of many creative hands upon study. Yet the individual artist is not a focus, rather the image takes precedence. A stress on abstract form makes Andean art highly sophisticated, but precisely in the direction away from specific appearances.

Reciprocity is a feature of a corporate worldview: one part is countered by and connected to another. This holds true on the social side, such as in the vertically-organized trade between altitude zones and in the state's obligations to provide for its members and vice versa. Reciprocal or dualistic thinking is so pervasive that it seems to have influenced visual perception: for example, the Incas saw in the night sky not only constellations made up of the twinkling stars but others made up of the dark, starless parts of the sky. They saw the light and the dark as equal opposites, not simply as light on a background of dark. Andean art has an emphasis on opposites interlocked, on pairs, doubling, and mirror-images of all kinds. Inca architecture sculpts the earth in oppositions of light and shadow, Chimú textiles dovetail identical birds, and double-headed creatures abound. The double reading (a single motif with two or even more possible identifications and hence multiple, sometimes opposite, interpretations) characterizes Chavín art but this subtle, intriguing tendency is also found in many other Andean styles.

Chavín art brings us naturally to the fundamental issue of transformation. Andeans, and indeed all ancient Americans, believed in a universe of potential and actual transformations from one plane of existence to another. Life and death were not seen as separate categories, but the constant natural cycling from one state of being to another. Shamans (priests) constantly metamorphosized from human to animal to supernatural forms. Thus, the world, although orderly, was in a state of flux, seasons continuously changing, planets moving, events taking place, and history repeating itself. Cyclical thinking was fundamental to their world and dynamic circularity certainly affected all aesthetic expressions. Art often served to unite planes, characterize change, and document transformation. Recurrent themes of animal-headed human beings capture the duality and transitional nature of the
179 human experience. The stages of corn growth are symbolically frozen and
23–26 images of shamans change into their animal spirit companion. Such a dynamic worldview posed difficult artistic problems; the many ingenious solutions by Andean architects, sculptors, painters, potters, and weavers continue to inspire awe today.

The concept that ties together all these tenets of worldview is that of 'essence over appearance.' Andean art favored the symbolic reality, the inner core, over outward appearance. This guided metallurgists to allow precious alloys to gild themselves, sculptors to depict two beings at once, and weavers to explore illegibility but stay true to their subject. Essence explains how
63, 64 the Nasca Lines are too large to be seen; it is not necessarily important that an image be visible for its essence to be obeyed. Andean art can de-emphasize the human audience because it was usually created for its own sake, for the supernatural realm, for the afterlife, and/or for ritual efficacy. Thus, a sacred image may be placed in the dark or a carving may be impossible to comprehend. Interestingly, humans are not necessarily central in the Central Andean worldview and the art they themselves created.

CHAPTER TWO

Early and Chavín Art

The Andes have been occupied for at least 10,000 years, as we know from objects securely dated as far back as 8600 BC. The first major style to be disseminated widely was that of the Chavín beginning around 900 BC. However, many important artistic traditions and stylistic components existed well before the Chavín 'synthesis,' most notably fiber arts as a central medium and composite beings (two as one) as an iconographic staple. Monumental architecture and sculpture were widespread, as was jaguar, snake, and bird imagery. These Lithic, Pre-Ceramic, and Initial Periods will be characterized briefly to set the stage for the later styles.

THE LITHIC PERIOD (10,000–3000 BC)

Ten-thousand-year-old fiberwork from Guitarrero Cave, the earliest so far from South America, and the later sophisticated textiles from Huaca Prieta, *5, 6* demonstrate an unusual sequence: in the Andes textiles preceded fired ceramics by thousands of years. It is only around 1800 BC that hardened clay becomes an important practical and aesthetic choice. While the basket fragments, cords, and simple cloths in a dry highland cave appear undistinguished, they mark the beginning of the longest continuous textile record in the world. At Guitarrero Cave – chosen for its strategic location near mountain passes to the coast, abundant flora, fauna, and water – plant fibers were twisted, looped, and knotted to make useful containers. Although there were no patterns in these first baskets, the cords are uniform and techniques well executed, suggesting these were probably not the very first attempts at fiberwork. By about 5500 BC here a stone scraper tool was carefully wrapped in a piece of animal hide and tied with a cord, thus establishing the pan-American practice of protecting, sanctifying, even personalizing objects by wrapping them in fiber. An extension of this propensity, *178* the world's earliest artificial mummification was invented in the northern Chilean Chinchoros area around 5000 BC. The deceased were allowed to decompose, then their bones reassembled and held in place by ropes and canes, the insides replaced by fiber stuffing and encased in a form-imitating

sewn casement, complete with delineated fingernails and a ceramic death mask.

There is something of a gap in the artistic record during the later Lithic Period, largely because the last melting glaciers caused the sea to cover most of the western South American coast *c.* 3000 BC. Thus, much was likely submerged and lost to posterity.

THE PRE-CERAMIC PERIOD (3000–1800 BC)

After the environmental stabilization of around 3000 BC, Pre-Ceramic sites such as Huaca Prieta demonstrate that enormous strides had been taken in the development of the fiber arts. Fishnets, found in abundance, are quite impressive: one is estimated at over 98 ft (30 m) long. The coastal openwork tradition established by functional nets and bags remained in aestheticized form from this time onward. More enigmatically, over 9000 twined cotton scraps, most used and discarded, were excavated from the midden at Huaca Prieta. When painstakingly reconstructed, they were found to contain some of the most graphically complex images ever twisted in thread. Twining is a non-loom technique, somewhat analogous to macramé, in which the vertical warp threads are diverted slightly to the left and right and held in position by twisted horizontal weft threads. Different colored warps trade places on the front and back faces of the cloth to form polychrome patterns with

5 (*Left*) A reconstruction of a twined textile from Huaca Prieta illustrating a raptor with a snake in its stomach. Over 9000 cloth fragments were excavated from this North Coast site. Pre-Ceramic.

6 (*Right*) A drawing of a Huaca Prieta twined composition featuring crabs that transform into snakes. Such sophisticated imagery was accomplished in this non-loom technique *c.*2500 BC. Pre-Ceramic.

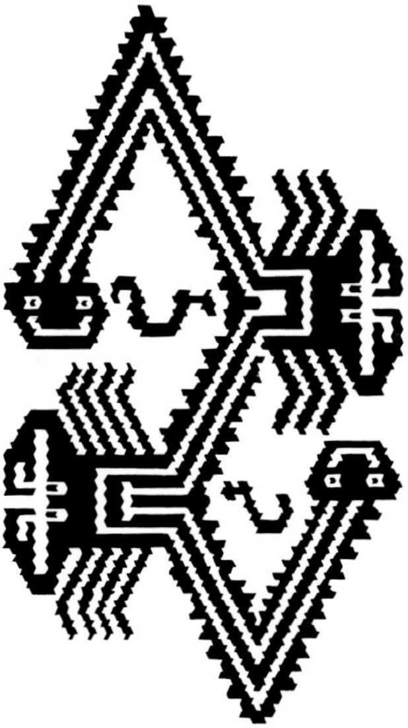

characteristic zigzag edges. Despite the simple concept of the technique, the resulting compositions are far from simplistic. Profile-headed raptors, double-headed birds, crabs whose claws transform into snakes and other fantastical and convoluted images abound. These are not the first attempts of weavers to add pattern to cloth, but rather represent the height of pre-loom fiber art virtuosity.

The Huaca Prieta textiles bear further comment, as evidence of extremely early Andean concerns with visualization, multiple readings, and composite beings. The image illustrated here, a photographic reconstruc- 5
tion, shows the outspread wings and characteristic hooked beak of a raptor with a coiled snake in/on its belly. The horizontal orientation of the zigzag edges betrays that the image was positioned *sideways* as the textile was being twined, thus underscoring the artist's power to visualize the final design. Presumably the twiner worked in this direction intentionally – it would have been considerably easier to work on an upright figure – probably so that the more dynamic zigzags could convey the movement of beating wings in flight. This piece is an excellent example of the typical Andean transcendence of technical limitations and denial of efficiency; aesthetic ends justified difficult and circuitous means.

The embedded snake shows how the artist has presented different layers of reality simultaneously in an 'X-ray' view. The essence of the devouring raptor is thereby succinctly communicated. In other Huaca Prieta composi-

tions multiplicities are even more complex, such as a recurring 'double' bird in which two identical heads are rotated to share a single body; the wings and tail assume their roles only depending on which head takes visual precedence at any given moment. Such two-headed images continue in
146 later Andean art as well. To a degree, the typically high value placed on formal exploration (the artist manipulating shapes and colors regardless of imagery) may provide the impetus to construct 'reversible' figures, again not an easy visual task. However, fundamental messages of embeddedness, interdependence, and duality are central to Andean art, thought, and survival strategies. This trend becomes most pronounced in the Chavín style.

6 'Multiple readings' means that one image turns into a completely different one: a crab, its large pincers and spidery legs jutting out, becomes a large, triangular-headed, poisonous snake. The entire crab-snake image is rotated so that the dual image is itself reversed and doubled. Such spectacular convolution betrays extraordinary preplanning, especially considering how threads recross within and between cloth faces in this technique. The characteristic twining zigzags are exploited in this case to convey scuttering crab and slithering snake movement. Here two separate species unite; perhaps the crab represents the sea and the snake the complementary realm of land; or possibly the aggressiveness of both, magnified by their pairing, transfer to the cloth's owner. The Huaca Prieta textiles may have held important ritual functions; however, they were recovered from a giant refuse heap 40 ft (12 m) deep. Evidently even such intricate examples as these were not saved for high status burial offerings (as in later times). In fact, social status differences in art and other material goods are not marked for about another thousand years.

Besides textiles, Pre-Ceramic sites have yielded small numbers of carved gourds (suspected to be imports from Ecuador), simple bone and shell jewelry, wooden earplugs and carved bowls, mirrors (one decorated with a double bird motif), feathers, and unbaked clay figurines (mostly female). These establish several Andean artistic forms that remain important: large
83, 84, 142 elaborate earrings, primarily for men; mosaic mirrors; featherwork; and female effigies. Other longstanding practices begun during this period include the taking of human trophy heads (evident at the site of Asia), the sacrificial burning of cloth as an offering (at Aspero), and the central importance of long-distance trade (of gourds, the highly-prized orange spondylus (spiny oyster) shells from the north, and tropical bird feathers from the east). Well before extensive agriculture, fired ceramics, cities, or social stratification, Andeans were exchanging a great variety of aesthetic products.

Pre-Ceramic monumental architecture, the oldest in the Americas by over a millennium, rivals portable art achievements. Artificial mounds, series of superimposed temples, large plazas, and sunken circular courtyards were combined in various similar ways along the coast and in the highlands at Asia, Aspero, Salinas de Chao, El Paraíso, La Galgada, and Kotosh. Several thousand people lived in each center, communally building and rebuilding them over time. Richard Burger calls this early public architecture 'the reification of human labor' because it consumed so much community time: El Paraíso, the largest, took an estimated 100,000 tons of stone to construct its nine enormous complexes. The huge works of public architecture present the unity and identity of one group to its neighbors. Constant renovation – there are least seven layers of buried temples at Kotosh – served to cyclically validate the community. The large plazas, found in Andean city planning from then on, allowed the populace to participate in open-air rituals. Later, restricted access to adjacent temples was established, as at Chavín de Huantar, but the communal ceremonial role remained strong. Andean architecture conveys corporate messages by enclosing outdoor space for public rituals, as elsewhere in the ancient Americas.

The highland site of Kotosh, first constructed *c.* 2450 BC, has typical Pre- *7, 8*
Ceramic features: mounds topped with freestanding, small, masonry temples; painted, mud-plastered interior walls often punctuated with niches and embellished with mud reliefs; plus centrally-located fire pits for the ritual burning of offerings. Earlier temple levels were carefully protected (layers of sand shielded the Kotosh reliefs), filled with mesh bags of stone rubble, and built over; archaeologists have called this 'temple entombment.' (Not only reserved for temples, many works of Andean art were similarly anthropomorphized; for instance, sculptures were dressed, ritually killed, and buried with or without their human counterparts.) Since sacred buildings represented the spiritual world, the collectivity, and were considered animate like everything else, they required proper treatment at their 'death.' Rather than underscore an individual's achievement by starting a new building campaign in a new location, Andean worldview dictated the reuse of a sanctified spot, the acknowledgment of the ancestors as an extension of the present builders, and respect for the building itself as a living representation of the group through time.

Kotosh consists of two mounds, the larger of which includes in its lower layers the Temple of the Crossed Hands, in which two adobe reliefs were sculpted below niches flanking a large central double trapezoidal niche. The duality of the mounds and of the reliefs, each emphasizing two arms, seems

7, 8 Interior view of the Temple of the Crossed Hands at Kotosh. Adobe reliefs below two of the niches personalize this room and were carefully protected with sand when the temple was originally buried. Pre-Ceramic.

consciously repetitive; it may signal the pervasive Andean interest in complementarity, or even the moiety social organization (a group divided into two interdependent though unequal halves), a pattern that continues to this day. One pair of crossed arms is smaller than the other and Seiichi Izumi proposed that they symbolize a female and a male. Clay figurines, found in niches elsewhere at Kotosh and other Pre-Ceramic sites, may betray such a concern with human fertility, a preoccupation in early societies. It is certainly tempting to envision sculpted human heads in the niches above the arm reliefs. With or without actual heads, the reliefs literally humanize the temple, whose entombment becomes even more literal. The reliefs, although technically and artistically rather rudimentary, do depict five digits and clearly show the superposition of arms, betraying an interest in accuracy and the visual world of specific shapes. While these choices in themselves may not seem extraordinary, they are by no means centrally important in other Andean art styles which, for example, rarely concern themselves with the correct number of fingers in a hand.

During the Initial Period Andean peoples began to farm intensively and live increasingly sedentary existences. They built larger settlements with more elaborate religious architecture, wove textiles more efficiently on looms, and fired clay (previously considered too weighty and impractical; but now receptacles were needed in which to boil agricultural products). Transhumance, herders' seasonal migration between highlands and lowlands, still played an important role in the mountains. Along the coast fishing continued to supplement inland growing of cotton, maize, chili peppers, and beans. However, in all areas larger groups of people coexisted, their combined labor producing portable art and public monuments on a massive scale. During this period many components of the synthetic Chavín style, from building layout to sculptural imagery, were set down; in fact, only recently have scholars determined that most of what was thought to be Chavín is actually dated much earlier.

Initial Period architecture features two distinctive systems, one coastal in origin and the other highland, which then intermingle, particularly on the North-Central Coast. U-shaped pyramids, often with flanking mounds that *9* embrace enormous plazas, characterize the coast for over 1000 years and even spread into the highlands to reappear at Chavín de Huantar centuries later. In the highlands, over fifty civic-ceremonial centers featured a different choice: sunken circular courts, often combined with rectangular plat- *10* forms themselves topped with sunken rectangular plazas. Combinations of these features continue in the later Initial Period and Early Horizon. *13, 17*

The artistic choices involved in both templates reveal fundamental Andean values. U-shaped structures, such as those at Huaca la Florida that

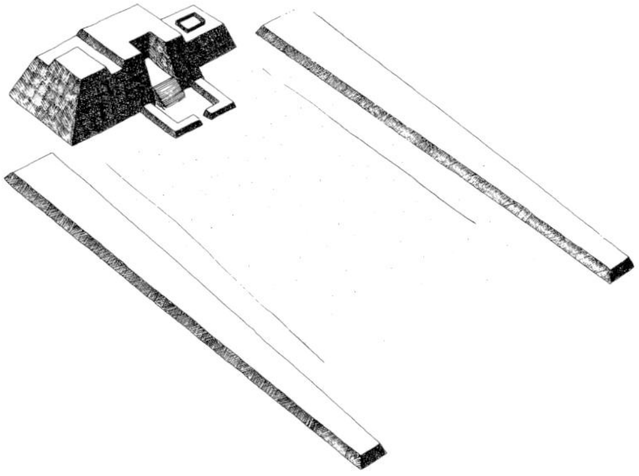

9 Reconstruction drawing of the U-shaped Huaca la Florida, Rimac Valley, dated *c.*2000 BC. Its arrangement of long mounds flanking a pyramid typifies early coastal architecture. Initial Period.

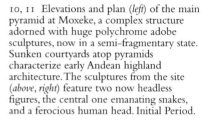

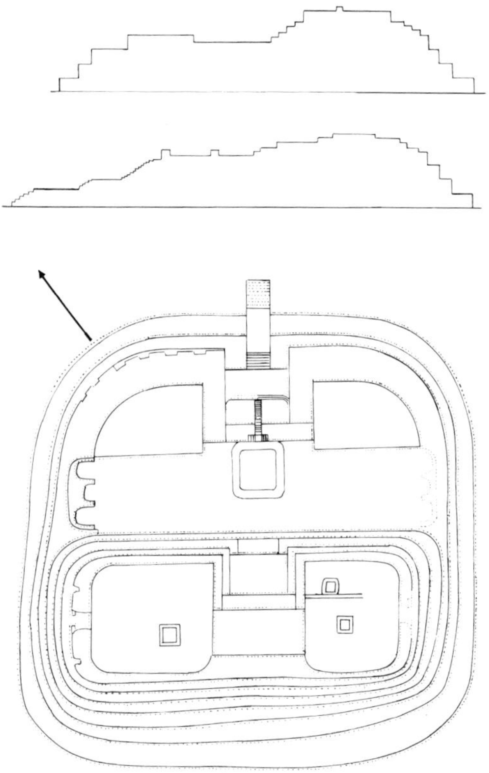

10, 11 Elevations and plan (*left*) of the main pyramid at Moxeke, a complex structure adorned with huge polychrome adobe sculptures, now in a semi-fragmentary state. Sunken courtyards atop pyramids characterize early Andean highland architecture. The sculptures from the site (*above, right*) feature two now headless figures, the central one emanating snakes, and a ferocious human head. Initial Period.

consumed an estimated 6.7 million workdays to construct, are designed to capture centralized ritual space near the temple. Thus, group cohesion through religious celebration is reified. However, while its axial and centralized form leads participants into its core, they proceed in increasingly smaller numbers, often through elevated or enclosed spaces and finally up a restricted staircase to the most sacred area. This hierarchical tendency to cordon off specialized, exclusive space reminds us that group rituals and corporate thinking are not to be confused with egalitarianism. Furthermore, the two arms of U-shaped configurations are characteristically slightly different, never mirror images, which at least suggests the importance of complementary parts, perhaps with the central building as mediator. These uneven halves may well signal the presence of the moiety system at this early date. The subdivided group could array itself along opposite mounds and representatives, or finally priests, proceed to the more rarified portions of

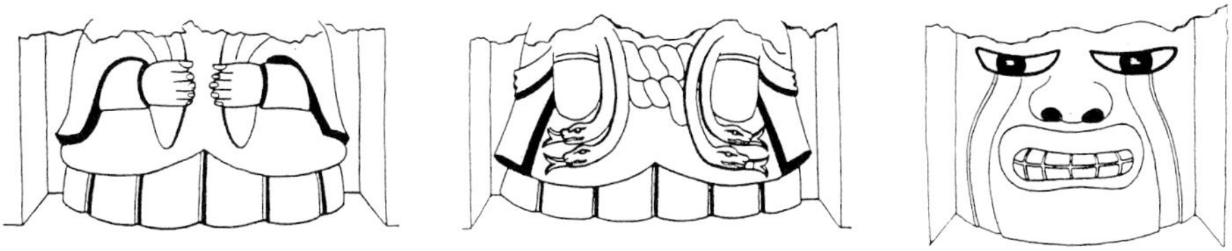

the complex, the message of the building being that religious intervention mediated social distinctions. Thus, dual symbolism of cohesion and constriction were successfully proclaimed in this arrangement of exterior and interior space.

The highland pattern of sunken courts, circular on ground level and rectangular on elevated platforms, can also be interpreted socially. Round courts seem to mark off intimate, more egalitarian space for gatherings, as in the kivas of the American Southwest. Circles do not favor any one direction, nor is any part differentially elevated, so all participants are at least potentially equal. These courts would seem to function as meeting places, possibly for kin or other less hierarchical groups. On the other hand, the tall
platforms with maze-like buildings, such as at Moxeke, are dwarfing in scale, 10
set apart and literally above. The tiered shape, most probably representing a sacred mountain, soars 98 ft (30 m) in height and covers 540 by 560 ft (165 by 170 m) at its base. The wide stair interrupted by a platform, continues as a narrower one that splits at the top, again emphasizing issues of ritual procession and limited access. The upper platform's rectangular spaces seem to compartmentalize special groups and direct attention toward leaders holding court.

Significantly, it is on these platforms and around their plazas that elaborate, colorful monumental sculpture, painted reliefs, and wall murals were placed during the Initial Period. At Moxeke, embellishment remains in the
form of nearly 13-ft-wide (4-m) painted adobe sculptures. Those remaining 11
on the third tier are two skillfully modeled, extremely high-relief, standing, now headless figures and a colossal head. While their exact identities remain unclear, the lower bodies' fluted edge may represent severed torsos and the head may be decapitated, by analogy with the gruesome images from Cerro Sechín (below). Snakes on one figure may symbolize streams of blood. Originally painted in pink, blue, and white, with incisions filled in black (one figure apparently painted entirely in black, possibly symbolic of death), these great sculptures would have boldly advertised the might of the Moxeke elites.

12 A huge sculpture of a feline head at the Huaca de los Reyes mound of Caballo Muerto on the North Coast. The adobe, probably originally painted, has not entirely survived the past three millennia or more since it was modeled. Initial Period.

12 Other coastal sites, such as Huaca de los Reyes at Caballo Muerto, had similarly impressive clay statuary with the new configuration of features: eyes with pendant irises, wide feline noses, fangs in drawn-back lips, and pronounced facial lines. Probably brightly painted, like the similar reliefs at Garagay on the Central Coast, these images of often anthropomorphized feline, reptilian, arachnid, and other animals were widespread on all media at this time.

Strong similarities exist between Moxeke and the most impressive site of
13–16 this time, nearby Sechín Alto. The largest ceremonial center in all the Americas, construction began around 1700 BC and continued until 500 BC. Its crowning twelve-story platform, faced in stones, supports a walled building known as Cerro Sechín (Sechín Hill).

The revetment of incised granite monoliths, alternating 10-ft-tall (3-m) uprights with stacked smaller slabs, forms a threatening litany of warriors and their victims. Well over 300 slabs depict dismembered bodies, severed

13, 14, 15, 16 (*Opposite*) Plan of Sechín Alto (*above*), Casma Valley, the largest ceremonial center in the Americas during the Initial Period, showing a series of rectangular plazas, sunken circular courts and the dominant pyramid known as Cerro Sechín (*center*). Cerro Sechín's walled temple consists of megalithic relief sculptures (*below*) depicting victorious warriors and the decapitated heads of victims. The arrangement of these figures, parading toward the entrance, would have given ancient audience members the sense of being part of this intimidating display. Initial Period.

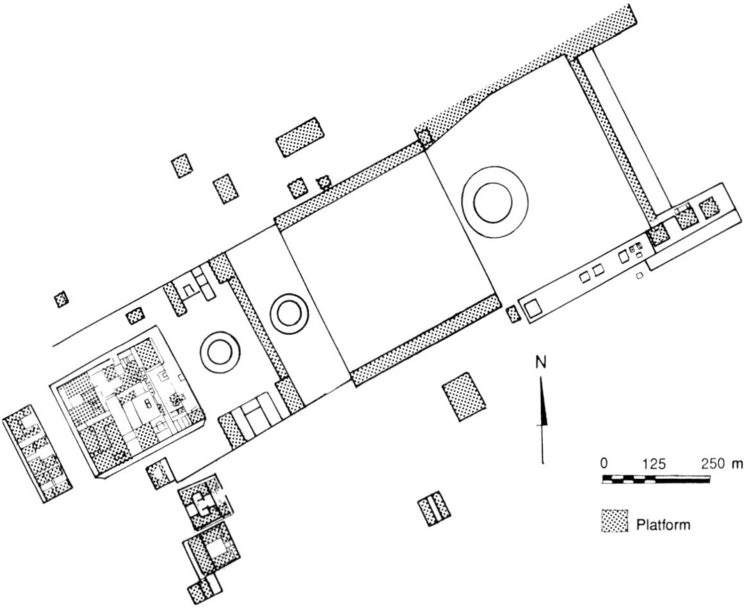
N
0 125 250 m
Platform

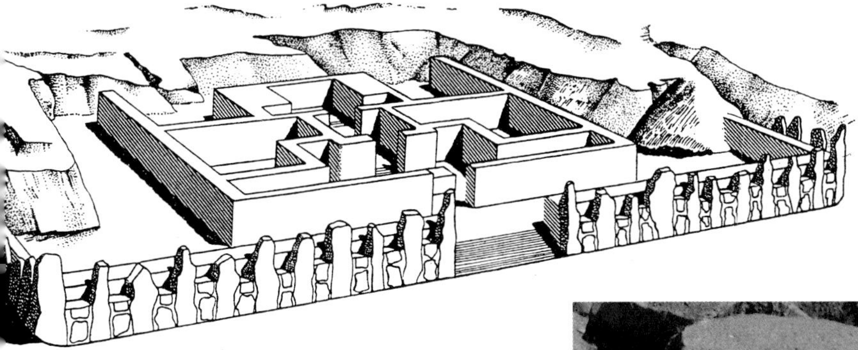

torsos, decapitated enemy heads, and even abstracted vertebral columns, interspersed with victorious warriors holding weapons who approach each other to meet at the single north doorway. Trophy heads appear in many contexts throughout the Andean tradition, as here, usually with crescent-shaped closed eyes and grimacing mouths to signal their demise and loose hair to indicate humiliation. While the Cerro Sechín array may suggest to some a mythological narrative, or even an historical event (though exceedingly rare in Andean art), it definitely sets up a procession in which viewers approaching the door actually become part of the macabre parade. The scale, reiteration, and participatory nature of the reliefs reinforce a powerful warning; conflict and conquest had evidently entered the ideological and certainly the aesthetic realms. Sculptors utilized deeply beveled incisions to catch the intense highland sunlight and create relatively wide outlines, while carving deep gouges to create strong interior lines. The play of inky shadows makes the gruesome display stand out graphically. The growing role of art as propaganda and an agent of social control is thus vividly underscored.

THE CHAVÍN STYLE

Chavín art can be divided into two phases. The first, corresponding largely to the late Initial Period *c.* 900 to 500 BC, includes the architecture and related sculpture of the Old Temple at Chavín de Huantar, the cult center. From around 500 to 200 BC the second phase corresponds to the Early Horizon New Temple construction and its associated arts. Other artworks not directly related to either architectural phase can only be generally dated by stylistic similarity to known monuments.

The Chavín synthesis unified the Initial Period aesthetic systems of both coast and highlands: the sunken circular courtyard, the U-shaped structure, and imagery of jaguars, snakes, and other animal-human composites come together. Yet, Chavín style also took a highly innovative stance in ceremonial center layout, materials, sculptural type, and sacred imagery. Along with presenting an innovative religious mix, the cult center also controlled commerce in ways that irrevocably altered highland village life. Chavín aesthetics, equally novel and powerful, altered the course of Andean art, influencing contemporary coastal styles, primarily by dissemination through textiles, and continuing as revivals in later eras.

Chavín is a very complex, 'baroque,' and esoteric style, intentionally difficult to decipher, intended to disorient, and ultimately to transport the viewer into alternate realities. Much of the cult's enormous success may be ascribed to the intense visual messages sent by buildings, their decoration, and the portable ritual objects. Their strong perceptual effect, certainly calculated by Chavín artists, inspires confusion, surprise, fear, and awe through the use of dynamic, shifting images that contain varying readings depending on the direction in which they are approached. The terms 'hallucinatory' and 'transformational' aptly describe much Chavín subject matter and artistic effect. An important component of the style has been termed by George Kubler 'visual metaphoric substitution,' denoting that certain parts, especially hair, fur, cords, or whiskers, are visually replaced by analogous elements, particularly snakes. Both a great deal of visual complexity and deeply symbolic religious concepts result from the Chavín solutions to the aesthetic problem of portraying two states at once. The iconography features staff-bearing deities, predatory animals, human-animal composites, and shamans in transformation. Most imagery is inspired by the tropical world to the east, another synthetic aspect of Chavín art. Its connection to the Amazon, while not completely understood, certainly relates to the location of the cult center itself.

THE CENTER: CHAVÍN DE HUANTAR

The impressive site of Chavín de Huantar lies at 10,330 ft (3150 m) of altitude in the Callejon de Conchucos, the easternmost basin between the Cordilleras Negra ('black,' snowless range) to the east and Blanca ('white,' snowy) to the west. Its intentional siting midway between coast and jungle, in a locale highly unusual for its near self-sufficiency, gave its makers access to the arts, architecture, environs, animals, foods, and ideas of all zones of the greater Andean region. Set at the confluence of two rivers and near two of only ten mountain passes, Chavín de Huantar constitutes a natural nexus point. (The Incas called such a juncture *tinkuy,* also denoting balanced harmony and governing the siting of Cuzco.) Chavín de Huantar was thus able to be equally centripetal, a pilgrimage center and importer of luxury goods from afar, and centrifugal, a disseminator of the first unifying Andean style. The expansion and changes over 700 years of Chavín de Huantar illustrate the longterm success of the cult and its aesthetics.

Architecture and Sculpture of the Old Temple

The first structure built at Chavín de Huantar, the Old Temple (in the past *17*
erroneously called the Castillo, 'castle'), was extremely large and impressive, measuring over 330 ft (100 m) across the back and 36–52 ft (11–16 m) high.

The temple faced the rising sun in the east, and the unnavigable Mosna River, turning its back to the trade route and secular buildings. The river and the lack of entrances on any side except the east meant that the approach to the Old Temple was purposefully circuitous; supplicants were forced to experience the formidable temple sides, then approach up a series of plazas and stairways. Inaccessible, introspective, enigmatic, the Old Temple and its surroundings were designed to embody the mysteries of the cult and its new message.

Yet novelty was carefully couched in familiar terms, as the Old Temple placed a sunken circular court in the arms of a U-shaped building. Additions, such as the east–west stairway entrances to the plaza being wedge-shaped, were not practical but can be seen as typical Chavín flourishes. Funneling stairs embellish processional movement, while also subtly winnowing the number of celebrants entering the plaza and thus reaching the temple entrance. Exclusivity continues as an important and insistent architectural message. Several other features of the Sunken Circular Court are equally unusual and significant. Archaeologists have discovered in its pavement remains of darker stones demarcating the human and solar east–west path, succinctly conflating architecture, human ritual procession, and cosmological phenomena. (A corresponding north–south line is suspected; if one existed originally, then the court also symbolized all directions, becoming an *axis mundi* or center of the world.) Another curious feature is a giant snail fossil set into the floor, perhaps acting as a graphic link with unknown areas to show the cult's control over exotic and mystifying natural wonders.

18 Around the edges of this circle sunk 8 ft (2.5 m) into the earth, and large enough to hold over 500 people, was a revetment wall of the very finest incised stonework. Courses alternate plain, smaller stones with rectangular and square carved panels, whose delicately and shallowly incised images seem to hover on the surface of the highly polished granite. Interestingly enough, these carved panels do not have to be easily seen from afar, they merely have to *be* in order to be effective. This is true to varying degrees of all Chavín art, and much of Andean art in general. These visually inaccessible but profoundly powerful images depict jaguars below and fanged humans above, marching in stately procession toward the temple. They obviously mirrored celebrants' passage through the court itself, a common congruence between the depicted and the actual world (as at Cerro Sechín). One can safely generalize that ancient American art is figured as an active, living presence, a permanent, elevated player in ritual reality.

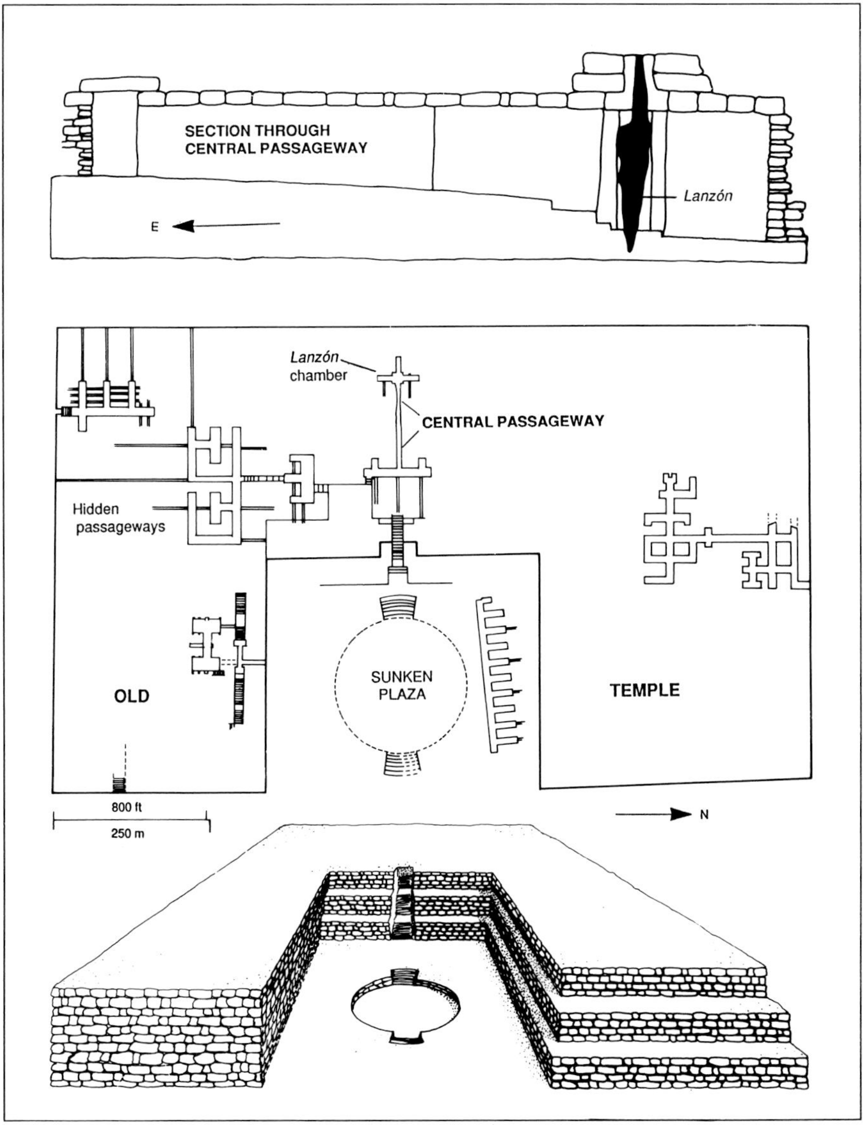

17 Perspective and plan view of the Old Temple at Chavín de Huantar, showing the U-shaped platforms and sunken plaza. The section through the central passageway shows the location of the Lanzón (ill. 21), which was probably the principal cult image at the site. Initial Period.

Yet the Sunken Circular Court panels do not simply reenact processions.
20 The profile jaguars are arrayed in identical pairs, probably seven or more pairs on each side originally. (Chavín de Huantar has suffered major disasters over the centuries, particularly landslides, and many sculptures are buried, destroyed, or out of place, and temple galleries are collapsed.) The jaguars have identifiable concentric spots, but bear the talons of the harpy eagle, to combine two of the mightiest tropical predators. The larger square panels above depict pairs of elaborately costumed walking figures, one of which blows a strombus (conch) shell trumpet, while another carries the hallu-
19 cinogenic San Pedro cactus as a staff of authority. Several wear hats with jaguar tails, and all have the crossed fangs of the jaguar, snakes for hair, and vicious eagle talons. These probably represent priests taking part in hallucinogenic rituals, beginning their transformation into the fully animal jaguars paired with them below. The sets of related pairs reiterate the importance of complementary dualism in Andean art and thought. This powerful imagery, when united with the actual priests moving toward the impenetrable temple to perform mysterious subterranean rites in animal form, certainly was extremely impressive.

Like the panel imagery, cult activities were mostly hidden from view. Priests disappeared into the windowless structure, honeycombed with labyrinthine unlit passages, only to reappear suddenly on the flat roof to perform public rites. Turned inward, like the priests were to the supernatural realm, the Old Temple was a disorienting place of narrow, indirect passages with a huge sacred sculpture at its heart. Luis Lumbreras has proposed that the many air ducts and water drains that crisscross the building, obviously of practical value in the absence of windows and given the heavy waterflow during the prolonged rainy season, could also have been manipulated to make the building roar with an eerie applauselike sound. Outside, at least
23–26 forty-one over-lifesize, monstrous tenon heads studded the upper walls, while cornices and wall plaques depicting fierce animals covered portions of the lower walls.

The entire structure was literally built around a centrally-located mono-
21 lithic sculpture. Erroneously known as the Lanzón ('Great Lance') for its bladelike form, its notched wedge shape probably actually refers to the high-
179 land digging stick. Its specifically local highland shape suggests that the supernatural inscribed on its surface ensured successful planting and thus human survival. In the Andes, ceremonial objects often retain a utilitarian shape which does not contradict their aesthetic component, but instills in them enhanced ritual efficacy and power. The Lanzón, the most important

18, 19, 20 The Sunken Circular Court at Chavín de Huantar. A view of the relief panels in situ (*above*), featuring parading shamans above (see also *left*), and their jaguar animal spirits below (see also *below*). Transformation of human into feline is also the theme of the New Temple tenon heads (ills. 23–26). Early Horizon.

early Chavín cult image, was located in a cruciform gallery deep in the center of the temple. Representing the four directions and sacralizing the spot as a world center, the floor stepped down and the ceiling was slightly corbeled to create an approximate cross in both planes. The gallery above was also cruciform and would have allowed priests to speak for the Lanzón as an oracle, according to Thomas Patterson (as at the later cult center of
148 Pachacamac).

Measuring 15 ft (4.5 m) high, embedded in the floor and penetrating the ceiling above, the Lanzón figure acted as a supernatural conduit. Its incised design includes four twisted strands branching out from the base, one of which continues up the back to mark the vertical path from earth to sky. Facing the rising sun and towering over a highly exclusive audience of priests and leaders, the Lanzón deity held sway with right arm up and left down. The all-encompassing gesture again controls and unites celestial and terrestrial spheres. A small channel carved down the front of the notch to the top of the head leads to a cross-shaped well with a circular depression at its center. Perhaps used to pour liquid offerings down from above like rain, the cross and circle motif reiterates the Lanzón's own gallery and even the Sunken Circular Court outside. In subtle ways the architecture and sculpture embed center within center. (This channel also points up the important ancient American tradition of finishing all sides of a work of art.) The Lanzón features all the components of the distinctive Chavín style, although its low-relief carving is exceptional, as other Chavín images are incised: round eyes with pendant irises, feline fangs and flat nose, upturned snarling mouth (not to be misread as smiling), and claws or talons as nails. Like other columnar Chavín sculptures, the image has been wrapped around the stone block, thus neither entirely visible from one standpoint nor fully three-dimensional in conception. It is withheld, creating its own reality regardless of the human perspective. In keeping with its supernatural character, elaborate repeating swirling elements ending in diminutive snake heads cover its body. These are visual metaphoric substitutions that function as puns: eyelashes, hairs, fur, or whiskers, are like, and therefore are shown as, snakes. In its belt fanged mouth bands with eyes to the right and left can be read as faces in either direction, illustrating another key stylistic device:
5, 6 contour rivalry. Already seen in Huaca Prieta twinings, contour rivalry denotes a situation in which the same set of lines belong to two images at once. Here a mouth forms faces with both the eye on its left and its right. Similarly, on the Lanzón's own face the eyelash near the eye is read as a hair, but switches to a snake reading further out. The surprising alteration of one's

21 The Lanzón cult image, a stone monument over 15 ft (4.5 m) high, set deep in the center of the Old Temple. This massive figure of the early Chavín supreme deity, gesturing up and down to encompass all realms, was probably an oracle. Early Horizon.

perception is at once a visual trick to disorient and a statement that one thing can be two 'depending on how you look at it.' Multiple religious entities also characterize other Chavín sacred images, particularly the Tello Obelisk and the later Raimondi Stela.

The Tello Obelisk, named for Julio C. Tello, the father of Peruvian archaeology, was not found in situ but rather in a corner of the rectangular Old 22

Temple courtyard. Despite its unknown original location, it probably dates from the earlier phases like the Lanzón. It is even more complex and seems to concern mythological origins, specifically tropical ones. Donald Lathrap calls its subject 'gifts of the cayman,' because it portrays a dual male-female crocodilian supernatural covered with the foods of the jungle. Two highly complementary versions of the same animal are incised on an 8 ft (2.5 m) tall obelisk-like shaft. As before, neither image can be fully grasped, much less the two together, as each is wrapped around two of the shaft's faces. Their vertical placement makes them even harder to read but presents them as conduits of energy between realms, as in the Lanzón. This arrangement again forces the viewer to change perspective, a trend that becomes increasingly marked in later Chavín sculpture.

The crocodilians' heads sport four large, overhanging teeth (in actual caymans these are prominent even when the mouth is closed) and an eye with a peaked outline upper edge, standing for the protruding crocodilian eye and body ridges. Above figure A's nose is a strombus (conch) shell, from the far-off Pacific Ocean off Ecuador, often used as a ritual trumpet and associated with maleness. Figure B has a harpy eagle, ruler of the skies, in the same position. Between the two is a small jaguar, king of the land, whose position and characteristics mediate these dual images of sea and air, coast and lowlands. The jaguar may once again represent the transformed shaman who intercedes between the animal deity and humans. (It is also interesting that the jaguar itself has a very wide range; though most comfortable in the tropical lowlands it is quite capable of existing in all other zones, making it an apt image of a Chavín priest bridging cosmic, ethnic, and environmental boundaries.)

The caymans' bodies are completely covered in plants, animals, and faces, their long backbones metaphorically replaced by fanged mouth bands, making an analogy between bones and teeth. The front and back legs splay in the horizontal reptilian fashion, but end in what look like human hands. Although certain Andean artistic choices appear to be 'poetic license' or anthropomorphization, this is really a quite accurate portrayal: they have five digits, only four of which appear on the outside. Such a similarity would have been easily noted when skeletal remains were seen. Caymans, which can stretch over 20 ft (6 m) in length, can also be observed invisibly floating, only eyes, nostrils, and scutes protruding above the water, then charging the shore with lightning speed, dragging prey back into the water, and ferociously devouring it. Stories of this, even though never experienced by highlanders, would have been enough to terrify and help ascribe formid-

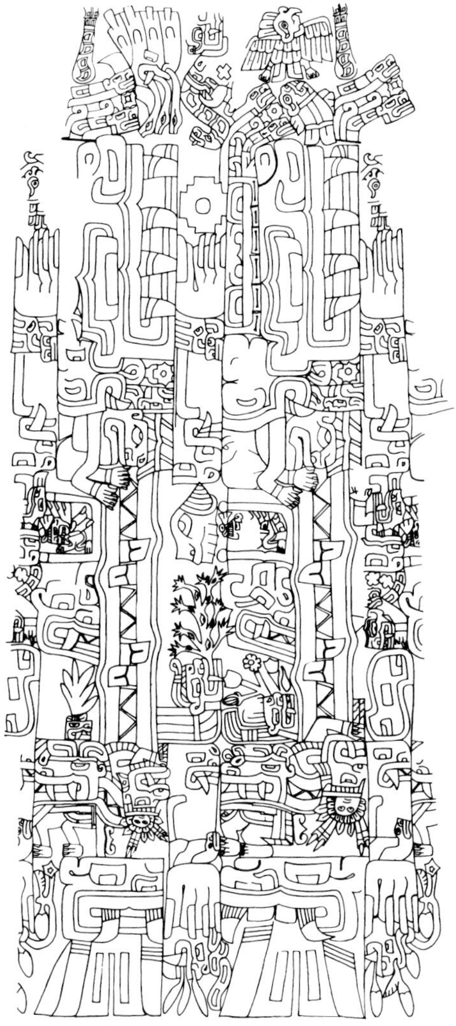

22 Rollout drawing of the Tello Obelisk. This complex late-Chavín highland image pairs male (A) and female (B) caymans covered with significant jungle plants. Early Horizon. Rollout drawing based on rubbings by J. H. Rowe.

able powers to priests claiming to control such hungry, vindictive beings. Both Tello Obelisk versions sport birds' tail feathers, perhaps to add flight to their supernatural abilities, to describe their attack speed, or simply to reiterate the shamanic trio of jaguar/crocodile/raptor.

Important additional fertility symbolism of this multivalent deity are suggested by explicit gender and association with plants. Figure A is male, his

penis metaphorically substituted by a serpentine animal whose fanged mouth emanates a manioc plant as sperm (note the tiny eyes; in this the manioc plant is potato-like). He also displays other root crops, such as the peanut seen behind his back foot. In the same relative positions, the female figure B has an abstract 'S' vaginal element and seed crops, such as the bulbous chili peppers, crucial to the Andean diet as sources of vitamin C and digestive aids. Thus, dualities of sex, plant type, ecological zone, and water vs. sky associations create an image seemingly dedicated to complementary fertility itself. Crocodilians, though deadly, also symbolize fecundity in most ancient American aesthetic systems because the animals breed in enormous groups. The intertwining of life and death is also central to ancient American thought. In the Tello Obelisk the specifically tropical lowland and distant marine references have several possible explanations. In general, the Chavín cult was based on combining the architectural forms of coast and highlands, plus the animals of all areas, in its universalist message. The efficacy of exotic cosmology (on the premise that the unknown is more frightening) would not escape the Chavín priesthood. Some argue for an actual origin of the Andean peoples in the Amazonian lowlands, a theory hard to prove given the lack of archaeological preservation there. More likely the jungle represents to the arid, high mountain cultures the epitome of watery fertility, abundance itself. In addition, the simpler Amazonian society may have been seen as closer to original sources of wisdom, as Richard Burger suggests. It was unquestionably an important source of the mind-altering hallucinogens that gave leaders direct access to the supernatural and their animal selves. (In the Americas there are over eighty natural hallucinogenic substances, in the Old World no more than ten, which is one reason for their prominence in indigenous religions.) For all these reasons,

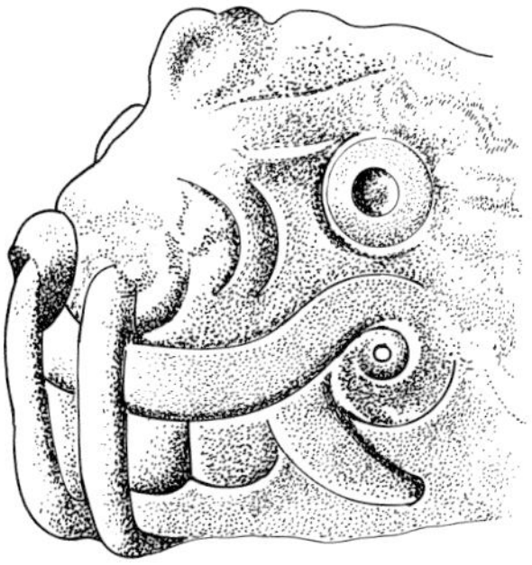

23, 24, 25, 26 (*Above*) Four of the over forty tenon heads that studded the high walls of the Temple at Chavín de Huantar. These four heads encapsulate the spectacular transformation of the hallucinating shaman into a monstrous animal spirit, a transformational sequence first proposed by Richard Burger. Early Horizon.

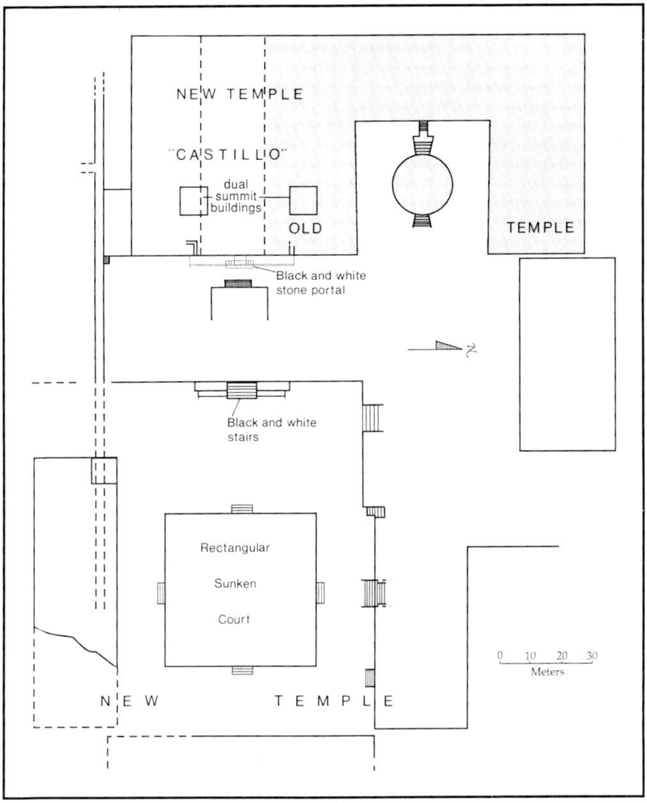

27 (*Right*) Plan of the Old Temple, New Temple and associated courts at Chavín de Huantar. Early Horizon.

far-flung items could figure in a highland image system, especially one located within reach of lowlands to both east and west.

Early Horizon Chavín de Huantar

The later phase of the site, 500 to 200 BC, featured extensive expansion and
a shift of focus for the ceremonial center. Renovated and enlarged, the New 27
Temple constituted a huge addition to the south side of the Old Temple, obscuring its now apparently outdated U-shape. However, the older building was neither destroyed nor ritually entombed, so presumably it and the sacred images it held remained symbolically valent. New larger plazas, able to hold three times the audience and reflecting both population growth and cult success, lead from the river to the New Temple entrance, now graced with a striking black and white stone portal. Themes of transformation and fertility continue in ever more succinct artistic statements.

23–26 The new addition was adorned with over forty large sculpted stone heads and numerous relief panels on the walls. Of the series of overlife-sized tenon (pegged) heads, only one remains in situ. Reconstructions place them high on the walls, one every few meters, and in a sequence from human to supernatural animal visages. As if in time-lapse photography, they document the dramatic process of shamanic transformation through hallucinogenics. Those with almond-shaped humanoid eyes and vertically placed features give way to heads with round, bulging eyes and flattened noses from which mucus, characteristic of drug reaction, streams. Finally, some heads display projecting muzzles and obvious fangs, as well as swirling snakes for hair and whiskers. Deep holes drilled for eyes and nostrils made them read well in the strong highland light and shadow, yet the tenon heads were physically inaccessible on the wall; again a powerful, frightening mystery is simultaneously announced and withheld. Typically, to fully comprehend the horrific changes, the viewer would be forced to circumnavigate the building.

28, 29 This illegible wrapping of image on building is even more extreme in the decoration of the Black and White Portal, which gets its name from the fact that the lintels (stones across the top of the doorway) are white granite on the north and black limestone on the south side. Duality and complementarity are thus underscored with natural color, and made clear in the largely invisible reliefs on the two columns to either side of the opening. When drawn rolled out, avian anthropomorphic figures emerge. Their heads have both beaks and fanged mouths, their tails appear split to either

28 The Black and White Portal of the New Temple at Chavín de Huantar. Early Horizon.

29 Rollout drawings of the incised figures wrapped around the columns of the Black and White Portal. An impressive gateway to the enlarged New Temple, it summarizes complementarity in a striking dark and light stone lintel as well as the female (left) and male (right) anthropomorphic avian figures. Early Horizon. Rollout drawing based on rubbings by J. H. Rowe.

side of their legs, and each has the outspread wings of a raptor in hunting flight. Yet important differences, as on the Tello Obelisk, become apparent: one is male (by metaphoric substitution for the penis of a central fang on a frontal agnathic (jawless) face), while the other is female (according to the two profile fanged mouths on her thighs leading into a fanged mouth band running up her torso which together represent a 'vagina dentata'). The male is identifiable as a hawk by the band running through his eye and the female as an eagle by her pronounced cere (the round nostril opening on the top of the beak). Myriad slightly different visual metaphoric substitutions appear on the two, such as the ends of feathers as intertwined snakes on the female. Eyes, snakes, and teeth motifs do double and triple duty to form faces throughout, especially at joints. For instance, notice the frontal face at the ankle which makes the foot like a giant tongue protruding from a mouth. Swirling, changing, yet clarifying after much visual study, these figures have upright parts at nearly every possible angle of view. Elemental male-femaleness inhabits non-natural space, defying gravity and so by definition are in the realm of the supernatural. Together they signify complementary fertile wholeness, perhaps in order to sanctify the new ritual center and demonstrate that the cult continues to represent completeness itself.

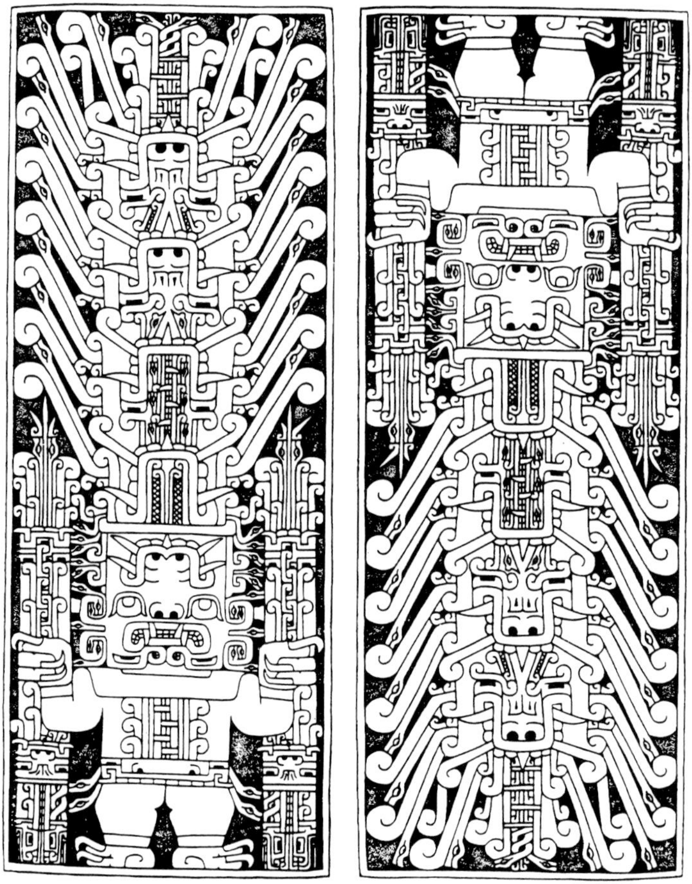

30 Two drawings of the Raimondi Stela, showing the upright and inverted readings embedded in this image of the staffbearing agricultural deity. Artists employed the perceptual effect known as 'contour rivalry' to allow the same incised lines to create different readings. Early Horizon.

30 The culminating expression of these ideas is to be found in the Raimondi Stela. Instead of two monuments adding up to the whole, this sophisticated incised composition embodies duality within a single figure. This 7 ft-tall (2-m) highly polished granite ashlar was unfortunately not found in situ, but its style is closely allied to that of the Black and White Portal figures, establishing it as late. Its image is barely perceptible, only lightly incised on the reflective stone surface, and is seen best in drawing. The illustration

shows two views of the monument, upright (left) and inverted (right) to clarify the double readings embedded within its one figure. Upright, the lower third of the slab depicts a standing figure with splayed taloned feet, arms to the side holding two vertical staffs made up of faces, snakes, swirls, and vegetation. The principal face has pendant irises hanging from the top of the eyes, a downturned fanged mouth, and is crowned by a huge elaborate headdress ending in alternating volutes and snakes to the sides. This supernatural being, known as the Staff God, has predominantly agricultural fertility associations.

However, when the inverted figure is perceived, the standing earth deity takes on a different face and character as it descends from above. The exact same lines are used to form a completely new image, by the extremely sophisticated use of contour rivalry. The same principal eyes, now with irises at the bottom, join with an agnathic mouth that formerly was on the forehead to form a new animalistic principal face. Another face above the principal one uses the original mouth, now upturned, and adds eyes and a pug nose formerly ignored as part of the chin. The body and staffs remain, but now appear to be plunging down from the sky. Most strikingly, the towering headdress suddenly becomes a series of animal faces: eyes plus mouths emanating one from another create a strange group of nested supernaturals. Through extraordinary, gravityless artistic visualization, the profound religious message of duality within oneness (not unlike the Judeo-Christian Trinity) is conveyed. Distinct earthly and celestial deities are one and the same, a paradox elegantly resolved in a transformational whole that betrays the real aesthetic and ideological genius of Chavín art. The Raimondi Stela could have been placed upright, in the ceiling or floor, we will likely never know. In any case, informed viewers could be taught to perceive the two versions through mental and physical effort, initiated into the mysteries by a visual challenge that successfully mirrored the sacred concepts.

Although Chavín de Huantar and its cult finally waned around 200 BC, it had enjoyed a phenomenal longevity and sparked a true creative revolution in the Andes. Its reverberations all along the coast via portable art speak to its successful translation into local vocabularies, as well.

PORTABLE CHAVÍN ART

The Chavín style was not only expressed monumentally, but in all media. Religious tribute, found under the temple at Chavín de Huantar, included: hundreds of ceramic vessels in various styles, exotic cut shells from far to the north, obsidian (volcanic glass) from far to the south, weaving tools, drug paraphernalia (snuff tubes and tablets), and reportedly goldwork. These materials and works of art came from near and far, all along the coast where the Chavín spread their distinctive religious message via portable art objects. Numerous local styles had preceded and run concurrently with it, but the powerful Chavín style and imagery often dominated. Local versions, never absolute copies, remained adaptations, variations on a set of themes. Yet it is remarkable that hundreds of miles away in environments and among cultures quite distinct from those of the highlands, items were produced that are instantly recognizable as Chavín inspired. Chongoyape gold of the North Coast, Karwa textiles of the South Coast, and two ceramic styles known as Cupisnique and Santa Ana represent some of the earliest Andean examples of sheet metallurgy, elaborately painted textiles, and the stirrup-spout vessel form, respectively. The Early Horizon was a time of explosive technological innovations in many media, seemingly fueled by Chavín expressive needs.

Gold had been worked into thin sheets as early as 1900 BC at the small village of Waywaka and copper sheets have been found at Mina Perdida dating to 1250 BC; however, these remained isolated, unconnected incidents to date. Sheet metal technology finally took off in the Early Horizon with three important technological discoveries: alloying (mixing of different metals together, necessary to lower melting temperature and help soft metals to hold their shape), soldering (affixing pieces of metal by melting a few drops of metal like glue at strategic points to convert sheets into three-dimensional objects), and repoussé (patterning metal sheets by hammering on the reverse face to raise relief). Chavín-style goldwork is known generally as Chongoyape for the far North Coast site where a wealth of beaten gold objects were cached and interred. Gold sheets were worked into tall cylinders, probably crowns, and adorned with versions of the Raimondi Stela staffbearer. Yet other crowns buried with these were decorated in a more representational style known as Cupisnique, showing that local and influencing styles coexisted. In the Chavín-style pieces, the tendency toward illegibility continues as the glittering, reflective surfaces create complex designs only by flickering shadows in the indentations. Burger suggests that the choice of gold itself was typically Chavín in its intention to impress, to be 'wholly other,' and so to immediately and suitably distinguish sacred messages. Gold, being truly immutable as well as seeming to contain the sun it so beautifully reflects, continued to be the choice for exclusionary, high-status, and sacred imagery from this time onward. Gold objects were almost

31 Repoussé gold alloy pectoral reportedly found at Chavín de Huantar, with a central frontal feline face emanating snakes and a braided encircling pattern. Early Horizon.

32 A gold repoussé crown, 9¼ inches (23.5 cm) high, found at Chongoyape on the far North Coast. This crown shows a representation of the supernatural Chavín staffbearer, also seen on the Raimondi Stela. Early Horizon.

all headgear, face masks, pectorals, or appliqués on clothing; by the concept of essences, the immutable and energy-filled gold worn on the outside reflected those inner qualities of the wearer.

Smallscale, often reductive versions of faces and figures are incorporated into this wearable gold art. Whether due to the limitations of space or the amount of detail possible in repoussé, or the need to convey new ideas to the uninitiated, on the whole, goldwork images are less complex than those in other media. On the circular pectoral reportedly from Chavín de *31*
Huantar, a fairly readable central frontal face has the characteristic upturned fanged mouth, pendant irises, and here a truncated pair of snakes as the missing lower jaw. Although simplified and isolated, the face necessitates decoding to those unfamiliar with the stylistic rules. Around the edge the simple yet finely wrought braid motif is a convention in Chavín-style textiles as well. Although it may serve primarily decorative purposes, the braid is an image of continuity and interrelatedness that subtly reinforces the cult's unifying message. The Chongoyape crown features the whole figure, its face *32*
erupting into snakey swirls above in a shorthand headdress, its torso sub-

33 Drawing of a painted South Coastal Karwa textile representing parading jaguars as in the Sunken Circular Court at Chavín de Huantar. Early Horizon.

stituted with a frontal face, and hands to the side holding modified staffs. While correct in its imagery, the combination of features is nevertheless unique. Neither pectoral nor crown exactly matches a cult monument or other goldwork; evidently technical creativity also extended to the local artistic interpretation of the sacred iconography, within limits. These artists must also be recognized for the great skill needed to create such small masterpieces: from alloying metals at over 800°C (1472°F), to alternately pounding and precisely heating the very thin, fragile metal sheets, to visualizing and executing the intricate designs in reverse.

Textiles in the Chavín style are known from the burials at Karwa, a looted South Coast burial site located over 300 miles (500 km) from the cult center. They recreate in a perishable, portable form a complete ritual environment, paintings resembling closely the layouts and sculpture of Chavín de Huantar. Yet they also betray a decidedly local emphasis on cotton and female imagery. Scholars presume that the Chavín cult spread by establishing secondary cult centers, probably described as wives or children, along the model of the later pilgrimage center of Pachacamac. Karwa seems to have been figured as a wife, sister, or daughter, given its stylistic and iconographic parallels plus its unique female emphasis.

The Karwa textile compositions were painted in shades of brown and rose dye on plain woven cotton cloths, a local coastal product. Some were

34 Drawing of a painted South Coastal Karwa textile, showing a female deity figure, specific to this satellite cult center. Chavín style was exported via cotton textiles over 500 miles from Chavín de Huantar. Early Horizon.

sewn together to form very large pieces, one in order to represent a circle of jaguars that rivals those from the Sunken Circular Court in relative scale, *33* certainly subject, and even the paired processional arrangement of figures themselves. Hung on the wall it would directly represent the main cult in two-dimensional, easily transported, and comprehensible form. Other Karwa textiles include belts painted very like that depicted on the Lanzón and cloths decorated with staffbearing figures and San Pedro cacti. Hangings, canopies, covers for altars, clothing – over 200 items – represent the full range of ritual items to recreate an entire Chavín cult center in cloth.

Yet, not mere copies, Karwa textiles illustrate many female figures. The *34* invertible supernaturals are always explicitly feminine, with eyes substituting for breasts and opened fanged mouths for vaginas, as on the Black and White Portal figure, and carrying vegetal staffs, as on the Raimondi Stela. Some of the staff goddesses hold intertwining strand staffs, perhaps textile referents, while other compositions depict animated cotton plants with characteristic trilobe leafs and cotton bolls. Profile attendants are portrayed as either male or non-gendered and do not reveal new images when turned, as do the females. This configuration of Earth Mother and lesser attendants made clear a familial relationship to the cult center, gave foreign imagery relevance to local concerns by linking Chavín assurances of fertility to a vital South Coast crop, and embodied an age-old association of females and textiles. As propaganda, the cloth ritual environment of Karwa was designed for effectiveness, impressiveness, and appeal.

Chavín-style ceramics were widely distributed along the coast, overlapping and diverging from a plethora of local styles. The working of clay at this time shares certain basic characteristics: particularly the stirrup-spout form, in which a cylindrical upright spout splits into two curved ones joining a globular vessel; and incising with selective burnishing, in which lines drawn into the moist clay separate raised pattern areas rubbed to a glassy sheen from background textured or matt portions. Vessel bodies feature three-dimensional standing jaguars, seated humans, plants or fruits, as well as simple globes with abstract incised patterns, such as double-headed fanged snakes or dynamic swirls. These images are again taken from the stock cult imagery, but even more reduced to essentials. Technically the pottery of this time is of extremely high quality, often with very thin walls, accurate and delicate incised outlines, and a high degree of burnishing (which is very challenging since it involves hard pressure exerted when the vessel is at its most vulnerable before firing). Aesthetically, Chavín-style ceramics epitomize elegance and power.

35 The best known ceramic substyle is named Cupisnique. Having gone through various changes, the later Chavín-related Cupisnique style of the Early Horizon has stirrup-spouts that are comparatively thick and sport a pronounced lip at the top. The diagnostic fanged faces covering the vessel body and traveling up the spouts are worked in deep relief of shiny on matt black. Low-contrast understatement once more challenges the viewer to decipher the complex image. Cupisnique ceramic sculptures achieve a bold
36 monumentality. Other related substyles abound, such as the earlier Santa Ana, distinctive in its red and black coloration and attenuated version of undulating beings. These two styles fall at extremes of a continuum from heavy to light, descriptive to abstract, demonstrating the variation inherent

35 Chavín-related coastal blackware stirrup-spout vessel of the Cupisnique style. Burnishing highlights abstract fanged serpentine forms like those of the cult center. Early Horizon.

36 Santa Ana stirrup-spout vessel. This substyle of Chavín-style ceramics is distinctive in its red and black coloration and highly abstracted imagery. Early Horizon.

in Chavín-related portable art. Yet, like the Black and White Portal figures, they follow the main style 'rules,' such as the wrapping of images around three-dimensional forms.

Chavín art had a long life after its time: the stirrup-spout form pervades many subsequent Andean ceramic styles, fanged heads play a role in the Paracas style and even later the Moche, staffbearers resurface with the Wari and Tiwanaku empires. However, the global vision of the cult was not recaptured for nearly a millennium as local movements took over during the Early Intermediate Period.

CHAPTER THREE

Paracas and Nasca

In different parts of the Central Andes, during the later Early Horizon and after the Chavín style lost sway, other important local styles emerged. The South Coast Paracas people developed one of the most recognizable, important styles out of the 'ashes' of Chavín, their vision reaching new technical and artistic heights. They spanned the end of the Early Horizon and beginning of the Early Intermediate Period, *c.* 600–175 BC. Chavín influence, strongly visible in early Paracas ceramics, nonetheless was filtered through local colors and techniques, and lent an unprecedented visual clarity. Soon the coastal artists went their own way, reveling in color effects, curvilinearity, and exploring local subject matter in one of the most naturalistic styles of the ancient Andes.

The Early Intermediate Period, *c.* 200 BC–AD 500, was a time of varied regional styles sharing different versions of naturalism. Paracas shaded into the Nasca style on the South Coast, while the Moche developed independently on the North Coast (Chapter Four). Both Nasca and Moche were subsequently conquered by the Wari (Chapter Five). During this time, when no single cult unified Andean art, several adjacent coastal valleys shared a regional aesthetic, their social ties not entirely clear. Paracas, a village culture with a high-prestige burial center as its focus, differed from Nasca, seemingly a loose confederation of clans or chiefdoms, while the Moche organized a small state with a permanent capital. All three preserved elements of Chavín art but in highly distinctive, new, and unique styles.

THE PARACAS STYLE

Paracas artists took a 'high-intensity' approach to the ceramics, textiles, and goldwork they created: concentrated and time-consuming labor, insistent repetition and variation of motifs, great visual profusion, extreme colorism, and attention to detail. Although internally varied, Paracas art tends towards curvilinear forms and superstructural techniques, from solid colors in wavy and circular patterns painted on clay *after* firing, to flowing figures meticulously embroidered on finished cloths. A secondary tendency towards

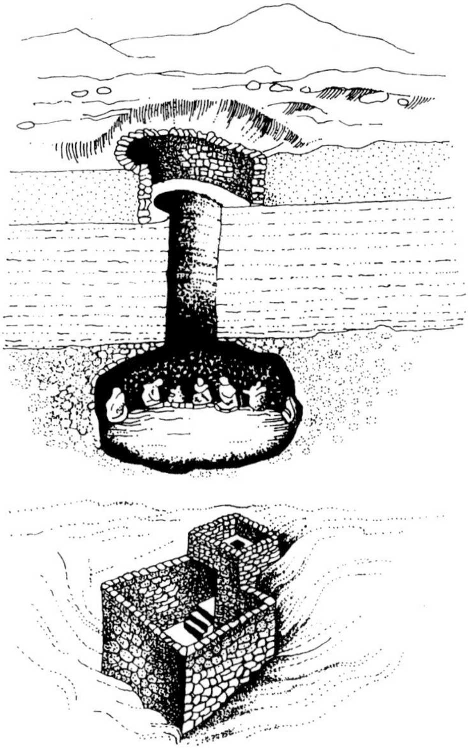

37 Drawing of the two types of Paracas shaft tombs: the earlier 'Cavernas' (above) and later 'Necropolis' (below). Both were filled with mummy bundles (ills. 40–43), over 500 in all, to constitute perhaps the richest ancient textile find in the world. Early Horizon-Early Intermediate Period.

geometry and structural methods can be seen (in the fiber arts in particular), showing that Paracas artists excelled at a variety of substyles and approaches. For instance, they adapted embroidery to two radically different artistic goals and achieved curves in an especially rectilinear structural fiber technique. The Paracas artists epitomize the Andean creative spirit in this disdain for technical determinism (the medium and working method necessarily determining the resultant look, such as a textile design being insurmountably governed by the warp-weft grid).

The culture that encouraged this expressive exploration was based on the Paracas Peninsula, the most jutting landmass on the South Coast, with bays above and below. Fishing these protected waters of the Humboldt Current, growing crops in the nearby Pisco Valley, and trading for distant luxury goods such as camelid fiber, feathers, and spondylus shells, these villagers built up a life of unexpected richness in the arid dunes. Not hospitable in the least ('Paracas' in the Inca language Quechua means 'sand falling like rain,' for the blasting late afternoon winds), the environment encouraged

37 subterranean architecture, particularly shaft-tomb burial chambers. Over time, the population grew to a height of several thousand and moved inland. They buried their dead bundled with fabulous weavings and offerings, first on the top of the prominent Cerro Colorado ('Red Hill') in bottle-shaped shaft tombs known as Cavernas ('Caverns'). When filled, they established cemeteries to the north of the hill near their village, Arena Blanca ('White Sands'). Finally they interred over 400 mummy bundles in the great Paracas Necropolis between the first two cemeteries. Found first at the time of World War I and excavated in the 1920s, these may constitute the world's richest burial grounds in terms of preserved ancient textiles.

38 However, the story of Paracas art begins with ceramics. An influx of characteristic Chavín imagery and stirrup-spout vessel form is obvious in the earlier Cavernas burial ceramics of this region. The familiar North Highland fanged faces with pendant irises appear on both intrusive stirrup-spout and local bowl forms. Even in these takeoffs there are noticeably non-Chavín features: blackware backgrounds adorned in swooping curves with multicolor post-fired paint and incised outlines for every detail, the hallmarks of the Paracas ceramic tradition. Chavínoid interpretations vary, some reaching an extreme of rectilinear reductivism, layering parallel lines crosscut with fangs until the referent is nearly lost. As so often occurs, an intrusive strain sparks experimentation, then becomes absorbed into a new configuration: Paracas ceramics quickly feature local subjects, especially

38 Early Paracas ceramic vessel showing strong Chavín influence (the stirrup-spout and fanged feline imagery in particular) as well as local curvilinear style and post-fired paint. Early Horizon.

39 This later Paracas ceramic mask of the 'Oculate Being,' probably a solar deity, includes double-headed serpent rays and a human figure incised and painted in the characteristic Paracas palette of green, ocher, orange, and black. Early Intermediate Period.

coastal foxes, owls, swallows, and falcons. The palette is firmly established as mustard yellow, olive green, terracotta, white, and black.

These colors – the yellow and green very unusual in ceramics – reflect the freedom inherent in applying pigments after firing. The process is as follows. A pot is formed from wet clay, partially dried, and its surface incised with the outlines of the complete design. It is then fired in a pit, the fire being smothered with ash partway through so that the smoke is driven into the pot's surface to produce 'smudge blackware.' Afterwards resin (probably from the acacia bush), mixed with mineral pigments, is painted on between the outlines and allowed to harden. As a final finishing touch, the whole pot may have been warmed slightly to remove all brushstrokes, since the color areas are remarkably smooth. Because plant resin remelts, these vessels were purely ceremonial. In fact, their fragile, slightly gritty surfaces can revert to a chalky residue over time. However, post-fired painting was evidently preferred for its capacity to produce bright, varied colors impossible to achieve by other means, as part of the overall Paracas fascination with the rainbow colors of their world. The ceramic artists' ability to sketch an intricate design, then accurately fill it in, is mirrored by the way in which textile artists approached the main embroidery substyle. Often the incised outlines themselves were painted with a contrasting color, another feat of manual dexterity that betrays interest not only in the possibilities of color but also in linearity, a powerful pairing developed further by the subsequent Nasca.

Later Paracas-style ceramics – masks, huge ovoid jars, bugles, and other boldly shaped and brightly decorated objects – become very idiosyncratic. The favored local vessel shape is the double-spout-and-bridge, with two upright, tapered, rimless spouts connected by a gently arching element. The vessel body can take on unusual forms, even crescent-shaped double-headed animals. Among the most imaginative and unusual are masks that portray a
39 large-eyed supernatural (the 'Oculate Being'), probably used for ritual impersonation, an important Paracas ritual activity portrayed in textile imagery. At times solar rays end in Chavín-reminiscent snakes; however, the typical Paracas upturned, square-toothed mouth is human rather than jaguar and humans often appear, as here at the top, in association with their deities. Trophy heads taken from enemies, playing a part in almost all Andean art from now on, are introduced. These human referents follow the new trend towards images of this world.

Later, with the Necropolis burials, a different strain appears of probably imported ceramics known as Topará. These plainer vessels, often imitating gourds, appear to have been the first on the South Coast to use slip (clay

40 Schematic diagram of a typical Paracas mummy bundle with the corpse in a fetal position seated in a basket and wrapped with layers of plain and embroidered textiles (the creation of which took from 5000 to as many as 29,000 hours to accomplish). Early Horizon-Early Intermediate Period.

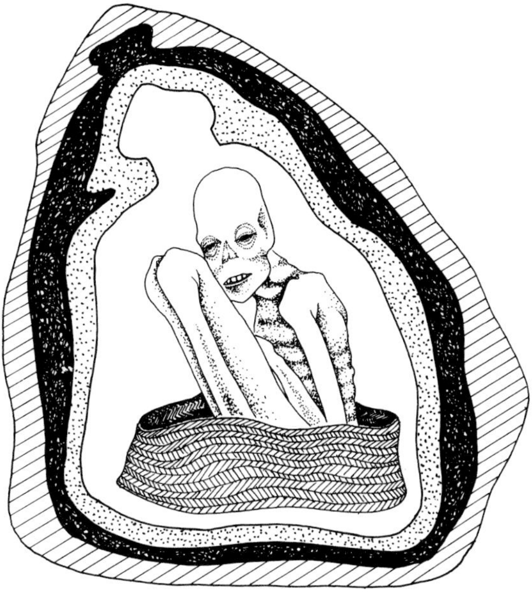

paint fired with the vessel). Slip covers the entire vessel, rather than being used to delineate designs as in Nasca and later styles. The exact relationship *56, 58* between the people buried, this new ceramic type, and the various textile styles remains unclear. However, both Paracas and Topará ceramics, found not just in Paracas, but in the Ica, Chincha, Pisco, and Nasca valleys as well, denote high prestige. Yet ceramics, beautiful though they are, were secondary in terms of quantity and time investment to the Paracas textile arts.

Paracas Textiles

Paracas burials range from the modest to the very sumptuous. Only a few *40* feet under the sand a lower-status person was wrapped in a rough cotton mantle, and surrounded by several simple pots. By contrast, a leader was wrapped in enormous numbers of plain and fancy textiles to form a mummy bundle up to 7 ft (2 m) high. Offerings of gold, feathers, animal skins, and imported shells accompanied him in a subterranean stone-lined room. The earlier Cavernas bottle-shaped tombs and later Necropolis square *37* chambers contained multiple burials (up to thirty-seven in one chamber), the variously sized bundles piled one on top of another. Some burials seem to have had the largest bundle in the center, with medium-sized bundles around it and smaller ones on top, as if the most important person were surrounded by his people. The proportionately larger numbers of everyday and

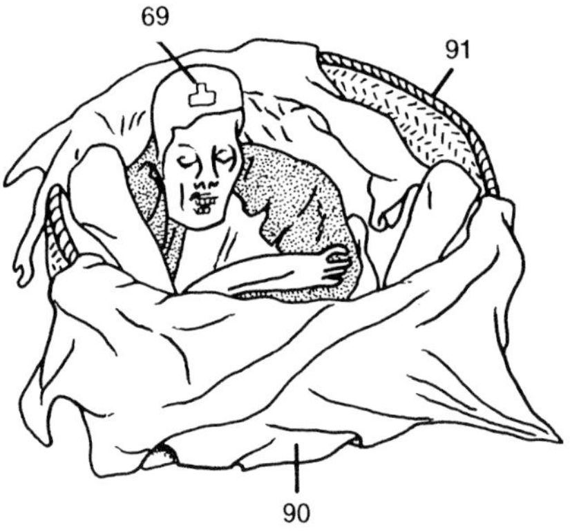

41, 42, 43 Drawings of three layers of an unwrapped Paracas mummy bundle. (*Left*) The corpse, placed in a basket (91) and wrapped in a deerskin (90), wears a gold forehead ornament (69). (*Right*) Many layers of embroidered garments encircle the bundle; shown here are two mantles (26, 27). (*Far right*) The outside of the mummy bundle is elaborated with a feather tunic (05), headband (02), feather-tipped staff (04), leather cape (03), and embroidered mantle (1), then encased in a plain wrapping cloth (01).

middle-class versus upper-class bundles describe a recognizable social hierarchy. Only large and medium bundles have been opened and all the skeletons inside were reportedly male; presumably the small ones contain mostly females. Not all bundles were interred in rooms; in fact, when first excavated the Necropolis cemetery looked 'like a field of potatoes' with the exposed tops protruding from the sands. The Paracas wound the fetal-position body like a giant bobbin with garments and wrapping cloths, and offerings inside the bundle. In this way, individuals maintained their integrity and associated goods in the mass burial. In fact, specific personalities come through the Paracas bundles particularly via their textile contents.

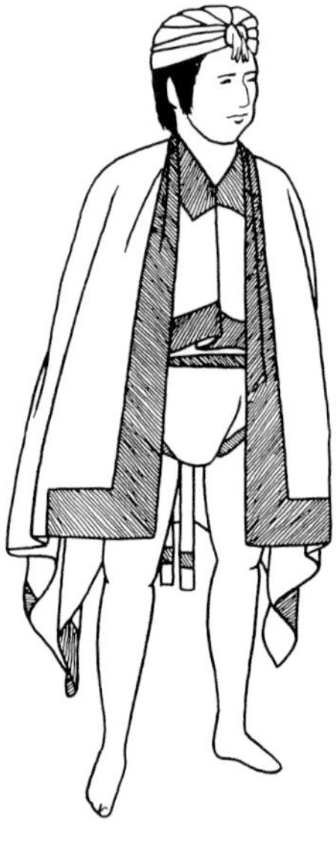

44 Elite Paracas men wore many layers and types of fancy clothing: turbans, shoulder mantles, short ponchos, and loincloths. These embroidered garments were also wrapped around their mummy bundles (ills. 40–43) at their death. Early Horizon-Early Intermediate Period.

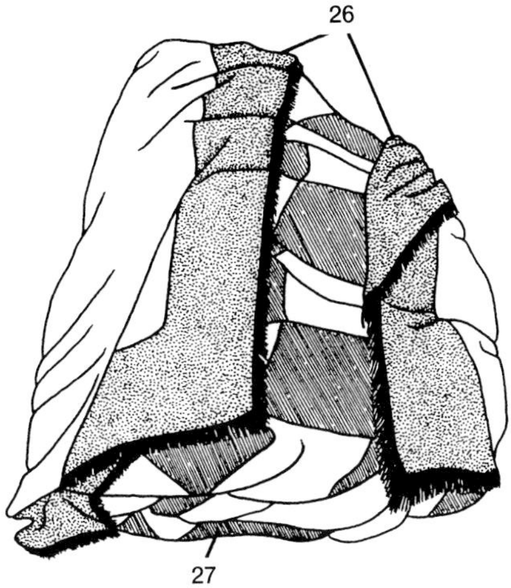

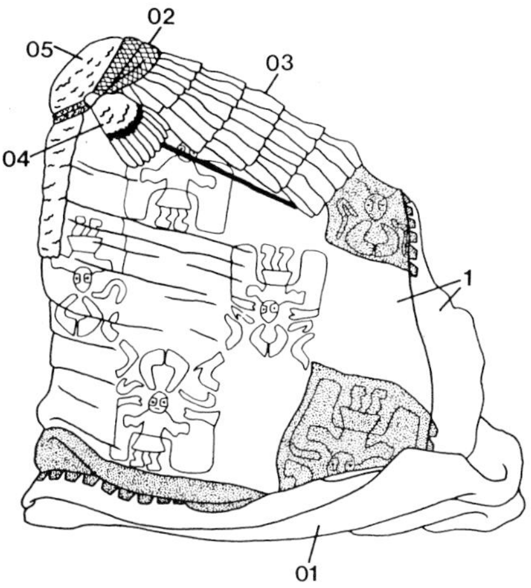

To understand these complex textiles it is important to explore briefly their context. The exact configuration of various bundles follows basic rules but each is unique. Anne Paul has researched one of the largest Necropolis mummy bundles, 5 ft 6 inches (1.7 m) in height and 4 ft 7 inches (1.4 m) *41–43*
across the base, containing 44 fancy and 25 plain cloths. Food offerings of maize, yuca (a potato-like tuber), and peanuts were placed around a large basket containing the body on a complete deerskin. Food offerings bespeak a belief that the body needed sustenance in the afterlife, and may have described the deceased as a fertile producer or controller of different zones. Deer seem to have been especially prestigious animals (among the Moche they were reserved for elite consumption and sacrificed as human substitutes). Around the body was unspun camelid fiber, a spondylus shell, a pouch perhaps with body paint, and a human skull. These imported and hard-won prestige items demonstrate the power of the deceased to command luxuries, take part in powerful rituals, and conquer enemies.

Next in the mummy bundle came layers of plain and fancy textiles, mostly wound around rather than dressed on the body. The first fifteen embroidered garment sets, many unfinished, were likely gifts because of their fragmentary state and distinctive iconographic themes. The whole thing, including the basket, was then wrapped in rough cloths. Plain textiles, some more than 33 ft (10 m) long, increased the bulk of the larger bundles, making the more important people 'larger than life' and better protected in death. High-status living people also appeared bulky, wearing layers of loin-cloths, skirts, tunics, and ponchos with large shoulder mantles, turbans, and *44* headbands. The outer bundle layers featured two staffs and an animal skeleton, six mantles, a leather cape, a yellow tropical bird feather tunic, a staff with feather top, and a final headband. These staffs, placed as if being held, reiterate authority, as do sacrificial animals and the prized feathers of the far-off Amazon. All this concentrated finery was then completely enclosed and buffered in a large plain wrapping cloth sewn up with long stitches.

Other bundles vary: although only average in the quality of workmanship, another nevertheless includes a plaid wrapping cloth, six unique hangings, and several embroideries with twice as many colors as usual. With so many variables – how many cloths, what type, what decoration, other offerings, positions of the various elements – the Paracas people could express a lot about a person, from hierarchical position to clan affiliation. These choices not only express the individuality of the deceased, but also that of the artists who devoted so much time to the wrappings. Textiles on such a massive scale (one measured an almost unbelievable 11 by 85 ft (3.4 by 26 m)) and with so much decoration (often as much as 75 percent of the surface is covered with minute embroidery stitches), demanded extraordinary planning, skilled execution, and time. According to Paul's estimate, bundles may have necessitated from 5000 to as many as 29,000 hours to produce. Seemingly whole families devoted their lives to making splendid garments for the dead.

For so many collaborators, Paracas artists developed an apprentice system, according to a 'training' mantle analyzed by Anne Paul and Susan Niles. A central column of well-embroidered, consistent figures among more tentative, error-filled flanking columns reveals the location of various learners' attempts to copy the master's example. It is fascinating that such a practice piece, as well as unfinished compositions, were interred. Perhaps there was the perceived need for as many fancy cloths as possible when the person died suddenly, or if a given piece were being made expressly for that person it must accompany him or her regardless of its state. Whatever the case, such partial compositions reveal the creative process, the various ways Paracas textile artists approached embroidery, and even fundamental beliefs and values.

45–49 The vast majority of Paracas textiles are embroidered and fall into two main stylistic groups, Linear and Block Color. The two styles differ greatly, from straight lines to curves, few colors in thin lines to a full palette in broad expanses, and from repetitive to innovative imagery. The creative process was almost opposite as well, despite both being versions of a simple running stitch. In Linear Style the thread is simply sewn in and out of the ground

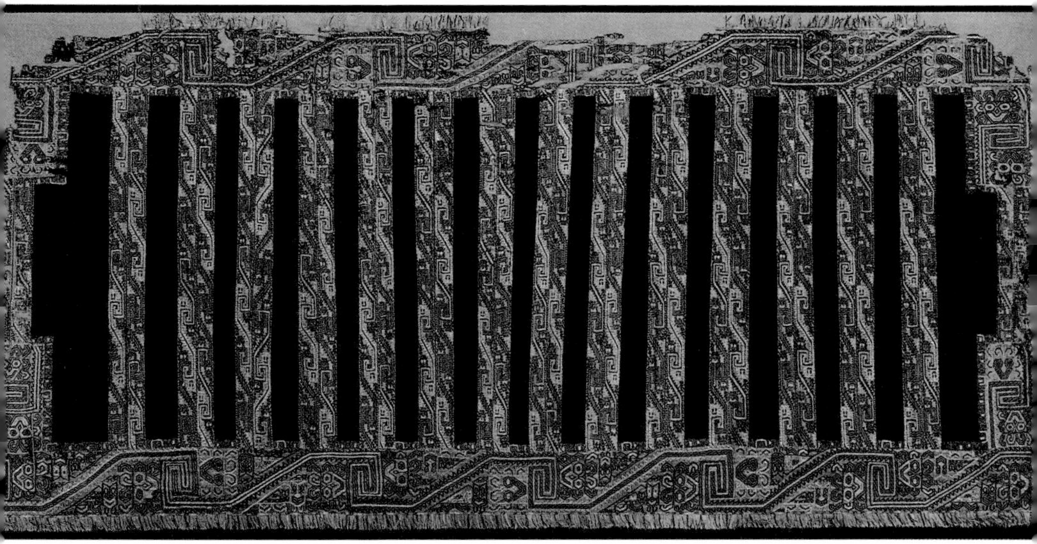

45, 46 (*Above*) A Paracas Linear Style embroidered mantle, measuring over 4 by 9 ft (1.3 x 2.8 m). All but the plain dark areas have been meticulously covered in tiny stitches in red, green, yellow, and blue. (*Below*) Detail showing the columns and border with 'Oculate Being' and feline motifs. Linear Style embroideries were stitched in rows as if they were woven, in contrast to Block Color examples (ills. 47, 48, 49). Early Intermediate Period.

cloth, always in a forward motion, leaving short lines of thread visible on the top, while in Block Color 'stem stitches' were taken (consisting of a forward stitch, half a backward stitch, then another forward stitch) forming a line of slightly overlapping diagonals. When massed up, both create strong color areas and were used to cover a large amount of the ground cloth. This in itself is an unusual use of embroidery, a technique rarely employed for coverage but rather for intermittent accents. Yet Andeans, particularly the Paracas people, favored intense solid color areas and lavished great quantities of time and materials on 'non-efficient' techniques. As burial items, excessive labor and resources themselves praise the power of the deceased.

45, 46 Linear Style, the first Paracas embroidery style to evolve, is first found with the Cavernas cemetery mummy bundles. It continued almost unchanged for 400 or so years, coexisting with the Block Color in most mummy bundles. Most probably the same artists worked in both widely divergent styles. As its name implies, it consists only of narrow straight lines on the horizontal, vertical, and diagonal. In nearly every case only four colors are employed: red, green, gold, and blue. Motifs typically fill borders, accent neckslits, and appear in columns in the center of mantles. Control, precision, and strict repetition are the rule, with only slight variations to add dynamism. The characteristic motifs are nested images combining felines, birds, snakes, and the 'Oculate Being,' all with upturned mouths. All available space is filled, with puzzle-like precision. For instance, on the borders of this mantle a serpentine spiral connects sideways faces, the triangular interstices filled with felines, themselves filled with and surrounded by smaller felines.

Such complex embedded series of images remain somewhat visually elusive, since images are built up of only thin lines and the background of the border is one of the body colors as well. This effect has been termed 'transparency' to call attention to the fact that figures appear permeable and insubstantial. The embroiderers have manipulated our perception of figure and ground (a solid clearly portrayed on top of a continuous backdrop); intentional confusion results from the ground invading the figure. Figures cannot be easily separated from their surroundings or from one another because visually the embedded versions lie in and on the same plane simultaneously. Linear Style artistic choices seem to communicate abstract, conceptual ideas, such as the traditional Paracas deities and the interrelatedness of all Nature. These concepts do not relate to the palpable, readable world of solid bodies in space and so tangible, perceptible images would have been inappropriate. (Albeit different in style, medium, culture, and place, this shares a common basis with the Chavín non-human emphasis.)

These abstract concepts, maintained largely unchanged over time, like the principal tenets of all religions, were highly controlled. Artistic innovation was rarely permitted (the extra colors in the one bundle represent a minor deviation that did not affect the shapes). In order to preserve images intact over time, they had to be communicated exactly from one generation to the next. Unfinished compositions tell us how Linear Style images were made and thus how they were transmitted. Interestingly, they were *not* made utilizing the inherent freedom of embroidery threads to move independently of the cloth's warp and weft grid, sketching out any chosen design. Rather, embroiderers built up patterns row by row as if they were weaving, counting the number of ground cloth threads to sew over and under. For example, at the mantle edge the embroiderer sewed over and under the ground cloth threads where the border's background red was to appear for at least one repetition of the entire serpentine design. The artist left the ground cloth showing where the lines would be filled in subsequently to form the feline's feet, emanations of the face, and zigzag border of the serpentine image. Then the next row of red was added, often sewing over and skipping a different set of cloth threads so as to leave spaces for diagonal lines. Only after the entire background was laid out were the lines filled with blue, gold, and green. Thus the design was approached negatively, i.e. the background defined the figure. Such a 'reverse' method could be expressed as a mathematical sequence (somewhat analogous to knitting instructions today). One artist passed to another only the background sequence, thus complex designs were easily learned and kept stable. The creative process also reveals that the figure was not built up separately from its background, just as it is not perceptually independent in the final product. The way it was made and the end result are one and the same, suggesting the ritualized and unified nature of sacred Linear Style images. Often in Andean art as a whole, the process is as important as, and instills the basic essence in, the work of art as it finally appears.

Although somewhat regimented for higher spiritual reasons, these compositions remain extremely challenging to create and impressive in design. Even broken down into rows, the complexity of the embedded images forced embroiderers to visualize the whole pattern, keeping track of their place in each detailed image (on the same row are the middle of a large feline's face, the top of a small feline's back, the edge of an 'Oculate Being's' ray, etc.). This requires great focus, on top of the technical skill, to make even stitches in consistent tension so as to prevent puckering. One mistake would necessitate taking out all subsequent rows, to keep the pattern regular.

47–49 Block Color embroidery was added to the Paracas repertoire slightly later than Linear Style, but persisted to the end and even appeared alone in the latest mummy bundles. It emphasized creative modification and variety almost as much as Linear Style restricted it. Block Color style features outlined, curvilinear figures whose elaborate costumes and accoutrements are solidly filled in with brightly-colored stitches. The palette includes nineteen different colors. Motifs typically fill borders, as in the Linear Style, but also the centers of garments in columnar and checkerboard arrangements. Great dynamism is conveyed by figures' arching, twisting bodies in varying color combinations that often match on the diagonal. In contrast to the Linear Style, Block Color compositions feature clearly legible non-transparent figures against the continuous ground cloth with which they contrast in color. This style eschews abstract concepts, to portray palpable humans ritually impersonating animals and composite beings; its subjects are of this world, although the religious referents are ultimately super-human. Block Color is therefore complementary to Linear imagery; it is understandable that they should both have been included in most Paracas mummy bundles. One provides the deceased's connection to the larger social continuity and shared religious beliefs, while the other shows the ritual activities constantly reinforcing the individual's contribution to society and spirituality.

Block Color compositions changed over time, varied one from the next, explored a multiplicity of ritual impersonations, and give us a lively glimpse into certain real objects and practices of 2000 years ago. There are nearly as

many different versions of figures as there are pieces, although only rarely more than one type of figure in a given piece. One, famous for its stunning 47
workmanship and telling clues as to process, features bird impersonators in outspread feathered capes carrying trophy heads and arching batons. Each tiny figure, only 5 inches (13 cm) tall, sports one of four distinct mask patterns and costume color combinations. Looking closely, between the two lefthand gold bracketing borders are two unfinished figures, the upper one with most of the top, the lower one only some of the bottom of a bird-man. From this we can tell that the embroiderer began by outlining the silhouette and important internal portions, as in a sketch. Within a border, the

47 (*Left*) Detail of 'Bird Men' mantle, upper right corner, with border bracket figures unfinished. These figures show that the embroiderers outlined first, then filled in the images. Apparently the owner died suddenly and his magnificent garment was interred with him, even though it was not quite complete. Early Intermediate Period.

48, 49 Paracas Block Color style mantle (*below*) and detail (*right*) with flying shaman motifs. Early Intermediate Period.

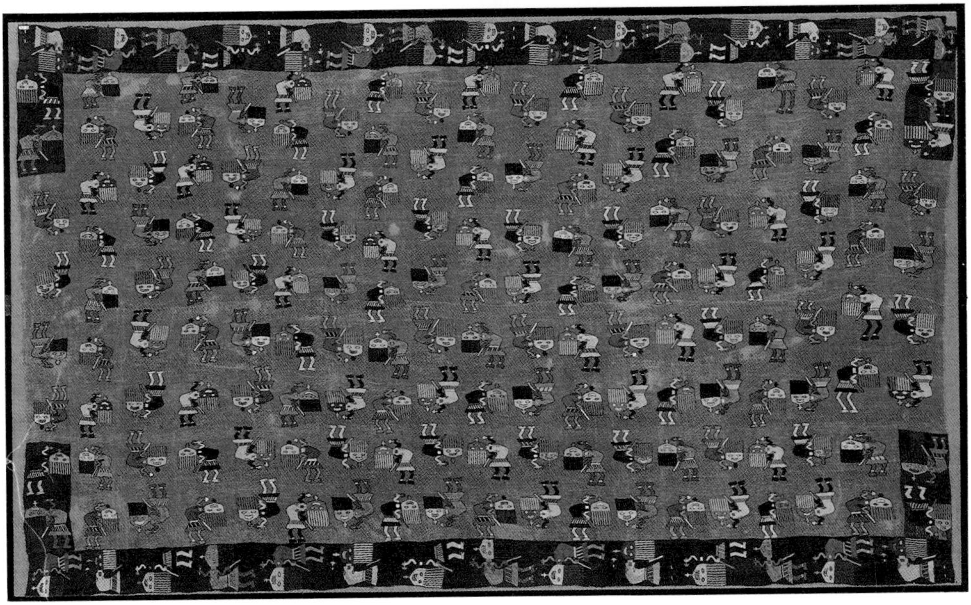

outline was the same color as the background, which was then filled in, and finally the internal figure colors were added. In the field just the latter was
47 necessary. As illustrated in the left-hand unfinished bird-man, not all of the inside colors were completed. On the other side of the mantle two figures that should correspond to the outlined ones were not even begun. This exquisite mantle's matching loincloth (many Paracas pieces are garment sets) has only its bird-men outlined and the border background finished. It is as if the embroiderers heard the tragic news of the patron's death, lifted their needles from the surface, and took the textile masterpiece to the graveside. This mantle betrays the opposite approach to that taken in the Linear Style creative process: the figure has precedence, both over the ground cloth and the background, which was only established after the figure had been delineated.

In keeping with the individualism of Block Color some outright formal irregularity was permitted in this substyle, especially in images of shamans who, as spiritual leaders, were in many ways 'above the rules.' The illustra-
48, 49 tion here shows the typical shaman, head thrown back, hair streaming, baton and knife in hand, and sporting a cross-shaped chin adornment. In this piece, the clear rows of figures break down (extra ones are added in to the right, throwing off the design). The shamans seem to dance or fly, just as shamans were believed to do during healing trance states. The exuberant sloppiness of the pattern accentuates the energy and barely-contained chaos of the priestly intervention into the supernatural. Again, the making of the piece and its intended message are completely congruent.

Even these few examples of the thousands of extant Paracas compositions show how one technique was applied in many different ways, towards divergent yet complementary goals. It must also be appreciated that these were not just static wrappings and offerings for death, but most had a flowing and brilliant life, being worn in the many rituals conducted on the Paracas Peninsula. Art in the Andes was made to be activated through pageantry. Just as artists were not bound by technical limits, so sacred garments transcended everyday practicality to soar as symbols of other realms and human attempts to access them.

50 In addition to embroidered garments, the talented Paracas fiber artists mastered a spectacular structural technique known as discontinuous warp and weft. Two magnificent fragments survive of hangings of huge mythical beings made in one of the most unusual and demanding techniques possible in fiberworking. In weaving, usually the threads in one direction are continuous, i.e. they pass vertically or horizontally across the loom unin-

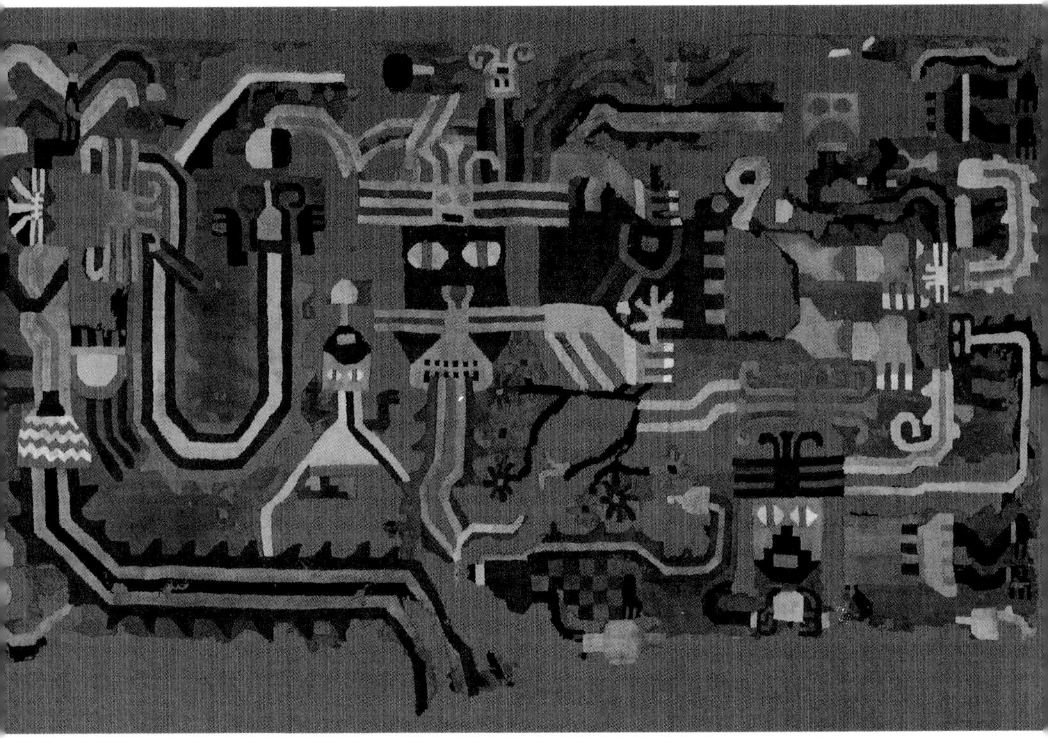

50 Late Paracas hanging created in the extremely arduous technique known as discontinuous warp and weft. A masked figure dominates this fragment. Originally the composition covered perhaps an 8-ft length (2.5-m) in intricate images.

terrupted. This is not only the easiest to accomplish but makes a stronger cloth, especially when the warp is continuous (the load-bearing threads placed on the loom first). But it is possible to create a pattern by making both the warp and the weft threads discontinuous, that is linking up various different colors along the way, though it is tedious and confusing work. It is necessary to stretch temporary scaffold threads across the loom to hold the intersections of one color warp and the next until all the colors are connected. Then the mass of multicolor strings can be drawn tight enough to weave in the wefts in matching color areas. The more complex the design, the more color changes, so the more scaffolds needed; in compositions as mind-bogglingly complicated as this, the number of scaffolds can be estimated by tracing the number of different colors along any one line. The actual design would have been almost totally obscured by the scaffolds; perhaps the weavers worked from the reverse side, one of the many working relations to the loom Andean textile artists employed over time. Evidently Paracas weavers chose such a technique because it achieved a contradiction – solid, rich colors in a lightweight, gauzey cloth – but it may also simply embody the height of artistic virtuosity demanded by the most sacred images.

50 Because of the fragile, incomplete condition of the cloth and the complexity of the design, individual figures may be difficult to read. The horizontal figure (with vertical head) slightly to the left of the upper center has large white eyes, a light blue mouth mask, and serrated mouth emanation. His yellow arm, with white-tipped nails, holds a scraggly bunch of flowers. The technical challenge increases our appreciation of the many curved shapes, such as these flowers, every tiny step of which needed a scaffold. His dark green tunic, yellow legs, and feet with white toenails are difficult to distinguish from the smaller figures all around them. These preserved fragments, the largest of which is 28 by 45 inches (70 by 114 cm), constitute only about a third of the original. It is impossible to estimate the amount of time lavished on the creation of these hangings and it is no wonder that so few of them are known, in comparison to the embroideries. They were obviously of the highest importance and symbolic power. They are also probably quite late in the Paracas trajectory, forming a transition to the Nasca style, which often featured large-scale versions of Paracas figures and employed dis-
60 continuous warp and weft widely in geometric patterns. The goldwork of the two, thin gold sheets cut out to form masks, forehead ornaments, and dance wands as seen on the textile figures, was likewise extremely allied.

THE NASCA STYLE

Nasca and Paracas are closely linked, especially by subject matter, but just as Paracas had veered off from Chavín influence, Nasca sensibility too developed independently. The Paracoid subject matter of ritual impersonators,
53–56 native flora and fauna, and mythical beings continued. Agricultural abundance was an even more major preoccupation for these irrigation agriculturalists living precariously by meager water sources. Nasca art shifted emphasis in two divergent directions: both to more partial, atomized figure parts treated as separate motifs, and to more simple, naturalistic representations. Colors remained varied and vivid, but colorism was equally matched by linearity and a whole new trend toward the boldly geometric.

51 Nasca double-spout-and-bridge vessel in the shape of a stepped fret. Painted in multicolor slip, on its surface is a complex battle scene. Early Intermediate Period.

Techniques emphasized painting and drawing more; slip painting replaced resin entirely in ceramics, many textiles were painted, and even the rocks of the plains were made into 'drawings.' Scale is often enlarged, up to the point of the gigantic Nasca Lines. Nasca art constitutes one of the true peaks of *63, 64* the Andean tradition with its flowing, enigmatic forms.

There is little agreement among scholars as to where Nasca social organization fits between the levels of chiefdom and short-lived, nascent state, but the architectural evidence points to at least a loose affiliation of many villages or clans. The strikingly ephemeral pilgrimage center of Cahuachi served as a capital for the region from the Cañete to the Acarí Valleys. Corporate labor was amassed to a new degree, seemingly by separate groups of related people rather than by forced conscription, as seen by the forty plus temple mounds of Cahuachi and the many hundreds of overlapping Lines. The banding together of groups for large-scale rituals and

projects (such as unique underground filtration canals to maximize water from rivers that run dry for months and sometimes years) betrays a common anxiety surrounding water, fertility, and so survival itself. Art also points up
51 increased levels of social conflict, including depictions of fighting, trophy
52 heads, and overtly bellicose objects, such as slings to hurl stones and fiber armor. A more complex society such as this expressed itself in many contradictory ways, from sensitive hummingbird portraits to chilling human trophy head burials. However, since death and life were seen as complementary aspects of the circle of life, these poles would not have necessarily seemed antithetical to the Nasca themselves.

Nasca Ceramics

The ceramics of the Nasca run the full gamut of life and death imagery and were in many ways the high point of Central Andean creativity in clay. Certainly their vibrant slip-painted surface decoration, displaying more colors than any other in the Americas, merits special recognition. Rounded vessel shapes with very complex compositions wrapped around all sides are characteristic, as are the glossy burnished surfaces and bright colors that look remarkably fresh in spite of their age. Nasca ceramics were strikingly uniform from one South Coast valley to the next, betraying a strong common religion and constant artistic contact. Forms include the double-spout-and-bridge and spout-and-handle continued from Paracas, as well as fairly simple bowl, plate, jar, and effigy vessels.

53, 54 Nasca ceramics feature bulbous overall shapes with slight three-dimensional details, as opposed to a fully-realized sculptural style such as the Moche (Chapter Four). Rather than stemming from a limited vision, the Nasca blend two-dimensional effects with volumetric ones subtly and elegantly; painted-on features complement protruding ones. The control over painting, from color placement to overlapping of shapes, gives the illusion of a layered body. Slight bulges for shoulders, chin, skull, and a sweeping concavity for the hair/turban work together with the painted outlines, such as the dark lines of the tunic edges, to form a seamless sense of corporeality, yet with very few bodily contours actually modeled. The illusion continues on all sides, with the fringed ends of the headband gracefully crossing and flexing. Also using the entire vessel, elaborate supernaturals
55, 58 or their components painted around cylindrical and globular vessels become visually subdivided by any one view. Depth and movement effects achieved by overlapping point up a growing interest in natural space and physicality.

At whatever end of the spectrum from two to three dimensional, Nasca 56
design is equally masterful. A hummingbird achieves calligraphic elegance 57
in sure lines and simple colors, seeming to hover in the air. An *achira* plant – a coastal tuber whose edible subterranean stem sends up shoots above ground – unites graphic and sculptural motion in a supremely dynamic composition. Shimmering optical effects come from the black-and-white zigzag surface, while the bulging sprouts spin pinwheel fashion. The artist exaggerates and modifies the actual plant shapes to encapsulate vibrant
vegetal growth, a constant absorption of the Nasca farmers. 51

A final culmination of aesthetic as well as literal balance, in a very innovative vessel shape, is the step fret-shaped double-spout-and-bridge vessel. The glossy smooth planes give a taut feeling, while the fret portion dramatically arches over negative space. On its front and back faces, contained by the signature Nasca black outline, is delineated a frantic battle scene: a pitched struggle taking place on the steps as if on terraces. A newly defeated figure lies prone toward the horizontal lower edge. The three main spaces of the step fret each have their own scene, providing an underlying order to the story. The introduction of narrative itself, also a characteristic of North Coast art at this time, adds another naturalistic, worldly concern. It certainly has political ramifications as well, allying victory over enemies with such fancy ceramics and especially the step fret motif (a high prestige design throughout the ancient Americas). All three vessels integrate the practical spout in graceful, seamless ways.

Beautifully made, with extremely thin, even walls, Nasca ceramics result from a range of handbuilding techniques, particularly coiling. Turntables gently revolved the pot so work and decoration could proceed on all sides evenly. (This low platelike implement is not to be confused with the potter's wheel, as it was not for throwing pots.) Such turntables, used from 500 BC to the present day in Peru, betray the interest in finishing all sides of an art work so as to encapsulate more fully its essence. Its long usage also demonstrates that Andean peoples were not ignorant of the wheel, but simply adapted it to their own cultural viewpoint in which a tool rarely if ever takes precedence over human manual and visual skills.

After construction, but before firing, painting with slip took place. Slip paints are simply water and mineral pigments, such as iron oxide for red and manganese for black, added to white or terracotta clays to make thin, colorful suspensions. Nasca artists were able to perfect up to thirteen different slip colors, all at relatively low firing temperatures. This extraordinary achievement – most ancient Americans discovered only the obvious shades

52 (*Opposite, above*) Nasca ceramic cup with abstract trophy head motifs. Early Intermediate Period.

53, 54 (*Opposite, below*) Nasca ceramic effigy of a man, front and rear views. Although the black designs on the face give the appearance of a moustache and beard, Amerindian males have very little facial hair so these markings represent body painting or tattooing. Early Intermediate Period.

55 (*Top*) Nasca ceramic bowl with a two-headed supernatural image wrapped around it. Among the finest work in clay of all the Andean traditions, Nasca vessels are thin-walled and so well painted that they appear newly made even after 1500 years. Early Intermediate Period.

56 (*Above*) Nasca ceramic bowl with a feeding hummingbird painted on the side. The calligraphic delicacy of this often naturalistic style goes well with the subject matter. Early Intermediate Period.

of red, white, and black – included rare blue-grey, maroon, and light purple. Color as a prominent aesthetic goal was perhaps inherited from the Paracas textile aesthetic, although it is a widespread Andean value. However, slip painting is a radical departure from resin painting, and binds colors to the vessel to become almost totally permanent. Nasca vessels were then burnished carefully, perhaps more than once, after the slip was nearly dried (to reduce friction and avoid smudging, the artists may have used an oily surface lubricant, which would have burned off in firing). These minute masterpieces underscore the fact that simple technology does *not* equate with crude artistry.

Nasca ceramics went through several changes during the 800 years of their creation. Archaeologists discriminate as many as eight stages, but four suffice here: Proto, Early, Middle, and Late. Proto Nasca ceramics have their roots in Paracas incised outlining, merely substituting slips for resin paint. Experimentation with the new slip painting technology meant that sometimes surfaces were 'crazed' (superficially cracked) from overly thick application. Only a relatively few colors were perfected, although grey already existed, proving innovation began early. The permanence of slip and its suitedness for delicate lines were also appreciated: often the incised lines are themselves painted in with white or red, a difficult feat. The counterpoint of sculptural and surface effects was already in place. Linearity and colorism became more emphatic as Early Nasca introduced the characteristic painted black outlines and a broader range of slip colors, most often on a white background. Bowls became deeper with more exterior designs, such as rel-
55 atively simple supernaturals. The one illustrated here shows two heads, either feline or feline-masked according to the rounded ears, a fantastical trident tongue, and a serrated body with abstract markings. Highly naturalistic birds
56 are also typical.

Middle Nasca marks the undisputed height of the style, with all thirteen colors, peak modeling, painting and burnishing quality, and extraordinary visual complexity. A brown background slip was almost universal during this phase, bowls and cups were built with higher sides, and designs show
58 increasing abstraction. Wrap-around images abound of heavily adorned, flying-position supernaturals sporting many trophy heads, while elemental
52 versions of portions of this imagery may also be isolated, as in the schematic trophy heads. As in many styles, the peak of achievement prefigured the more dispersed, reduced final versions in which coherent figures became a series of repeated elements. Late Nasca phase ceramics revert to fewer

57 Nasca ceramic double-spout-and-bridge vessel in the shape of an *achira* plant. Its pinwheel sculptural movement, along with the graphic black-and-white surface patterning, epitomizes the dynamic Nasca aesthetic. Early Intermediate Period.

colors, typically no longer feature a brown background, and the vessel forms
58 become even taller, the images more abstract. Tentacles, emanations, and pointed protrusions nearly obscure the flying figures with their repetitive elaboration, while both the geometric and evocative strains of earlier phases are integrated. Thus, Nasca painted ceramics trace a fairly familiar route from limited, tentative experimentation through mature complexity to shifts between reductive and effusive elaboration. In the final decades, Wari conquerors of the South Coast created interesting hybrids, drawing inspiration for their pan-Andean abstraction from the richness of the Nasca heritage.

59 One of the enduring Andean aesthetic traditions that first appears in permanent form during this time is the panpipes. Music was evidently a central component of rituals, as can be seen in wall decoration at Cahuachi (see below). More ancient clay panpipes differ from later versions in that they are a series of sealed tubes, rather than open cylinders. The musician blew precisely across the tops to produce the familiar, haunting, windy sound. As an ethereal entity, sound seems to have been believed well-suited to communicating with the spirits.

58 Late Nasca ceramic beaker with typical faces, geometric patterns and disembodied elements from flying supernaturals (see ill. 55). Early Intermediate Period.

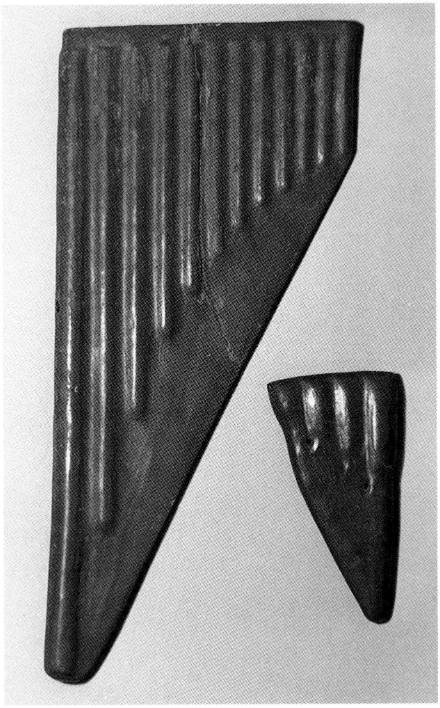

59 Nasca ceramic panpipes of different sizes. Unlike modern examples, musicians blew across the top of closed pipes to produce the haunting, breathy sounds associated with the Andes.

Nasca Goldwork and Textiles

Goldwork also typically has celestial associations since it reflects the sun and is immutable, like the supernatural arena. Paracas and Nasca goldwork is virtually identical: extremely thin, even sheets cut into elaborate silhouettes with few repoussé details. Forms include shaped noserings hanging from the septum (often large enough to be called mouth masks), face masks, forehead ornaments, clothing appliqués, and dance wands. The metal objects are exactly as worn by ritual impersonators and mythical beings in other media, although details such as whiskers ending in trophy heads cannot be accurately portrayed at such small scale. While technically not an improvement over the sophisticated repoussé work of Chavín, Paracas/Nasca goldwork achieved maximum glitter and shine by emphasizing less interrupted surfaces. Such thin sheets used smaller amounts of gold, which was purer as it did not have to hold much pattern (copper alloying strengthens gold). It is by no means easy to take a small lump of metal and produce a thin and even sheet without breakage or melting; exact knowledge and supreme manual skill are required to hammer and anneal (heat to just below melting) repeatedly so the gold will not become brittle. As always, only stone tools were used.

Textiles of this style, like ceramics, often feature curvilinear and naturalistic painting; however, the Nasca also explored many rectilinear and geometric patterns in structural techniques. The artists took advantage of the large surfaces of plain-woven cloth to paint larger-scale figures and extensive, multifigure compositions. The palette tends to be red, black, yellow, and green, with some subtle blues and purples in painted examples. The black outlining characteristic of ceramic painting is a constant feature here as well. Certainly the Nasca debt to Paracas cannot be denied, yet the interpretation – more continuous, flowing, and momentary – is definitely distinctive.

Fewer Nasca textiles survive than Paracas, and many have no indication of being garments. Like the Chavín-style Karwa textiles, hangings could have functioned to set up temporary ritual spaces; as we shall see, Nasca ceremonial life at the capital was based on intermittent gathering rather than permanency. Subjects range from very sensitive renditions of animals and harvesters to bolder depictions of ritual impersonators and supernaturals. They reflect the preoccupation with crops seen in the other media: in the
60 textile illustrated here the leftmost pampas cat impersonator carries two *jicama* (yam bean) roots below a gourd rattle, the central one a stalk of maize, and the rightmost two bean pods above a gold forehead ornament; in the
62 'Harvest Festival' textile all kinds of crops are presented.

60 (*Left*) Painted textile fragment in the Nasca style, depicting figures carrying agricultural products, such as maize (center), and ornaments, such as a forehead mask (right).

61 (*Above*) Detail of a Nasca discontinuous warp and weft textile in gold, red, and black. Nasca art ran the gamut from highly naturalistic (ill. 56) to boldly geometric. Early Intermediate Period.

61 Structural textiles differ strikingly from painted ones and may have played very different, perhaps non-ritual roles. Continuing the arduous technique of discontinuous warp and weft, but in a strictly rectilinear manner, bold, monumental stepped patterns fill mantles in red, yellow and black, and even in one singular case, pale shades of maroon, light blue and lavender. Internal differences among Nasca textiles may suggest that the continuation of Paracas religion was largely in painted form, while secular and novel ideas were played out in other techniques. The many technical accomplishments and wide variety of styles make the Early Intermediate Period a time of exploration and individuality in the textile record.

Nasca Earthworks

For a long time only the great Nasca Lines were known as the grand communal expression of these people and they continue to be the most famous and 'mysterious' remains of ancient South America. First located in the 1920s from aerial reconnaissance, they have provoked scholarly disagreement and popular speculation, from the breathlessly mystified to the patently absurd. However, recent excavations have uncovered Nasca cities, principally the capital of Cahuachi and surrounding ground drawings, filling in our knowledge and dispelling apparent mystery. Nasca earthworks, as both the subtractive drawings of the Pampa de Nazca and the modified hill temples of Cahuachi may be loosely termed, show their concern for the earth, equal parts reverence and propitiation. They also show a lack of preplanning and centralization that demonstrates the importance of different social groups expressing themselves over time. Yet the internal similarity of the Lines and temples bespeaks a strong religious and ethnic identity. Thus, architecture expresses two complementary aspects of Nasca communal effort, the dispersive and the cohesive.

The city of Cahuachi is unusual. Located to the south of the Lines, along the banks of the Río Nasca, it falls among natural hillocks and on top of a natural water source. Rare in this arid land, the presence of water made this a sacred spot, a *huaca* (Quechua for special place or thing). In the 1950s it was thought to be a large (150-hectare) walled capital of substantial population; however, excavations in the 1980s by Helaine Silverman found forty or so temples in no apparent pattern along the riverbank, vast plazas (over 75 percent of the city is open space), burials and cached offerings, but no domestic housing or refuse to suggest much population at all. The city wall turned out to be only 16 inches (40 cm) high, not a defensive structure but another Nasca linear outline, this time of a sacred space. Posts and postholes

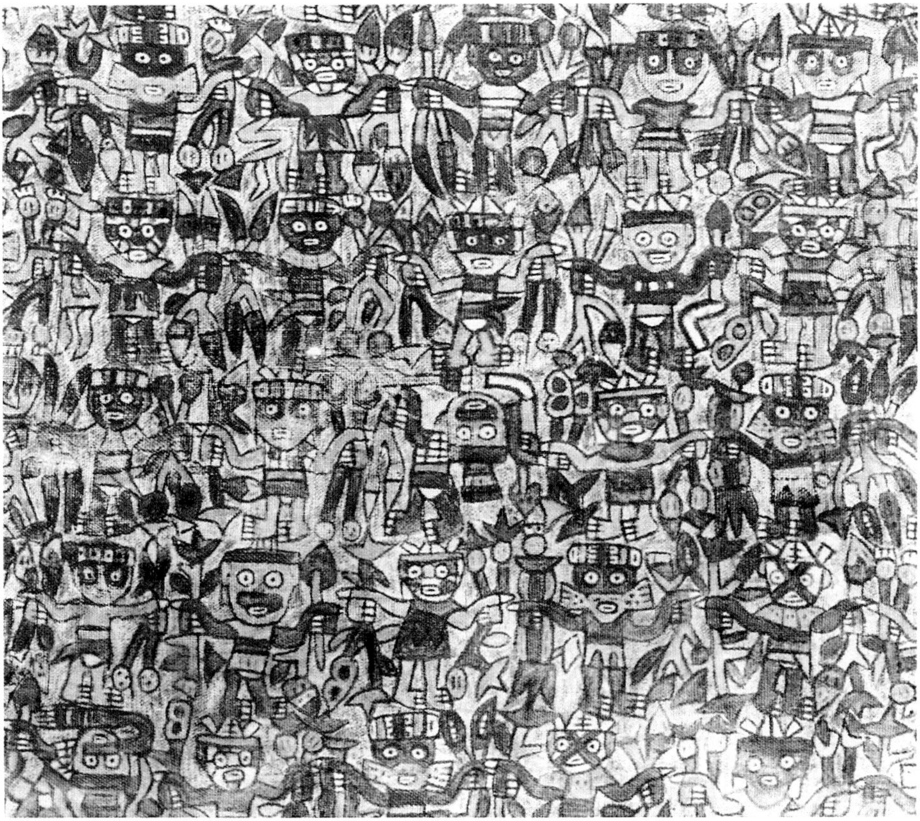

62 Detail of the painted Nasca 'Harvest Festival' textile with hundreds of figures displaying agricultural products. In the dry coastal valleys concerns about survival and Natural abundance were paramount. Early Intermediate Period.

were found in various parts of the city, as if temporary canopies were erected rather than permanent walls. These findings were puzzling to Silverman until she visited a modern Catholic pilgrimage center and witnessed a transitory city erected and torn down in a matter of days. Likewise, Cahuachi, its vast plazas suitable for huge gatherings, but with almost no living quarters, could have been filled periodically by all the Nasca people, the temples built onto the existing hills, then swept clean as a ritual gesture and abandoned. The windswept sands would remove other remnants of the celebrations, which may well have been harvest festivals as depicted in textiles. *62*

Temples, each a modified hill topped by adobe walls and fill, follow a

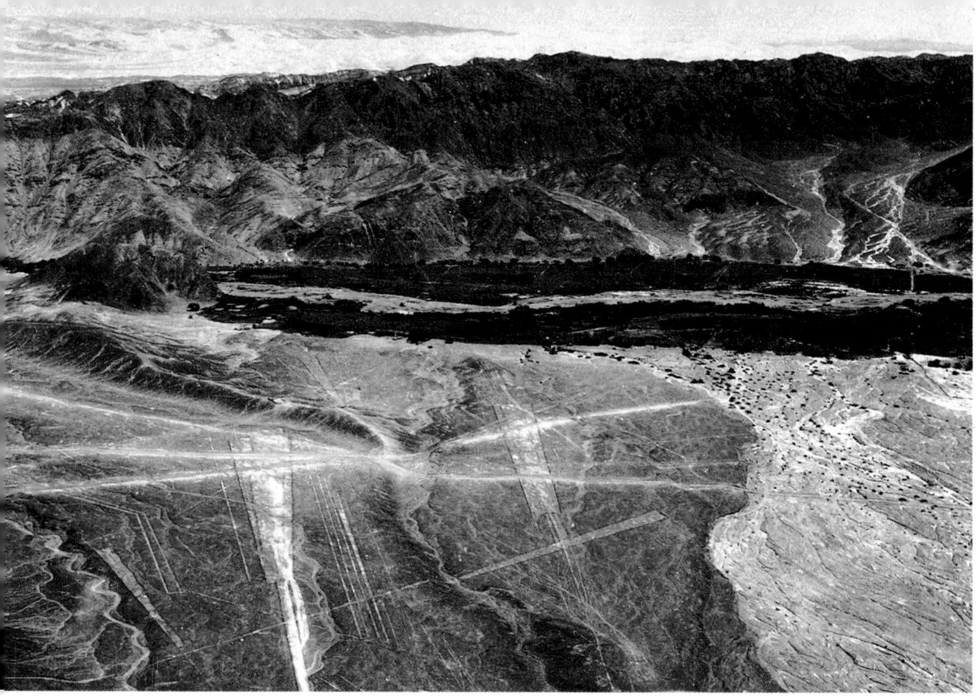

63 Aerial view of the plains of Nasca, a 'natural blackboard' with hundreds of overlapping lines, trapezoids, and figures (see ill. 64). The Nasca Lines were made over a period of several centuries simply by selectively removing dark stones to reveal the light ones below. Early Intermediate Period.

similar pattern of construction, face the same general direction, but vary in size, elaboration, and detailing. The largest, known as Unit 2, is part of an aggregation that may be a central acropolis, although the additive nature of the city makes for no true center. Its step fret-shaped terrace and abundant ritual paraphernalia remains suggest it was a focus for large group religious activity. To the southeast, however, a fully intact buried structure known as the Room of the Columns reveals a bit more about the nature of Nasca rituals. A central altar was protected by a roof or textile canopy erected on
59 columns, while rather crudely incised images of panpipes and rayed faces adorn adobe walls. Certainly the clay panpipes figured prominently in rituals performed here, perhaps dedicated to deities with solar associations typically important to agriculturalists.

The celebrants who filled these empty rooms and huge plazas almost cer-
63 tainly arrived at the ceremonial capital by traversing the great Lines drawn on the adjacent plains. The 193-square mile (500-square km) natural black-

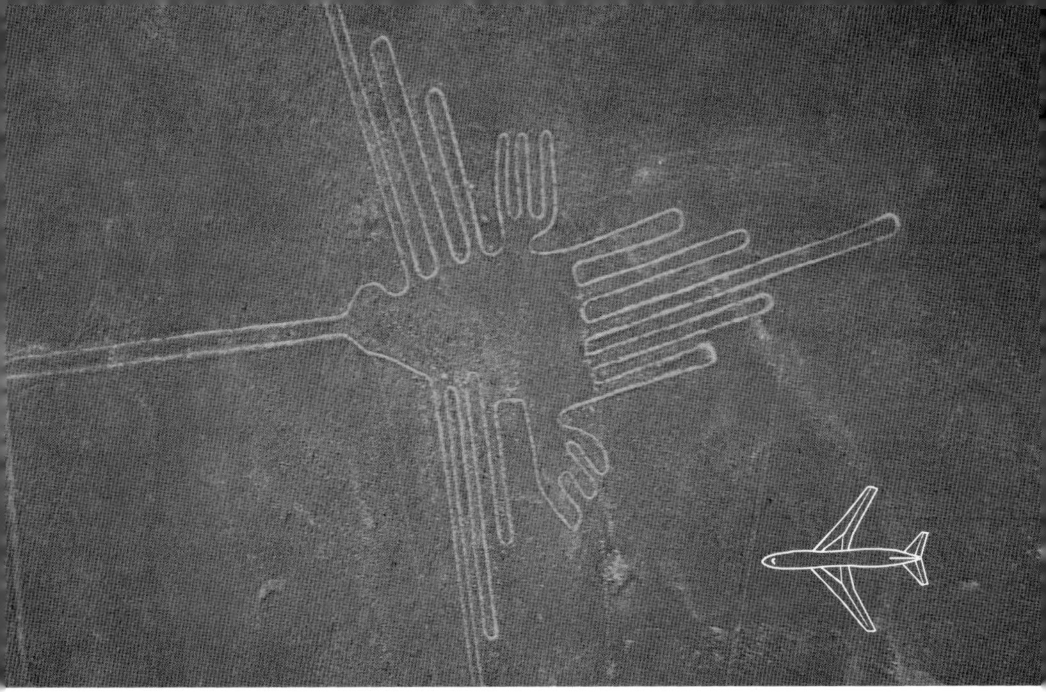

64 The Nasca Lines hummingbird figure with a jumbo jet for scale. These enormous ground drawings were made for the earth, the deities, and perhaps the constellations, rather than for a human audience, since the Lines are too large to be comprehended from the ground or the low hills around the plains. Early Intermediate Period.

board, essentially a layer of dark over light stone, was filled over the generations with hundreds of lines, trapezoids, radiating lines (called ray centers), as well as thirty immense figures of animals, humans, plants, and fantastical *64* patterns. They overlay one another to create a giant palimpsest, like the cave paintings of Paleolithic Europe. Their significance, while multi-faceted, may not be totally foreign to the latter, in that the Lines may have served primarily ritual purposes, sympathetic magic to help ensure a good harvest. Other theories regarding their meaning have included: astronomical sightlines (although a recent study shows that they point to significant celestial happenings no more than allowed by chance); water source pointers (many do so but many do not); invisible line systems, later known to the Incas as *ceque* lines, that delineate different groups' water rights (suggested by the ray centers, but not fully accounting for other types of lines); evidence of group labor tax (again as per the Inca *mit'a* system; a heavily economic approach that ignores both content and form of the Lines); and ritual pathways (some connect, for example, the plains with Cahuachi). All of these explanations may together be true, with certain lines more related to sky, others to water, and yet others to landmarks. They can all be encompassed by the idea of repeated ritual action, which explains why so many were made then overlaid. Certain groups may have 'owned' and reused certain areas of the plains, recognizing current lines by their relative brightness (oxidation gradually darkens the exposed sand; unfortunately all the Lines have been swept to brighten them for tourists, thus erasing evidence of relative chronology).

Lack of a single explanation should not contribute to maintaining the illogical 'mystery' of the Lines. One source of their popular enigma has been
64 their enormous scale: the hummingbird is six times longer and five times wider than a jumbo jet, while one line goes perfectly straight for 13 miles (20 km). These dimensions are difficult to grasp conceptually and are equally elusive visually; they are simply too large to be perceived by humans on the ground. The Nasca sense that a human audience is not necessarily the only or primary one comes as no surprise, given the values of Andean art as a whole. Their immensity was scaled to that of the earth itself and implies a celestial supernatural audience. The fact that we enjoy their full beauty from low-flying aircraft does not mean that the ancients were incapable of making them. (This has given rise to the insulting idea that they were created by space aliens. Medieval European cathedrals were erected in the shape of crosses largely invisible to the populace who made and used them, yet no one attributes them to little green men!) Technically the Lines are quite simple to create and it has been proven repeatedly that the Nasca were the ones who did so. Scientific dating of the wooden posts that mark the ends of some, the style of the many potsherds found on the surface, and the
56 almost identical motifs on the ground and in Nasca painted ceramics, demonstrate without a doubt who constructed the Lines.

To reveal the light layer in contrast to the dark overlay of rocks, the Nasca carefully swept an area, leaving a line of displaced rocks along the edge (another outlining tendency). Geometric thinking and surveying techniques allowed them to place poles and sight along them to generate straight lines, create circles with strings tied to those poles, and measure out other units according to the human body (such as the average hand width or forearm length). This can be done without an aerial perspective, to any size desired. The particular climatic conditions of the plains prevent almost any natural destruction of the Lines once made, although modern depredations – such as the Pan-American Highway that now bisects the Pampa de Nazca – are a current threat to this magnificent monument to human effort.

CHAPTER FOUR

Moche Art and Architecture

The Moche culture was first referred to as 'Early Chimú,' as if part of the later North Coast state. It has also been called Mochica for the language spoken in this area at European contact. However, currently Moche, the modern town near the ancient capital, designates the culture, people, and state that held sway over the North Coast for the first 500 years AD. Because 'Moche' has so many referents, the capital will be known here as Cerro Blanco, as it is currently in archaeological circles.

Moche was the first identifiable state of the Andes. With a few gaps, it stretched from the Piura Valley in the north to the Huarmey Valley in the south. From the administrative and religious center of Cerro Blanco, the Moche consolidated many distinct coastal groups, unifying art styles, building methods, beliefs, and rituals and erecting Moche settlements often over earlier ones. A defensive conquest state, constructing forty fortifications in the Santa Valley alone, its bellicosity was probably inspired by the lack of new agricultural land, since it was easier to usurp that of others. Its successful control was based largely on extensive water canalization (one Moche canal reached 70 miles (113 km) in length, an aqueduct 4600 ft (1400 m)). Such engineering feats as well as the enormous adobe pyramids for which the Moche are justifiably known, necessitated a huge outlay of organized corporate labor. Moche subjects erected the largest solid adobe building in *75, 76*
the Americas. They also produced thousands upon thousands of ceramic vessels, through the revolutionary use of press molds. These were exported throughout the state; identical pots have been excavated hundreds of miles apart. Such concerns with scale, warfare, standardization, and control certainly betray a state mentality. Yet Moche art is one of the most expressive and unique of the Andes, with a personalism and dynamism rarely equaled anywhere. Since the late 1980s the Moche have been the focus of some of the most exciting archaeological finds of artistic masterpieces as the gold-filled royal tombs of Sipán are being excavated. The grave offerings allow *79–84*
scholars to identify actual people known from Moche painted depictions.

Shared characteristics abound in the Moche corporate style: the solid molded adobe brick architecture of fortifications, palaces, and pyramids, with platforms, ramps, and gabled buildings; the extended burial in cane or wood caskets filled with finery and accompanied by sacrificial burials; correspondingly bellicose imagery and practices depicted in painted ceramics, massive goldwork items, a few surviving textiles and murals; and a wide variety of natural subjects, myths, and rituals expressed in an energetic, outlined graphic style. Moche products of all kinds were largely mass-produced, presumably to reinforce identification with the state and promote social cohesion.

Certain components of Moche style can be found in previous and con-
current styles. Located near Caballo Muerto and Chavín centers along the
coast, the Moche were aware of the earlier broadly disseminated North
Coast styles. The Moche consciously revived Chavín elements, such as the
88 fanged mouth for priests and deities. Chavín emphasis on incisions, processions, crucial moments (such as those of transformation, as in the tenon
heads), as well as overall visual power and persuasiveness, all figure in the
Moche style. In three-dimensional forms (modeled ceramics and buildings)
and certain types of imagery, Gallinazo predecessors in this area were also
influential. Built directly on top of Gallinazo centers, Moche architecture is
more extensive, its bricks molded slightly differently, but the two remain
markedly similar. The contemporaneous North Highland Recuay likewise
77 overlap with the Moche in certain mural designs. Finally, in late Moche
times the Wari conquerors imposed their style, succeeding in further
formalizing and geometricizing it toward their own ends.

Even taken together, however, these foreign styles could never constitute
the highly recognizable, distinctive Moche aesthetic. It is composed of a
new, transcendent blend of the graphic and the volumetric, greater variety
of imagery than in any other Andean style, an unprecedented and unparal-
leled interest in individuality – to the point of true portraiture – and a high
degree of legibility until the very final phase. The simple, easily readable
color scheme for ceramics is limited to white and red, with only a very occa-
88 sional yellow. (Murals, seen by fewer people, are multicolored.) This color
contrast is used to great graphic advantage, whether to describe a figure
boldly or tell a complex tale accurately. Three-dimensional effects are
equally important, ranging from truly sculptural vessels and sheet metal
objects to massive mountainlike structures. Often two- and three-dimensional imagery is combined on a single vessel, though quite distinctly from
the Nasca approach.

65, 66, 67, 68 Drawings of a now-destroyed mural known as 'The Rebellion of the Artifacts' at the Huaca de la Luna, Cerro Blanco. The imagery includes an animated shield taking a human victim and a club-wielding headdress ornament chasing a warrior. In Moche art nearly everything may be portrayed as actively alive. Early Intermediate Period.

A more complex, enlarged perspective perhaps resulting from incorpo-
rating diverse peoples into a single state, is evident in the vast range of new
subject matter. Especially in clay, the Moche depicted nearly every animal
and many significant plants in the natural landscapes of sea, coast, and highlands. They illustrated great numbers of activities, from royal burial to sha-
86, 91, 93 manic healing, from sea lion hunting to sexual intercourse. They flaunted
the physiognomic idiosyncracies of their leaders and other special people.
89, 95 This pervasive interest in 'the individual' extends even to internal emotional
states, to narrative – as many as four events in one composition – and to the
85, 87 depiction of the moment, such as that of a war victory or a successful hunt.
These details are legibly rendered with precise detail and infused with an
extraordinary animation: limbs cocked at sharp angles, Moche figures
plunge, dart, flee, and collapse with great, almost frantic energy.

In such pronounced personalism and underlying naturalism, Moche art
runs somewhat counter to the Andean tradition. Nonetheless, it does belong
firmly within the Andean aesthetic and worldview. As informative as the
ceramic images are and as tempting as it is to see them as an encyclopedia
of Moche life, they nevertheless feature *ritually* important subjects: a fairly
limited number of ceremonial events, portraits of only specific types of
people, plants with shamanistic uses, animals exclusively hunted by the elite,
and so on. To date none have been found that portray such basic tasks as
agriculture, pot-making, or eating everyday food. Besides, as throughout the
Andes, a warrior may have a fox's head, boats can have legs, and fanged
65–68 people abound. Even weapons and ornaments become alive and attack
people. This is obviously not a purely realistic mentality, despite the fact that
the person's fangs may be incorporated into their facial muscles in a believ-
able way. In addition, the exaggerated animation of people and things,
although extreme, is also central to the Andean worldview that everything
is alive in a dynamic universe. In spite of artistic attention to appearances,
the style thus still betrays a marked interest in essences, especially in accentu-
ating what is inside, physically and spiritually. From eyes that are sculpted as
88, 89 round eyeballs in sockets and bodies bulging inside garments, to emotional
94 states such as tenderness, the internal manifests itself externally. Such artistic sophistication is easy to appreciate as it more closely corresponds to our
own concerns; however, its intentions are to show the symbolic and invisible just as in any other Andean style, only via representationalism. Even a
specific moment of suspense, terror, or violence is frozen, formalized in
keeping with the importance of the subject. The Moche style is not simply
naturalistic but represents selective naturalism at its height, with decidedly

69 One side of a Moche vessel showing a stepped wave with sacrificial victims on the wave crest and lowest step. On either side of the vessel stands an officiant, here a lizard-headed man and on the other side a wrinkle-faced man. This composition sums up complementarities such as mountain-ocean and priest-victim. Early Intermediate Period.

more attention given to faces than bodies, for example. It is this striking interplay of moment and essence that gives Moche art its enduring power.

Stylistic duality is also reflected in subject matter, especially on the more abstract level occasionally featured. Living on a barren desert, in simultaneous view of the fierce and fertile sea as well as the dangerous and life-giving mountains, the Moche people internalized a particularly Andean interest in complementary opposites and mediating rituals. Contrasts range from red and white on a vessel or gold and silver in the same ornament to the constant juxtaposition of victor and victim or the equation of wave and mountain, seashell and land snail. Through art the state's diverse subjects comprehend the new ritual requirements and values such as aggression, sacrifice, religious observance, offering, and the perceived differences between social classes. One can even find propaganda in the agitation and restlessness

69

of the style; it exhorts action in a very commanding, 'verbal' way. The art's degree of standardization displays and promotes similarity, to the point of identical pots in farflung valleys, yet also celebrates the individual, or at least the individual role. Creativity of the artist was also a strong component of this state style, and remains so in later Andean imperial aesthetics. Personalism balanced with corporate effort seemingly gave the Moche state a flexible, appealing humanity perhaps responsible for some of its longevity and success.

PRECURSORS AND CONTEMPORARIES OF MOCHE

The major precursors to the Moche style in the last two centuries BC were
70 Salinar and Gallinazo, relatively unknown due to scanty archaeological attention and in some cases the direct overlay of the Moche. Of these, the later Gallinazo is the more direct antecedent, establishing such patterns as building on hills using mold-made adobe bricks (although theirs had impressions of the cane form while those of the Moche were smooth). Like all North Coast ceramics, fully sculptural animal and human images are predominant; however, like many non-Moche styles of the north, negative painting was favored for the surfaces (resin painted on the surface reserves the slip color underneath, so a light on dark look is typically achieved). The extent of Gallinazo social organization may have been great: an estimated 30,000-room complex in the Virú Valley could have been the center of a large-scale confederation perhaps like that of the Nasca.

Two contemporaries deserve mention: Vicús and Recuay, both also producers of sculptural ceramic styles with negative painting. Vicús, seemingly limited to the far north Valley of Piura, produced vigorous, but rather technically crude ceramics featuring humans with hooked noses and slit features and more rounded animal visages. Gold was also worked, perhaps influencing the Moche. Recuay, more widespread and definitely interacting with the Moche, created more technically advanced clay vessel sculptures. Geometric patterning and a less naturalistic but fully three-dimensional treatment of animals, humans, and architecture appear in thin-walled
71 complex spouted jars. The vessel shown here features a man's enlarged head
72 between two grain storehouses. Tapestries with frontal rayed faces bear affinities to the later Wari. Thus, the northern context of the Moche was not entirely limited to their impressive and widespread domain.

70 Salinar-style stirrup-spout vessel of a monkey. Earlier sculptural mastery of complex hollow forms set the stage for Moche achievements in clay. Early Intermediate Period.

71 (*Above*) Recuay ceramic vessel depicting an enlarged head between two storehouses, decorated in typical negative painting. Early Intermediate Period.

72 (*Left*) Recuay tapestry fragment showing characteristic rayed faces. These contemporaries of the Moche strongly influenced the makers of one mural layer at the Huaca de la Luna in Cerro Blanco (ill. 77). Early Intermediate Period.

75, 76 Moche architecture completes a progression in coastal building: early U-shaped structures were oriented toward the mountains, then centers were built in or on the foothills, finally the Moche basically erected their own mountains on the coast. Their primarily pyramidal and often stepped constructions were not only shaped like, but nearly on the scale of, natural formations. Originally the Huaca del Sol, the main temple at Cerro Blanco, stood as tall as 165 ft (50 m). In this grand scale Moche building recalls the contemporaneous Nasca Lines; enormity may be seen as a widespread Early Intermediate Period trait, realized not only by the vision but also the labor of large, diverse groups of people. These giant structures were constructed of millions of adobe bricks, made of molded, smoothed, and sun-dried mud. This traditionally coastal process was only possible on such a scale because the Moche could pool large amounts of water from multi-valley sources and control countless work parties. The building process and the recognized contribution of labor groups are known because of the inscription of
73 makers' marks on the bricks themselves. The adobes were amassed in 'segmented construction' technique: tall sections, about four bricks wide, were mortared internally but not joined with adjacent sections. A cross-section of the Huaca del Sol can be likened to a loaf of sliced bread. More than 100 different geometric symbols, each found within a particular area, indicate a

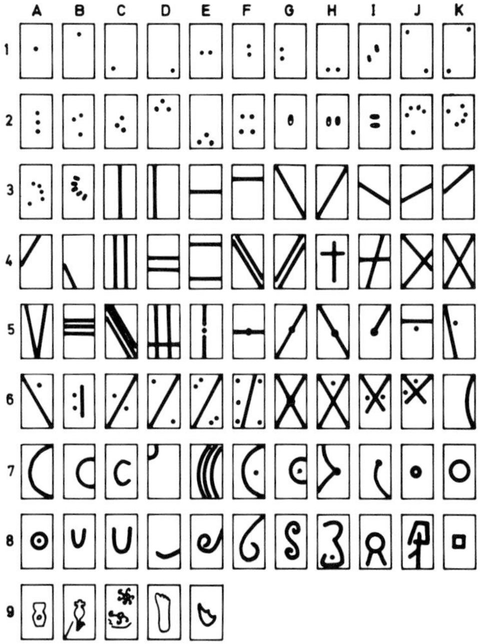

73 Diagram of the various makers' marks incised on the adobe bricks in particular sections of the Moche Huaca del Sol, the main pyramid at Cerro Blanco. These identifying patterns prove that work units documented Moche subjects' contributions to the staggering 100,000,000 bricks laid in this mountain-like structure. Early Intermediate Period.

74 Moche ceramic vessel depicting a tiered platform with a staircase topped by an elite structure. An important figure is shown seated in a typical many-gabled building with war clubs along the rooflines and pierced walls for ventilation. Unfortunately actual buildings, made of adobe and other perishable materials, do not survive. Early Intermediate Period.

particular labor assignment. By this additive approach an astounding 100,000,000 bricks were accumulated for the most important structure in the realm, billions for Moche architecture as a whole. These marks are true signatures, like those of European printmakers except that they represent a low-skilled group identity rather than that of a highly skilled single artist. They clearly express how pervasive Moche personalism was nevertheless dedicated to state interests.

Because of the profligate use of water they entailed, adobes were reserved for elite Moche architecture. Not only giant pyramids, but small structures, complex palaces, and fortifications were constructed of mud in high-status Moche centers in nearly every North Coast valley. The stepped-pyramid form featured multiple levels, with segments of varying heights and sizes, not necessarily symmetrical in layout. The different slant-sided platforms were connected by long sloping ramps and topped by small structures themselves with angled rooflines. According to the clay depictions of architecture, elites sat atop tall, terraced pyramids (as indicated by sometimes inset *74* red and white bands and connecting steps) under gabled roofs. Typically open on three sides with a solid and/or decorated back wall, these buildings had a single- and/or double-pitch roof, held up by wooden columns (another prestige item in the desert). To draw attention upward, rows of stylized warclubs created roofcombs, or the gables overlapped. In the absence of precipitation and cold, high-status buildings seemingly provided shade, windbreak, and focus on the elite inside. These structures have not survived the ravages of time and the desert; periodic El Niño flooding, sand deluges, and relentless winds have taken their toll over the centuries.

Palaces, such as the Huaca de la Luna at Cerro Blanco, also had several platform levels, ramps, and likely the same sorts of roofs, but had lower,
77 walled series of rooms. Probably most were decorated with murals, of which a handful remain, and adobe patterned friezes are depicted, such as at Huaca del Brujo in the Chicama Valley. Traces of color on many buildings' exteriors imply most were highly decorated and supremely visible in the monochromatic landscape. Cities had large walled areas that suggest large controlled gatherings, even the amassing of prisoners. Surrounding Cerro Blanco were standard-sized fields dotted with platforms for the supervision of coercive or tribute-type farming. Concentric, high-walled fortifications guarded crucial water sources, passes, and other strategic points.

The architectural record shows that the Moche state offered religious intervention, administration, defense, and the concerted control of water and land. Through massive projects and walled exclusivity it created impressive and highly salient symbols of subject loyalty and elite prerogative. Again, one must not forget pageantry in reconstructing the look of the Moche constructed world. The royal burials at Sipán tell us that the elaborate scenes depicted on small-scale art really happened: prisoners were paraded, arraigned, and sacrificed, leaders interred with unbelievable finery, and other lavish rituals took place on and in these colorful structures. Here Cerro Blanco, Pañamarca, and Sipán will exemplify Moche architecture, adornment, and burial practices.

Cerro Blanco, the capital city, only partially survives. All but destroyed by a series of natural disasters *c.* AD 600, it suffered depredations 1000 years later by the Spanish, who mined the Huaca del Sol for its gold offerings by diverting the Moche River. Colonial and modern looting continue. Thus,

75 The great Moche pyramid known as the Huaca del Sol ('Pyramid of the Sun') at Cerro Blanco. Before the Spanish diverted the river in their attempt to find hidden gold, this truly monumental structure stood over 135 ft (41 m) tall. Ritual use and royal residence, as well as burial, were its evident functions in the Moche capital. Early Intermediate Period.

76 Reconstructed cross-shaped plan and four-leveled elevation of the Huaca del Sol, Cerro Blanco. Early Intermediate Period.

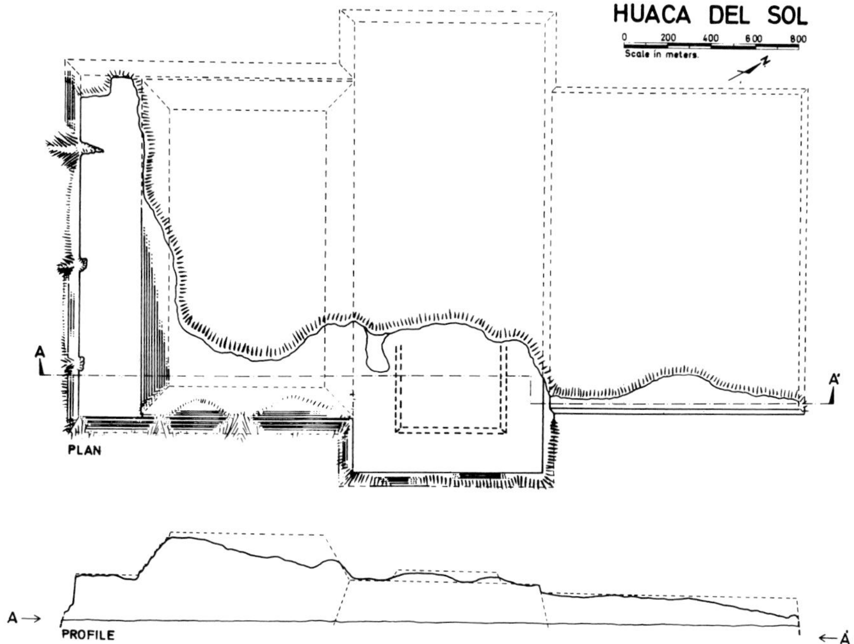
HUACA DEL SOL
0
200
400
600
800
Scale in meters.
N
A
A'
PLAN
A →
PROFILE
← A'

the once-great city is reduced to two hulking mud-brick ruins, even now impressive in their fragmentary state. The city held an advantageous location: on the river, near the sea and mountains, and along both north–south and east–west routes. The hill which gives it its name was held sacred, as offerings on its summit from this period and later evince.

75, 76 The Huaca del Sol ('Pyramid of the Sun,' the traditional name but not necessarily accurate) still stands 135 ft (41 m) high, and 525 by 1115 ft (160 by 340 m) at its base, although it is less than half of its former span. It was built in eight construction phases over a long period of time, ultimately rising to four levels: from right to left, a long low platform probably with a ramp to the uppermost level; a taller, wide platform giving a cruciform shape to the whole; the tallest small platform (heavily looted hence probably with the most burials and structures); and finally a lower, smaller level. Traces of red on the façade, remnants of elaborate burials, and considerable refuse suggest this pyramid served as a supremely important center of state life. Both religious, probably with a main temple on top, and political, most likely with the royal residence and tombs, it was rebuilt and enlarged by different rulers as the theocracy evolved. Originally there were elite buildings all around it, but these lie under the sands if traces indeed remain. Visually its power to command, to dwarf the commoner while elevating the noble, was unambiguous.

As a counterpoint to the Sol, the Huaca de la Luna ('Temple of the Moon') was built on the side of Cerro Blanco itself. This considerably smaller and lower palace-type structure was walled all around. Inside were three interconnected platforms, like the Sol not arrayed symmetrically. In the absence of any refuse whatsoever, archaeologists conclude this functioned solely as a temple. It originally had many interior murals in multiple colors with incised outlines on white ground. Several layers of murals exist, as if changes in the religion were marked here, but its role as highest temple endured. Two murals are of particular interest. One – unfortunately now
65–68 known only from rather inadequate and contradictory copies – was located in a throne room and showed people being conquered by animated implements, a shield, helmet, and war club. This same mythical scene is found on ceramic vessels as well. To have been featured in the main temple program it must have held great significance, although its interpretation remains somewhat tentative. Suggestions range from a creation myth in which a doomed race of people are attacked by their own weapons (by analogy with sixteenth-century accounts from both Peru and Mexico) to a more general propagandistic message that all things defend the Moche state. The imple-

77 Detail of one of the murals at Huaca de la Luna, the palace buildings at the Moche capital of Cerro Blanco. These faces with serrated emanations are closely allied with Recuay textile imagery (ill. 72). Early Intermediate Period.

ments' spry mastery may stand for that of the Moche over their enemies. War and religion were certainly unified realms. If nothing else, these images show that the Moche personalized wrought objects as much as other aspects of their culture.

The other mural, around a high platform, was repainted probably four times in various checkerboard compositions. Its earliest incarnation of small squares with staffbearing figures is very Wari-like, suggesting that this mural was quite late in the Moche trajectory. A second repainting is clearly Recuay, and the fourth again features staffbearers, this time in a more curvilinear version. These static, repetitive symbols suggest that the state religion's relationship to foreign imagery was perhaps seeking to incorporate, rather than be seen as yielding to, other systems. Rather like the two substyles of Paracas embroidery, Moche murals seem to feature both abstract concepts and lively ritual-mythological themes. *77*

One of the most repeated, and now substantiated, rituals was the Sacrificial Scene (previously called the Presentation Scene). This formed the subject of Mural E at the southern Moche center of Pañamarca and many painted ceramics. In the mural, now completely lost, a truncated version of this ceremony was shown. The large figure to the left is a Priestess, wearing a distinctive headdress and feathered tunic. The smaller celebrants bring her goblets, seen amassed in a large bowl to the right, while she may in turn be offering her goblet to someone else. We know from elsewhere that the *78*

goblets contain the sacrificial victims' blood (they are to the left of the bowl), and that a male high priest is likely the intended final recipient of the offering. A warrior procession along another wall fills in the gap as to how
92 the victims were obtained. In the full recounting on clay, the bound victims are being drained below, near their captured weapon bundles and a litter that brought the most important figure, the Warrior Priest. The Bird Priest to the right and this same Priestess serve him, while his faithful dog and other warriors are in attendance. Every element is meaningful: the paisley-shaped item behind the Priestess is an *illuchu* fruit, a known anticoagulant almost certainly consumed by the victims to ensure blood flow.

Recent excavations in the Moche realm have now identified the graves of the three most significant figures: the Priestess buried at Huaca de la Cruz has the diagnostic headdress and clay goblets with her and both the Warrior Priest and the Bird Priest are interred at Sipán. Like Karwa in relation to Chavín de Huantar, Pañamarca and Huaca de la Cruz may have been 'daughter' or 'wife' and Sipán 'brother' or 'uncle' subsidiary religious centers in relation to Cerro Blanco.

The breathtaking graves at Sipán give us a wealth of information and reveal new heights of Moche metalwork, a crowning Andean aesthetic achievement. Sipán includes three typically Moche adobe pyramids, the smallest one replete with lavish tombs still being discovered. Tombs 1 (the Warrior Priest), 2 (the Bird Priest) and 3 (the Old Lord) contain large wooden plank coffins, surrounded by dedicatory burials of warriors, women, and llamas, and containing layer upon layer of unbelievable finery inside. Elites commissioned great quantities of precious gold, silver, turquoise, imported shells, textiles, and vessels. Artists must have been constantly occupied, stimulated to greater and greater heights of technological and artistic innovation to satisfy their royal patrons. Not only the main celebrants of the Sacrificial Scene but large numbers of sacrificees and even the spotted dog have been located at Sipán. These finds prove that the events portrayed in the art actually took place, validating the historically-specific realism of the style.

The tomb of the Warrior Priest is the most lavish of all. Top to bottom, the offerings include: copper-appliquéd figural banners, numerous shell bead semi-circular pectorals, a stunning necklace of huge gold and silver
82–84 peanuts, three sets of spectacular earspools, a gold scepter (shown tied to the litter in painted Sacrificial Scenes), a massive gold crescent backpiece (also
79 prominent in depictions), 'Decapitator' theme bells and oversized knives, and imported spondylus shells. The peanut necklace is one of the many half-

78 Drawing of Pañamarca Mural E, showing a portion of the Sacrificial Scene featuring the Priestess (left), attendants and victims (center), and bowl of goblets (lower right, center) for blood offerings presumably to the Warrior Priest (not preserved, far left). The grave of an actual Priestess with her characteristic ornaments has been found at Huaca de la Cruz.

gold, half-silver ornaments found in the tombs, expressing duality in yet another form. The two strands of beads, each double strung, were held in position by spacer bars so that the peanuts would not overlap or twist (indicating that doubling and clarity were valued). They are sheet metal beaten into fully three-dimensional hollow forms, the largest peanut being 3.5 inches (9 cm) long. Peanuts may seem an unlikely subject for such an important personage to flaunt, but scientists have determined that around this point, *c.* AD 300, a new type of peanut was domesticated. The premium on protein sources in a marginal environment made such a foodstuff politically valent, its representation symbolizing a leader's power over natural fertility and people.

Triplication of gold and turquoise earspools, like the multiple layering of other objects, reiterates the Warrior Priest's supreme status. The three pairs are truly some of the most beautiful of all Moche art. They feature cut-out *83, 84*

deer, solid mosaic ducks, and projecting warriors with attendant warriors, measuring 3.3–3.7 inches (8.4–9.4 cm) across. The turquoise deer have the eyes, antlers, bellies, hooves, genitals, and tails picked out in gold. With the background cut out, they seem to be bounding in space, just as figures run lightly over the ground in paintings. The ducks are outlined in gold, the turquoise shades carefully contrasted so the ducks are darker than the background. The characteristic gold spheres around the edge are repeated around the center to create a unified composition. The warriors are diminutive masterpieces, with movable warclubs and removable noserings. Attention to detail is such that the owl-headed necklace beads are double strung with minute gold wire. Off his belt, the central warrior wears the same semi-spherical bells as the Warrior Priest himself, which in the large versions
79 feature the 'Decapitator,' a figure holding a trophy head in one hand and a knife in the other. Huge gold and silver knife-shaped backflaps also have this same intimidating image, reminding all that the Warrior Priest drinks sacrificial blood. Finally, the gold scepter with silver handle has a hollow upper chamber like an inverted pyramid, all sides displaying a low-relief scene of a warrior thrusting his warclub at a restrained prisoner. The elaborate garb suggests this is the Warrior Priest, again reinforcing his domination. Cast weaponry decorates the handle as well. Thus, threatening power exudes from his every accoutrement.

79 (*Left*) Gold bell depicting the 'Decapitator,' with a knife in one hand and a trophy head in the other, from Tomb 1 at Sipán. The Warrior Priest was buried with several sumptuous ornaments showing this gruesome image, proclaiming him to be a formidable warrior. Early Intermediate Period.

80 (*Right*) A gold spider bead, one of ten, from the earlier Tomb 3 at Sipán. A human face on the back of a spider, itself clinging to a web over a bowl-like backing, creates a particularly complex object, both technically and artistically. Early Intermediate Period.

81 (*Below*) Gilded copper necklace of the Bird Priest (Tomb 2) at Sipán. The inner strand of characteristically double-strung beads has upturned mouths, the outer strand, downturned mouths, suggesting complementary emotional states (although both can be seen as variants of ferocious grimaces). Early Intermediate Period.

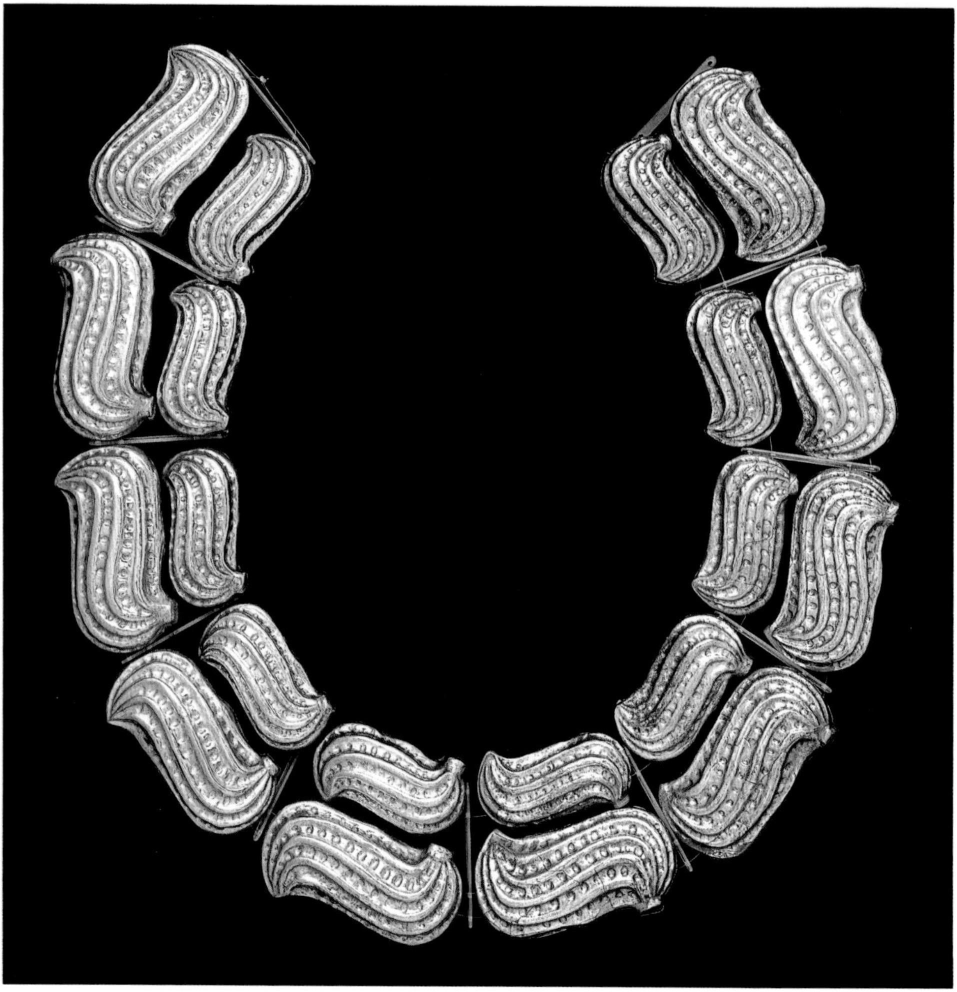

82 (*Above*) The gold and silver peanut necklace from Tomb 1 (the Warrior Priest) at Sipán. The largest hollow bead is nearly 4 inches (9 cm) long. One side of silver, the other of gold is a typical Moche arrangement, bespeaking a great concern with complementarity and dualism. Early Intermediate Period.

83, 84 (*Opposite*) Two of the three gold and turquoise earspools of the Warrior Priest (Tomb 1) at Sipán. (*Above*) A warrior figure with flanking attendants. He sports a removable war club and a minute owl head necklace. (*Below*) A running deer with golden antlers in cutout. These intricate earspools demonstrate consummate Moche metal artistry in three-dimensional, planar, and negative space. Early Intermediate Period.

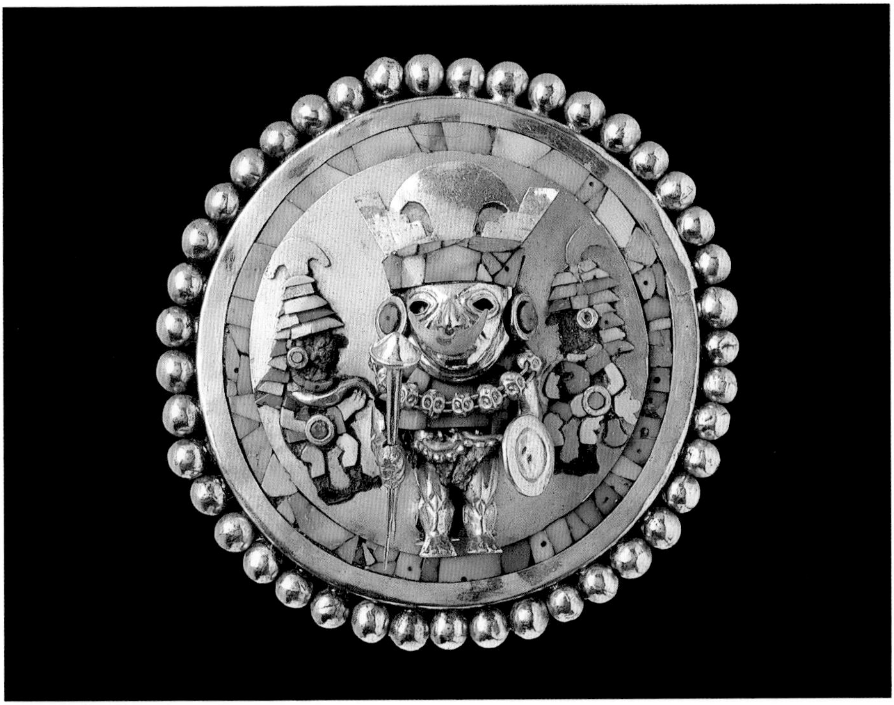

One notch down the hierarchy is the Bird Priest interred in Tomb 2. His only somewhat lesser finery included an extraordinary gilded copper owl headdress almost 24 inches (60 cm) across. Off the frontal bird's body arched a treelike structure from which metal bangles and long feathers hung in three tiers. Imagine the glittering and tinkling of this assemblage on the Bird Priest's head in the sacrificial ritual! Several of his ornaments – a backflap and a nosering – were joined half-silver and half-gold, more economical than the Warrior Priest's separate gold and silver ornaments. A final crown-
81 ing example of complementarity is a two-stranded, human-headed bead necklace, one set with upturned and one with downturned mouths. Although both look rather fierce, they may represent smiling and frowning visages; in any case they are uniquely oppositional and may represent emotional polarities, as part of the Moche internal perspective.

From Tomb 3, earlier in date by perhaps 200 years, the most spectacular
80 object is a necklace of ten gold spider beads. These elaborate assemblages combine beaten gold sheet for the dish-like back and spider body with a human face and soldered wires for legs and web. These beads show the ingenuity, virtuosity, and technological sophistication of Moche metalwork, even at its earliest phases. Primarily built up, in an architectonic manner, Moche metallurgists achieved full three-dimensionality from flat parts. They could cast, solder, alloy, bind separate metals into single objects, and gild, encompassing nearly every technical possibility. One of the most important and revealing Moche discoveries was a gilding process, reconstructed by Heather Lechtman from objects from the northern site of Loma Negra. Rather than the application of gold to the exterior, the Moche developed depletion gilding in which the piece essentially gilds itself from within. By bathing the finished alloy object in naturally-occurring acids, the outermost layer of non-gold metals, particularly copper, is depleted, leaving only a very thin layer of pure gold visible. Lechtman coined the phrase 'the technology of essence' to describe this pervasive approach to materials in which what is inside is revealed outside. Hidden gold on the inside is not wasted but rather crucial to the piece, for it to be 'truthful' (gold on the outside stands for gold on the inside). The overarching Andean value placed on essence is encapsulated here.

MOCHE CERAMICS

Nearly every type of object found in the grave offerings is depicted in paintings on Moche ceramics, plus a wealth of other clues to their art and world-

85 (*Right*) Early Moche battle scene with victor grasping the loser by the hair, the universal ancient American symbol of dominance. Notice the chevron-patterned scarf tied around the neck of the vessel, as depicted in ill. 91, to anthropomorphic effect. Early Intermediate Period.

86 (*Below*) Moche vessel of an owl-headed woman shaman (see ill. 93) in the process of curing a patient (right top) with her herbs, drugs, and ritual implements all around her. Modern shamans can identify nearly all the tools of the trade, which are still in use today. Early Intermediate Period.

87 (*Below, right*) Moche stirrup-spout vessel with the scene of a hunter in a tree shooting a bird with a blowgun. Ceramic artists defied the technical problems associated with unsupported solid portions to capture the dramatic moment before the kill. Early Intermediate Period.

view. Tens of thousands of such ceramics exist and scholars have barely made a dent in this amazingly varied corpus. Artists employed two-piece press mold technology so that more vessels were produced than ever before. Replication, the creation of exact copies, fits with state goals to disseminate a message widely and consistently. In fact, images painted on ceramics show clay bottles and bowls being transported on boats, the preferred long-distance mode of transportation. The Moche left offerings as far south as the Chincha Islands which they reached by reed boat in order to garner the bird
91 *guano* used for agricultural fertilizer. Another way in which the Moche were unusual within the Andean tradition is that their style was disseminated via clay rather than textiles; however, since textiles rarely survive the saltpeter-rich North Coast sands, the exact extent of Moche fiber arts remains unclear. Certainly the complicated stories told on some Moche ceramics would not translate well into weaving. Equally important, the Moche unquestionably spent a great deal – perhaps the majority – of their artistic time on ceramics, given the extraordinary number of compositions generated. And most are by no means exact repeats, despite the use of molds: even utilizing a mold, a handbuilt original model must first be crafted from which the mold can be taken, and all appliquéd, modeled, and painted decoration must be done freehand. Thus, the rigid standardization that could result from molding was avoided, technical excellence was routinely achieved, and artistic license is quite prominent. Through close visual analysis of painted pieces individual artists' hands have even been detected.

Vessel types are as varied as artists' hands and subject matter. While the traditional stirrup-spout bottle remains the most common form, particularly for elite use, the Moche also made spout-and-handle vessels, double-chambered whistling vessels, flaring bowls, dippers, and long-necked jars. A few other forms are illustrated but have not yet been located archaeologically. Diversity seems to have been of importance to the Moche, no doubt stimulated by complex ritual needs.

The characteristic stirrup-spout vessel was a technical challenge to create, with its closed body and complex spouts. Given this, its practical and symbolic advantages must have been important to the Moche. It was especially well adapted to the dry environment because the small top opening allowed only minimal evaporation of liquid, probably the high-status corn beer. The stirrup-spout pours smoothly because air enters one spout as liquid passes from the other. The spout is ergonomic for carrying and easy to suspend

88 Moche ceramic vessels with the typical red, white, and occasionally cream slip painting. Top left: an anthropomorphized peanut playing a flute. Top right: a goblet with rattling base and Chavín revival fanged head. Lower left: a barn owl with a snake in its talons and a conch shell trumpet on its back. Lower right: a survivor of the disfiguring parasitic disease leishmaniasis. Early Intermediate Period.

from a belt or rope. Beyond such concerns, since these were not primarily practical items, it was doubtless crucial to announce membership in the North Coast visual tradition. Similarity of the vessels to the previously hegemonic Chavín style helped to proclaim that Chavín was the ancestral culture, and perhaps even sanctified Moche state religion. (Yet artistic revival always introduces a strong element of change: the Moche spout tends to be oriented front to back in relation to the main image whereas the Chavín was typically placed side to side. Kubler points out that the Moche arrangement creates a more urgent need for the viewer to turn the vessel. Even this choice can be seen as part of the general exhortation to action, the 'verbal' Moche approach, with the premium placed on restless movement.) The underlying duality of the two spouts probably had symbolic significance as well.

All types of Moche ceramics have added decoration, either in the form
87 of three-dimensional appliquéd or fully modeled elements, two-dimen-
91, 86 sional painted patterns, or both. Moche sculptors were often boldly virtuosic in their modeled additions, casually defying the risks of solid suspended clay parts drying, shrinking, and breaking off. They were equally talented at painting terracotta red and creamy white slip accurately, and burnishing surfaces to a satiny sheen. The occasional blackware is found, but the vast majority were fired in an oxidizing atmosphere with few mistakes; grey splotchy fire clouds are rare. In many cases, although it has abraded off most, after firing an organic black pigment was scorched on to emphasize details,
88 such as a barn owl's radiating eye feathers. On occasion ceramics were even inlaid, as in metalwork. Thus, a great number of steps and skills were involved in each of the thousands of pieces produced.

Moche ceramics did not remain static for 500 years. Both modeled and painted fineline types existed from the earliest phases. The fineline tradition began with geometric patterns painted in broad brushstrokes, then featured
85 filled-in silhouette figures, very like Greek Black Figure vase painting (except in red). Simple scenes preceded complex ones, for instance, a battle conveyed through two pairs of struggling figures rather than a multitude. The silhouettes were nevertheless full of energy, utilizing the dynamic asymmetry of profile figures, legs in leaping position, arms akimbo. Some overlap of parts in space was allowed, if the clarity of the action was not compromised. Again like the Greek trajectory, Moche artists, desiring more detail, added thin lines in white slip over the red figures and/or incised through the red layer to the white background below. *Pentimenti* (evident changes of mind by the artist from sketch to final image, called 'ghostlining' by Christopher Donnan) reveal

the creative process of fineline painting. Apparently many vessels were incised lightly with the plan for the overall composition, difficult to envision on such round surfaces, then the painted lines followed (or sometimes the design was adjusted, since preliminary and final versions do not always coincide). Sketch lines were burnished out in most cases.

As mastery grew and painted compositions became more complex, such preplanning must have been increasingly necessary. Thinner and more precise linear outlining replaced silhouettes and only a few elements were filled-in, such as clothing and ornamentation. This artistic trend may correlate with the increasing complexity of the state and its rituals (as the contrast between the Old Lord and later Sipán burials attests). With the increasing elaboration, painted scenes approached illegibility. Although earlier fineline unfilled outlines had been transparent, numerous small figures had kept their integrity as figure against ground. However, over time the addition of filler elements (smaller figures, plants, animals, even dots), *93*
crowding of figures, description of background, inclusion of several different scenes, and exploration of minute detail gradually made late Moche finelines almost impossible to decode. Perhaps the visual pace quickens in a larger and more complex state. This type of late 'baroque' phase does nevertheless form part of an artistic cycle the world over. Once an iconographic code is totally understood, artists take more liberties with it. In addition, illegibility can be exploited by a political hierarchy for its exclusivity; an esoteric or mysterious image may be read only by the privileged few.

Of the many classes of imagery, we can touch on only some here: Chavín revival, mythohistorical scenes, figures, portraits, certain animals, sex, death, and art production.

Many ceramic objects had ritual uses, the goblet in the illustration here *88*
being at once a drinking vessel and a rattle (clay balls reverberate in its hollow stem). When one drank from its frankly Chavín-revival fanged head with a jaguar headdress, the rumbling feline sounds would be activated, another way in which the internal configuration of the object manifests the subject's essence. Like most Moche ceramics, this piece was boldly painted and modeled to be comprehended from some distance. Goblets feature prominently in depicted ceremonies such as the Sacrificial Scene and are found in graves such as that of the Priestess.

A well-known Moche stirrup-spout depicts an owl-headed shaman *86*
identified as female by her shawl, kneeling amongst her curing paraphernalia with a patient to her left. Her owl attributes express her transformation during trance; like the nocturnal hunting owl, she hunts out malevolent

89 (*Left*) Moche ceramic portrait head vessel of an important man wearing a regal expression. When compared with ill. 95, it becomes obvious that the idiosyncratic physiognomies of distinctive individuals were recorded. Early Intermediate Period.

90 (*Above*) Moche ceramic stirrup-spout vessel (now missing its upright spout) depicting a scene of a woman giving birth, assisted by a midwife, a moment rarely illustrated in ancient American art. Early Intermediate Period.

91 Rollout drawing of the painted scene on a Moche fineline vessel depicting the violent clubbing of sea lions near a *guano* island. A gabled structure and ceramic offerings illustrate the actual Moche presence in the South Coast islands, which were important sources of agricultural fertilizer. Early Intermediate Period.

spirits during night curing rituals. The tools of her trade, some modeled and some painted, are nearly all familiar to modern shamans. These include strings of mind-altering espingo seeds, perhaps a section of hallucinogenic San Pedro cactus in her left hand, and a sacrificial llama. The patient sports crossed fangs, so again this is not an 'ordinary' daily life depiction.

Seemingly more quotidian, some scenes nevertheless relate exclusively to
87 elite activity, especially hunting. In an ingenious artistic solution to the stirrup-spout bottle format, a hunter pursues a bird with a blowgun. He is modeled precariously on the side of the vessel body, his long blowgun (in the Amazon region actual ones reach 7 to 10 ft (2 to 3 m) in length) connecting him inexorably with his prey. Although technically such a suspended, interconnected structure is very difficult to accomplish, the artist overcame the problems to convey action and suspense. Painted on the rest of the chamber are the delicately waving branches of the tree, adding a graceful, energized surface to the frozen movement of the scene. Other probably ritualized hunts undertaken by well-dressed elites involve high prestige land and sea animals, the deer and the sea lion. In one hunt scene, the patently exhausted male deer, his tongue lolling, dies from the spear wound in his neck. Elements include a modeled deer in a net – in another deerhunt composition the net is drawn encircling the pot as it did the deer themselves – the helpful dogs, other dead deer and their attackers, and the main hunter, larger than the rest to reinforce hierarchy. The command over the painted line to record salient details of a dramatic moment makes this
91 one of the many outstanding Moche compositions. Another is a sea lion hunt taking place in the waves around the mountain-like South Coastal

guano islands (which are shown with a slant-roofed building and ceramic offerings, just as have actually been found, as propitiation to the source of fertilizer that formed the basis of successful coastal agriculture, and hence the Moche state itself). A specific landscape forms the context as hunters club the animals whose varied poses convey the chaotic violence of the hunt. The top volumetric figures emerging from the melee restate confrontation in elementary pairs.

Moche artists also conveyed events and ideas on an abstract level. One *69*
formally and symbolically masterful vessel combines a stylized wave with a terraced, mountain-like form and features four figures: two officiating on the sides and one each as a sacrificial offering on the crest of the wave and the lowest tier of the mountain. Similar naked, prone victims with loose hair (a sign of subjugation, as victory in war involves grasping enemy hair) are also found in mountain sacrifice rituals, perhaps carried out to ensure water flow. The officials are a lizard-headed figure and a wrinkled character that are known important ritual actors in other scenarios, especially the Burial
Scene (see below). By inextricable pairings (wave and mountain, two *93*
victims and officiants), the analogy is made between life-giving sea and mountains, both believed to need reciprocal donation of human life force. Duality, complementarity, reciprocity, cyclicality are all summed up in this creative composition.

Victims such as these were obtained in battles, according to abundant Moche depictions of struggles and their aftermaths. Combat – personalized hand to hand fighting – is usually arrested at the most dramatic moment of
victory. The aggressive Moche fought the sea and the land for food, and each *85*

92 Rollout drawing of the Moche fineline Sacrificial Scene in which prisoners of war are bled (lower register, right) for blood presentation to the Warrior Priest (upper register, left) by the Bird Priest (upper register, left center) with the Priestess (upper register, right center) in attendance. These three priests' graves have been located, two at Sipán (see ills. 79–84) and one at Huaca de la Cruz. Early Intermediate Period.

other for resources and power. Heroes vanquishing sea monsters allay the fears of nighttime sea fishing people, while warriors dressed as beans may signify battles with or over the food-producing land, or even harvest portrayed as conquest. The entirely animated world appears potentially dangerous as well.

92 The literally blood-thirsty events following battle, such as the Sacrificial Scene, have been discussed; however, its artistic aspects deserve comment. Narrative has been reduced to key players, signal actions, and descriptive accoutrements. Before and after, low and high status, near and far are suggested in the use of the two registers and differential scale. It is also crucial to keep in mind that these stories are being fitted onto the small, curving surface of a bottle, quite an artistic feat in itself. A complex, multipartite composition like the Burial Scene further underscores this achievement. Three or four discrete events are portrayed on each of a series of late fineline bottles. The different related scenes are separated by double lines; however, the order of the events is unclear. Two large, elaborately dressed
93 figures are instrumental in nearly all the scenes on the various Burial Scene pots: 'Lizard' and 'Wrinkle Face' from the wave/mountain vessel. One interpretation could organize the events as follows. Scene one (lower left) is a ritual of conch shell presentation conducted on a pyramid, perhaps after the death of the person, as conchs are found in the most ornate tombs. In scene two (upper left) a denuded woman is sacrificed and staked on the ground

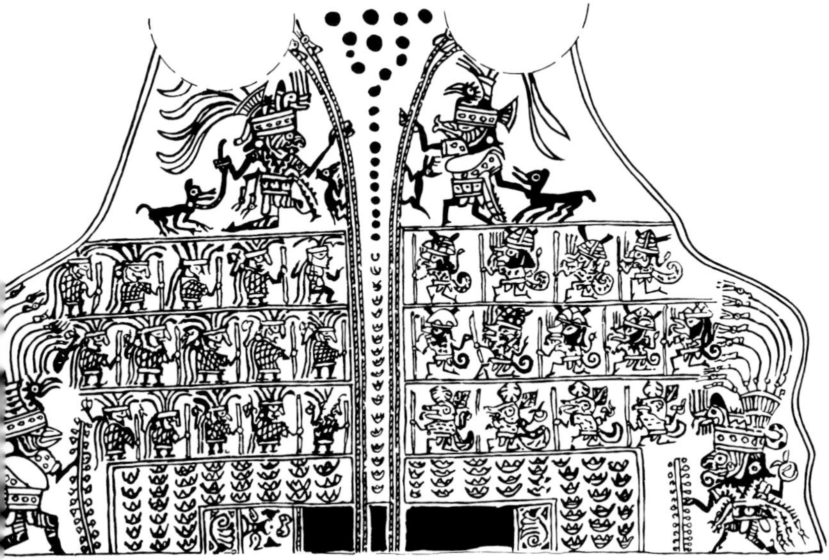

93 Rollout drawing of a late Moche fineline vessel with elaborate Burial Theme scenes. Upper register, left: the punishment of a female shaman by staking (she was perhaps held responsible for the death). Lower register, left: a ritual involving conch shell presentation (perhaps before the burial). Right: the lowering of the casket by 'Lizard' and 'Wrinkle Face' (see ill. 69) in the midst of rows of warriors (perhaps at the funeral). Early Intermediate Period.

for birds to peck. Donnan and McClelland have drawn attention to later ethnohistorical accounts of this punishment if a leader died as a result of the shaman's ignorance. Recall the female shaman in the owl pot discussed *86*
earlier. This gruesome scapegoating could take place before, during, or after the other two scenes. Scene three involves the assembly of many distinct people, perhaps at the funeral, their rows bracketed by large 'Wrinkle Face' and 'Lizard.' One side of mourners are animal warriors (notice the deer antlers in the lower right register), while the others wear net shirts (seen repeatedly, usually in boats, thus perhaps fishermen). This may be a complementary gathering of 'Lizard's' land and 'Wrinkle Face's' sea people, to show how everyone came to pay homage to the fallen leader. In scene four (above and in the center of scene three) 'Wrinkle Face' and 'Lizard' lower the casket down into the ground with long, snake-headed ropes while grasping the sacrificial animals. In and around the casket the burial mask and offerings are like those found at Sipán. This elaborate tale may be a specific historical event serving as an oft-repeated cautionary tale, since it appears on at least nine vessels. Such intricate narration describes the kind of pomp and cir-

cumstance, as well as ritualized deaths, that accompanied the incredible finery at Sipán. Even without documents Moche history can be partially reconstructed because of the specificity of their art.

Individual figures are equally prevalent in Moche ceramic art, showing true sculptural mastery and underscoring the personalistic approach of the culture. These run the gamut from leaders to composites, animals to skeletons. Yet, like the rest of Moche art, subjects do not seem to have been chosen casually to illustrate daily life.

The Moche portrait head vessels are unique within the Andean art styles
89, 95 and paralleled in the ancient Americas only by a handful of Maya works. The physiognomic characterization of features and even personality simply are not the overwhelming priority in images of important people; usually role, status, and generic qualities such as keen sightedness prevail. These certainly factor in the Moche portraits, all of mature, elite males, but nevertheless their specificity cannot be denied. Probably they immortalize local leaders at the peak of responsibility; so many individuals were portrayed as to suggest they are not all rulers. One might have been placed in a commoner's grave to indicate his/her undying loyalty and service to the chieftain. All the portraits show the subject looking slightly upwards, perhaps to embody higher purpose, spirituality, and leadership abilities. Each wears distinctive large earspools and a decorated headdress. Expressions range from formal and regal to mirthful, while facial features range from aquiline to decidedly corpulent (a desirable trait in pre-industrial societies only possible for the most successful elites). The different set of the eyes, areas of wrinkles, flare of the nostrils, play of musculature, and deposition of fat are quite distinct one from another, especially the more examples one sees. Engaging and individualistic, these are comparable in their convincing naturalism to portrait traditions anywhere in the world.

People were depicted who were otherwise special, in particular victims
88 of normally fatal diseases such as leishmaniasis, a parasitic condition. Their ravaged faces and missing lips, noses and eyelids are fairly common Moche images. Rather than some fascination with disfigurement, or a purely encyclopedic desire to document all the citizenry, these probably indicate the significance of these people as survivors. To carry the evidence of having defeated death, like victorious warriors, may have lent them almost supernatural powers on a par with shamans. Equally, the evocative image of a
90 woman giving birth may not only seek to portray the most momentous event of a woman's life but may have been the equivalent of warfare for men, as it was to the Aztecs of Mesoamerica. Certainly the internal made

manifest applies to this powerful image. These female and male images, not necessarily of important individuals but of important states of transition and heightened experience, also show the sheer variety of postures, activities, and states successfully explored by the Moche artist.

There are an almost as unique series of Moche figural vessels that concern perhaps the most fundamental transitions of all, combining eerie skeletons and sexual acts in provocative juxtaposition. While skeletons may be shown singly, or as a macabre group of dancers, they are often ithyphallic males with a female consort. The dead are connoted by a skull and prominent ribs, but an otherwise living human body. While they remain somewhat enigmatic, they do suggest the theme of regeneration by conflating graphically procreation, the beginning of life, with its end. Their own bodies are both living and dead, encompassing the entire cycle. The depiction of sexual activity is not limited to death images. Singular within ancient American art, these stirrup-spout vessels depicting explicit acts, and other vessels frankly shaped like genitalia, remain enigmatic. Scholars have put forth hypotheses ranging from birth control propaganda, to ritual acts, to erotica. They do fall within the bounds of the naturalistic, varied Moche approach and seem to stress the important concept of fertility, a constant Andean concern.

The fertility of plants and animals, a prerequisite to human survival, surfaces as another preoccupation. Different foods were conflated with certain human characters: maize, a traditionally important protein source, was anthropomorphized as a fanged being; beans, also high in nutritional value, were made into warriors; potatoes and diseased people were allied; and peanuts apparently could be musicians. These combinations could have *88*
been based on overlapping meanings (such as high prestige), visual similarities (the lumpy eyes of potatoes being like distorted, pocked human bodies), and/or patron relationships (musicians as the ritual benefactors of the peanut). Peanuts, the high-status foodstuff at Sipán, were further immortalized in a clay figure both dressed as and being a peanut. In keeping with Moche 'internalism' the human head is like one nut inside the husk clothing, his body another. In addition to the accurately lobed shape, the artist has captured the characteristic ridges, pointed tip, and yellowish color of a real peanut.

Animals' successful reproduction was also immortalized, as in the tender *94*
scene of a mother llama nurturing her offspring. Camelids as sources of food, fuel, fiber, and the transportation of goods made them central to Andean culture. On the coast they additionally represent access to valued highland resources. Although not native to the coastal regions, camelids

94, 95 (*Above*) Moche stirrup-spout vessel with a mother llama tenderly nuzzling her offspring. Although extremely rare in ancient Andean art – and ancient American art in general – emotional states were communicated in some Moche works of art, including this portrait head vessel of a laughing or smiling man (*right*). The llama vessel also celebrates the fecundity of the Andes' most crucial species. Early Intermediate Period.

were kept on the coast, according to the many images made of them, as well as other archaeological evidence. One camelid image with a man on its back has been particularly puzzling since llamas are not strong enough to be ridden. However, the backwards rider sports beans on his headdress and thus can be interpreted as a personified load of beans. In such cases the literal style belies the more symbolic meaning. Alternatively, some have suggested this incongruous scene could be a joke. Humor may well be one of the
95 many possibilities in Moche art, as suggested by the laughing man and another composition in which a jealous infant squalls as his father seduces his mother. However, jokes remain one of the most difficult of crosscultural identifications.

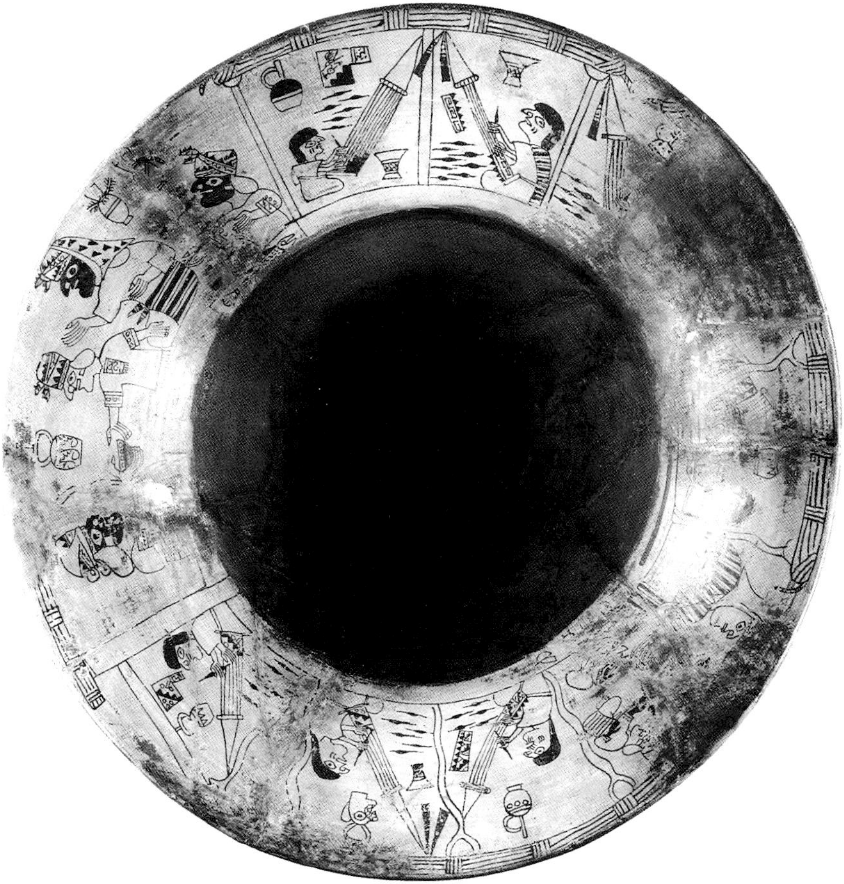

96 Top view of a tall flaring bowl with a rim design of weaving workshops and ritual presentations. Female weavers are shown in accurate detail with backstrap looms, bobbins of thread, and either models or finished products matching their work. Males in elaborate dress perform what may have been considered analogously important actions, perhaps in courtyards outside. Early Intermediate Period.

Certain animals may even be illustrated primarily for their analogies with humans, returning us to the issue of Moche aggression. The barn owl carries *88*
a conch shell trumpet on its back and holds a snake in its talons. Barn owls, fierce and accurate nocturnal hunters who must have been attributed the keenest of eyesight (although they actually hunt by sonar), were probably revered as warrior animals. The owl-headed shaman also suggests that their *86*

battles may be supernatural ones. The snake is the victim and the shell, represented elsewhere and found as actual trumpets, may have had a ritual role in healing and/or warfare. The conflation of the three – the shell as if part of the owl's rounded back, the snake tail sinuously connecting shell and bird – is particularly masterful. The levels of metaphor and juxtaposition in Moche art necessitate further study to unravel.

Finally, there are isolated images of art-making, metal smelting and textile
96 weaving. Metalwork and fine textiles, being reserved for the elite, again are elevated images (ceramic mass-production is not recorded). Corporate and informational, these scenes show collaborative effort and control over artists. In a complex, technically difficult sculptural assemblage, male metalsmiths blow into tubes to heat the ore and extract the pure metal. Along the rim of a flaring bowl weavers in a workshop setting create textiles on their backstrap looms. Finished garments, or the models from which to weave them, as well as elaborate ceramics, fill the workspace. Outside the workshop males offer these ritual items to important personages, demonstrating the goal of this controlled creativity. As in the later Inca empire, highly-policed women weavers seem to have been responsible for the most prestigious textiles. Actual Moche textiles have not survived in any number, although the powdery remains of them are found in fancy graves and images of men holding up elaborate tunics seem to represent tribute payers. At Sipán, metal appliqués were definitely sewn to simple ground cloths, now disintegrated. The few extant fabrics are complex structural cotton cloths that use colorful, imported camelid fiber sparingly. In late Moche times tapestries with distinct Wari influence feature angular warrior and staffbearer figures.

THE MOCHE DEMISE

A multitude of other beautiful objects were made by these people, but like all great and creative cultures, Moche civilization eventually came to an end. Around AD 600 a major El Niño event decimated the city of Cerro Blanco, and as soon as repairs were made, a massive sandslide reburied it. This double calamity caused the capital to be abandoned and may have brought about a widespread loss of faith in the Moche religion. Without centralized authority the state soon collapsed in the face of Wari expansion. Not until several centuries later would the North Coast be united again, this time by the Chimú.

Tiwanaku and Wari Imperial Styles

While we are certain that the Moche was a state style, during the subsequent Middle Horizon we have clear artistic evidence of empire. In the period approximately AD 500–800, the diverse people from the far North Coast to the far south highlands, modern-day Peru to northern Chile, shared an iconographic system referred to as Tiwanaku-Wari or Wari-Tiwanaku. It emanated from two distinct highland centers, Tiwanaku near Lake Titicaca in Bolivia and Wari in the southern highlands of modern-day Peru. Previously 'Tiahuanaco' stood for the site, known since the sixteenth century, and 'Coastal Tiahuanaco' for the Peruvian area (both 'h' and 'w' spellings are approximations, the latter more in current use). However, twentieth-century discoveries of other cities have prompted scholars to agree on two separate but related spheres, a northern and a southern empire.

These two spheres share the same complex iconographic system, spelled out on the sculpture at Tiwanaku but seen in a variant interpretation in Wari portable arts, especially textiles. Tiwanaku and Wari ceramics and metalwork are fairly similar, yet their architecture is almost totally dissimilar. It was first postulated that Tiwanaku was a peaceful theocracy and the warlike Wari adopted its powerful imagery to their bellicose ends. Now these roles, while retaining a kernel of truth, are modified: each had religious and military aspects as well as being the hub of a thriving economy. They apparently overlapped at only one place, the mineral-rich far South Coastal Moquegua Valley, and indications are that the two colonies did not coexist there as in a unified empire, but rather exchanged hostilities and the Wari group left. Thus, current theories propose either an initial missionary or pilgrimage contact, Tiwanaku always the influencer and Wari the influencee, or a common separate origin and subsequent divergence, with Pukará as the likely progenitor.

The fascinating artistically distinct characters of the two spheres were perhaps responses to different political styles. Wari and Tiwanaku art and architecture share common subjects but express them in fundamentally divergent ways. Tiwanaku imports, but not architectural outposts, are found far to the south, as many as 500 miles (800 km) from the capital, thus betraying a centripetal economic/religious strategy. The Tiwanaku style emphasized curvilinear elaboration yet kept clarity as a priority, perhaps in the interests of promoting a new religious hierarchy. By contrast, although parts of the northern sphere were merely influenced, most others seem to have been brought under Wari sway directly, according to imposed administrative and military architectural statements. The Wari aesthetic system took certain portions of the same complex subject matter and allowed artists to deconstruct it into almost pure abstraction, usually in rectilinear forms. If largely imposed, perhaps legibility was less a concern than the exclusivity and mysteriousness conveyed by these marvelously abstract images.

Comparison between the two aesthetic interpretations points up different crosscurrents of imperial goals in relation to artistic means and ends. Ritual objects and spaces, with their implications for the movements of people and water, bring out particularly interesting contrasts and commonalities. Both Tiwanaku and Wari developed important agricultural strategies, ridged fields and canalized terraces respectively, that – like the Moche coastal canalization – gave them extraordinary advantages and changed the character of later Andean organizations. This allowed both to prosper and control vast territories at a time when ecological adversity had dismantled earlier unifications. Powerful ideology, packaged with economic advantages and encapsulated in many widely disseminated artistic media, at least partially included another revival of the Chavín religious images, adapted for new highland propagandistic ends. Middle Horizon patterns also prefigure a number of important choices adopted by the Late Horizon Inca megaempire.

PRECURSORS AND ORIGINS

The seeds of the Middle Horizon accomplishments were sown in the Early Intermediate Period, when Tiwanaku began its climb from village to imperial capital, Pukará had a brief but important florescence between the northern and southern spheres, and the pre-Wari Huarpa culture began terracing formerly unused levels of the highlands. As is typical, the scale, motivation, administration, and persuasive goals rather than the innovative idea itself set the successful state apart from local phenomena. Art, the powerful graphic communication of the new synthesis, exported beyond the actual reach of the group, encourages and maintains participation in the new social order.

97, 98 The site of Tiwanaku is located just southeast of Lake Titicaca, a large and deep inland sea, on wide high plains known as the *altiplano*, at 12,600 ft (3840

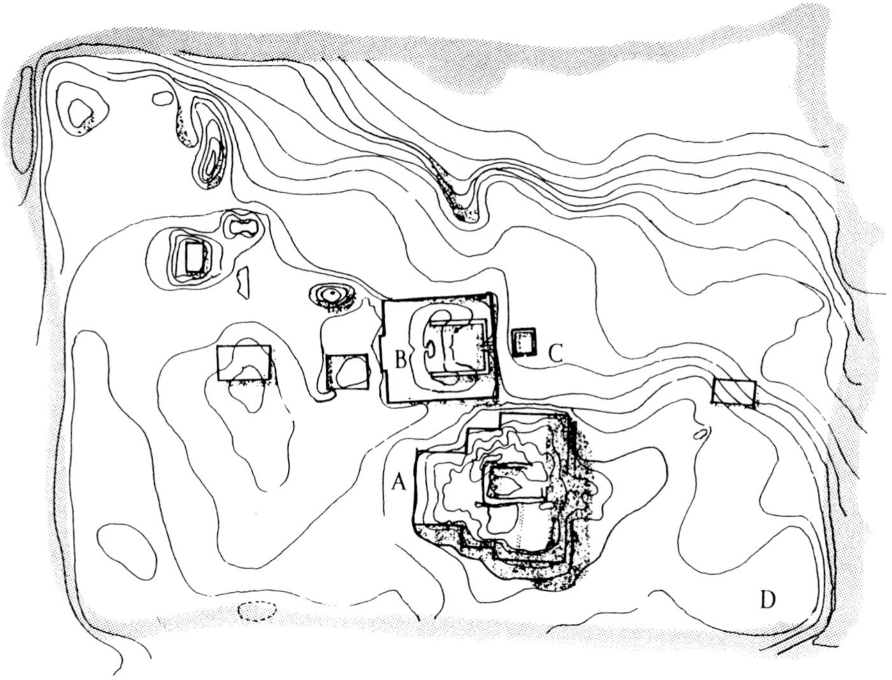

97 Plan of Tiwanaku, the capital and ceremonial center of a sprawling empire from the Lake Titicaca area principally south and eastward. Dominated by the Akapana pyramid (A) and Kalasasaya enclosure (B), it also features a Semi-subterranean Temple (C) and moat (D) and to the south a secondary center, Puma Punku (shown in ill. 98). Early Intermediate Period-Middle Horizon.

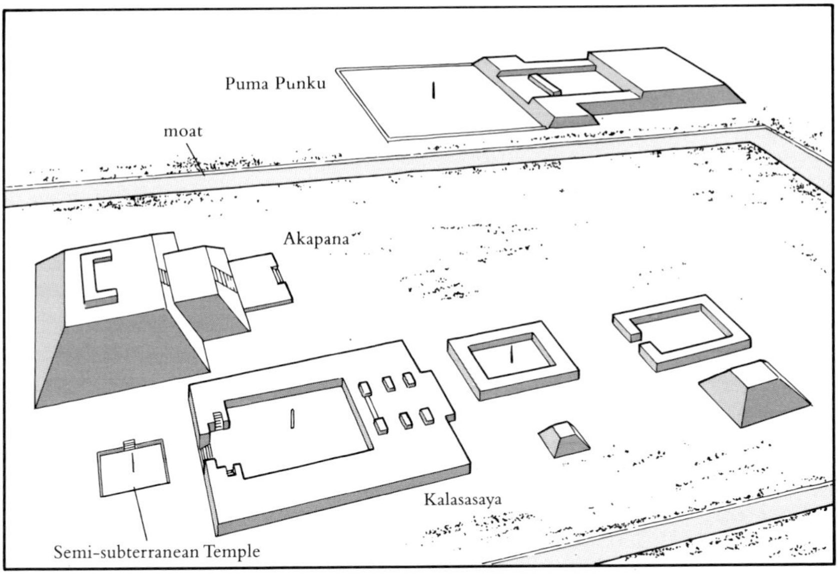

98 Reconstruction drawing of Tiwanaku seen from the north, showing the site's principal buildings and their relation to nearby Puma Punku (top).

m) of altitude. To the east are sacred mountain water sources, dominated by Mt Illimani, and the paths down to the fertile *yungas* or mid-altitude agricultural regions abutting the jungle. To the west are the lake and the dry highland herding areas. Anthropologists agree that Tiwanaku was sited to mark the nexus of these two fundamentally complementary zones (wet/dry, low/high, east/west), and that its highest building, the Akapana, relates the two. Yet to exist here, on prohibitively salty land beyond the lake shores, the people had to develop a new agricultural strategy: a long canal from Titicaca plus a system of raised fields. Long strips of mounded earth direct canalized water to deep trenches on either side, so that salt leeches out, water levels stay constant, the soil resists frost, and silt forms a perfect fertilizer that, periodically spread back on the ridges, nourishes and restores their elevation. A superbly productive method of farming, modern experiments show many times usual yields and the ability to withstand extreme droughts.

The earliest secure date of the village of Tiwanaku is around 400 BC. As this agricultural innovation was implemented, population grew accordingly and the village became transformed. Fabulous stonework, in the form of carvings (often of the staffbearer, long revered in the Andes), and cut stone buildings, united with cosmic location and prosperity to proclaim an imperial message. Tiwanaku hit its peak during the late Early Intermediate Period and Middle Horizon between about AD 375 and 700, but by 1000 it had collapsed.

Where Tiwanaku, and Wari as well, got the new version of the old staffbearer is not completely clear. It could have come from the coast, from highland travelers, or perhaps even been reinvented independently. However, the timing, location, and look of Pukará make it a prime candidate. Located on the northern tip of Lake Titicaca, this small, shortlived site existed between 100 BC and AD 100, predating the Wari and coinciding with early Tiwanaku. Its buildings were adobe on stone foundations, as at Tiwanaku, and its tombs were built of large stone slabs, a feature found at both Tiwanaku and Wari.
99 But its sculpture seems the most influential to both imperial styles, with its large-scale, blocky columnar figures with huge, flat, squared oval eyes. Pukará pieces are, however, characterized by more prominent ribs and movement of limbs in space than their probable descendants. Ceramics are also quite similar, in the modeled *qero* form, stepped patterns and bright colors, as well as in the subject matter of herders, effigies, trophy heads, sacrificial victims, and felines. Yet the Pukará style features more oval eyes,
100 deeply incised outlining of features and geometric patterns, and greater overall curvilinearity than Wari or Tiwanaku. In later versions the formal-

99 (*Left*) Pukará stone sculpture of a man holding a trophy head. Obvious similarities between these and later Tiwanaku sculptures (ill. 105) lead scholars to see Pukará as seminal. Early Horizon-Early Intermediate Period.

100 (*Above*) Pukará ceramic fragment showing incised outlining, bold features, and polychromy that seem to have influenced later Wari and Tiwanaku styles. Early Intermediate Period.

ism typical of empires elevates and constricts Pukará images to more hieratic and hierarchical expressions. However, if Pukará was not the sole or primary transmitter of this imagery, then this new look was at least widely shared in the southern highlands from this point onwards.

North of Pukará, in the Ayacucho Valley where the Wari would later dominate, the Huarpa culture set the stage with strong ties to the South Coast, especially the Nasca area. The two areas traded camelid fiber for salt, among other products. As cultural exchange, the Nasca style heavily influenced the ceramics of the highland area, as it continued to do in the Middle Horizon and vice versa. However, Huarpa art remained rather rough and undistinguished compared with other Andean traditions. Practically speaking, the Huarpa began the very successful land reclamation program based on terracing the *quichua* zone, the steep but lower-altitude lands farther from

101, 102 Tiwanaku's Semi-subterranean Temple (*right*) and view from it of the reconstructed entrance to the Kalasasaya (*below*). Numerous monoliths interspersed with smaller stones, grand portals, and tall sculptures are found throughout this capital city. Early Intermediate Period-Middle Horizon.

the highland river sources of water (equivalent of the *yungas* to Tiwanaku). Terracing and canalization allowed new, vast areas of flat irrigable land to grow maize, a high-protein crop capable of feeding large populations, easily transportable, and vital to a state desiring to store quantities of food to redistribute to subjects, armies, or the nobility. (Continuation and expansion of Wari terraces allowed the Incas to feed as many as 10,000,000 subjects a millennium later.) Terrace agriculture certainly gave the Wari an edge at a crucial moment, providing the survival advantage that allowed their arts to flourish and be spread far and wide. As a stepped modification of the landscape it also may have increased the potency of the stepped outline and the zigzag in the arts of the Middle Horizon.

Scientific analysis of glaciers shows that a major, generation-long drought took place in the sixth century. This probably helped destroy the Nasca and the Moche hegemonies, while propelling the innovators of Ayacucho and the *altiplano* into greater prominence, as their water-miserly systems were nearly drought-proof. The power to sustain life during such a global disaster, attributed no doubt to supernatural sponsorship, must have added persuasiveness to their growing cults and communities. The solar emphasis at Tiwanaku and the agricultural one in Wari images, betray the everpresent Andean interplay of belief and survival. Water, both ritually moved and consumed as corn beer, maintained a significant role in aesthetics. Fertility and its corollary sacrifice are also strong artistic themes stemming from the same, somewhat anxiety-ridden, relationship to the environment and the supernaturals 'responsible' for it. The art and architecture of the Middle Horizon empires thus explore polarities of unity and struggle, growth and demise, and the individual and the group.

TIWANAKU

97, 98 Tiwanaku grew to be a large city, especially in the context of tiny *altiplano* herding villages. Its environs covered at least 4 square miles (10 square km) and housed an estimated population of 30,000–60,000. Tiwanaku's special nature was first signaled by an artificial, non-defensive moat containing the ceremonial and civic center within a rounded rectangle. Not of any practical use, this shallow moat is best understood as symbolically subdividing the vast plain into secular and sacred zones and probably transforming Tiwanaku into an island, like those in nearby Lake Titicaca. Later recorded Andean myths place human creation itself in these islands (the world envisioned as a rocky island protruding from the water succinctly characterizes the actual water-encircled, mountainous American continent). In any case, the moat cordons off ritually important space controlled by the Tiwanaku elite who built their palaces alongside ceremonial architecture, the giant
101, 102 pyramid (Akapana), sunken courtyard (Semi-subterranean Temple), huge shrine enclosure (Kalasasaya), and other structures.

Scholars argue that the demarcation and elaboration of the sacred precinct also makes Tiwanaku symbolic of an *axis mundi*, or center of the world. According to a sixteenth-century chronicler, the actual name for Tiwanaku was Taypikhala, Aymara for 'the stone in the center.' The city is not only at the mediation point between vastly different ecological zones, it also marks the sun's path, both east and west horizons being visible from the summit of the Akapana, itself oriented eastward. In the midst of flatness, to see is to participate in cosmic phenomena and perhaps to control them, or at least

103 One of many finely carved architectural fragments at Puma Punku to the south of the main ceremonial precinct of Tiwanaku. The stepped diamond pattern also appears in Middle Horizon as well as later Inca textiles. Early Intermediate Period-Middle Horizon.

knowledge about them. The iconography found on the monuments, featuring gods, humans, and composites, reinforces the self-conscious position of this place as a cosmic interpreter, if not the city's self-proclaimed role as a point of human genesis itself. Tiwanaku, both a cult center and the thriving capital of a broad empire, had a grandiose image to project. Internal hierarchy, both supernatural and human, was definitely reinforced by the city plan, its architecture and monumental sculpture increasingly impressive and sacred as one reached the center of the center.

In keeping with its inclusive (cosmic) and exclusive (social distinction) roles, the city had buildings of all kinds, creating a sort of small, complete world. Its dominating pyramid, the Akapana, was built vertically in direct imitation of the Andes beyond; as a counterpoint the Semi-subterranean Temple reached down into the earth and was filled with sculptures from various periods and/or places held captive. The Kalasasaya embraced a large surface plane apparently to contain numerous other shrines, also possibly subject peoples'. Thus, to signal cosmic and social power, all directions – up, down, and across – were embellished and references made to natural and cultural landmarks beyond the city itself. Tiwanaku also had a secondary sacred center about half a mile (1 km) away, a smaller terraced mound known as Puma Punku (now almost entirely in tantalizing fragments). Thus, *98, 103*
the north-south axis of the 'island' and Puma Punku may have divided the metropolis into two unequal halves, typical of Andean moiety social organization (still practiced in that area until the nineteenth century).

The ceremonial architecture as a whole often repeats a terraced platform mound around a sunken court. Masonry consists of fine ashlars, dressed

104 Ceramic incense burner in the form of a jaguar, found in a secular building in the northern part of the ceremonial precinct at Tiwanaku. Middle Horizon.

andesite and sandstone monolithic slabs, often interspersed with smaller stones set without mortar. Stonework at Tiwanaku is so fine that the Incas imported all their stonemasons from there to build Cuzco centuries later. Elaborate stone carving even extended to below ground carved drains, many more than were practically necessary. The ritualized movement of water was obviously a priority, as is especially apparent at the Akapana (see
102, 106 below). There was also a marked emphasis on post-and-lintel or monolithic carved doorways found throughout the ceremonial center; therefore, it seems that processions, both depicted and actual, were central to Tiwanaku ritual and the demarcation of ever more sacred spaces. Other carvings, such
103 as the elegant stepped diamonds found at Puma Punku, show consummate carving skill in their crisp corners and deep shadows delineating symbolically loaded abstract shapes. Sculptors also excelled at shallow, intricate relief
106, 105 carving of the lintels and friezes above doors, as well as the surfaces of figural sculptures.

The Akapana stood 56 ft (17 m) high and reached over 650 ft (200 m) on a side. Its seven terraces were made of earth, clay, and gravel faced with cut stone revetment. The lowest terrace has the most beautiful revetment, complete with the beveled edges of the monolithic slabs meeting precisely at the mortarless joins to form dark shadow lines (this feature adopted directly by the Incas). Vertical monoliths were placed at the corners and at about 12-ft (3.5-m) intervals, and small stones between were precision joined as well. This alternating pattern was also used for the wall of the Kalasasaya; it augments stability with variety, and subtly highlights virtuoso carving and stone placement. Creativity and death go hand in hand, however, because underneath the pyramid lie mass dedicatory burials and ritually smashed *qeros* probably used in the dedication rites. The upper terraces were covered more simply with large stone panels and human and feline tenon heads, as well as other now-lost ornamentation, no doubt colorful and complex. The terraces themselves were not necessarily empty; on some levels were adobe structures from this and later times.

On top of the Akapana was a large sunken courtyard, approximately 165 ft (50 m) on a side, and secular structures (presumably priestly residences). The elites were buried under their central patios along with ornate ceramics, such as the jaguar incensario and other cached ritual items (including *104*
disarticulated llamas, metal, obsidian, and probably some of the large sculptures now scattered about the site). Beneath the sunken court, almost certainly the ritual center of the empire, and within the pyramid as a whole, ran a complex and highly symbolic system of drains and spouts. During the heavy rains the court would need to be drained; however, Tiwanaku engineers designed a decidedly symbolic solution to the problem. Draining water entered the body of the pyramid to re-emerge on each terrace, cascading from one and disappearing into the next. This made the pyramid into an enormous fountain, and perhaps a calculatedly noisy one, much like the Temple at Chavín de Huantar. But Alan Kolata and Carlos Ponce Sangines point out that this play of water directly imitates the sacred water source of Mt Illimani with its subterranean and above-ground streams. Thus, through manipulation of water and earth the architects made an artificial mountain in their artificial island, to state their control over the most crucial natural place in their world. The link of water with life itself on this high, dry plain is obvious and the mysterious beauty of a waterfall pyramid would have impressed all who saw it.

Just to the east of the Akapana lies the Semi-subterranean Temple, a square *101, 102*
sunken courtyard. The walls, studded with tenon heads in slightly different

styles, suggest that it was re-used over an extended period of time. These human heads, most somewhat coarsely carved out, have the characteristic large squared eyes and relatively little detailing. They may represent trophy heads, but do bear some revivalistic relationship to the Chavín tenons (although not conveying a process of transformation). In the center of the courtyard were found a number of large sculptures, including the monumental Bennett Monolith, named for Wendell C. Bennett, an important early excavator both here and at Wari. The grouping may be another example of the shuffling of objects over the centuries since the collapse of Tiwanaku. However, it could also represent a collecting mentality: documenting stylistic change and hence imperial longevity (like the tenons) or holding sacred images from subject peoples 'hostage,' another traditional Andean custom. In any case, ritual objects set in its center suggest that this was an important elite gathering place for ceremonial actions, possibly conceived of as a counterpart to the sunken courtyard atop the Akapana. Its theme may well have been revival of earlier religions and those from elsewhere brought under Tiwanaku sway.

The Bennett Monolith stood an impressive 24 ft (7.3 m) tall and is the
105 largest Andean stela. The Bennett Monolith and the Ponce Monolith represent classic Tiwanaku figural carving in their square columnar forms softened slightly by rounded edges and limbs tightly bound to the block. Towering, taut unities in shallow relief, the figures hold *qeros,* shells, batons, and other ritual objects. Thus the stelae likely represent priests, perhaps the Bennett Monolith even the High Priest himself, his height a measure of his relative importance. Delicately and precisely etched into the surface, barely visible in fact, are elaborate tunics, belts, and headdresses. The patterns correlate exactly with actual Tiwanaku textiles. These images are particularly finely observed, complete on all levels and all sides, as befitting important figures.

The other dominant architectural feature is the enormous Kalasasaya enclosure to the west of the Akapana. The monumental Kalasasaya portal has been somewhat uncertainly reconstructed, but carved steps, uprights, and lintels were definitely combined to make majestic processional
101, 102 entrances throughout Tiwanaku. The Kalasasaya's two-story walls, measuring over 328 ft (100 m) on a side, were reconstructed from where the monolithic slabs fell down, with the current arrangement of smaller intervening stones not specifically original but generally correct. The tall slabs each have their own distinctive silhouette, generally trapezoidal but without standardized proportions or even size. The top outlines vary as well, with a pre-

105 Detail of the Ponce Monolith, from Tiwanaku. Characteristic of sculptures in this style are the square eyes and detailed shallow relief.

dominance of steps but no overriding pattern. This exemplifies a dynamic, organic, abstracting side of the style that was embraced by the Wari. The stepped forms may also refer in a generalized fashion to the mountains, in a manner somewhat analogous to the Akapana. Such monoliths deeply influenced the Incas whose architectural style is consciously and closely allied.

While the Kalasasaya was definitely a large-scale gathering place, its original contents are not yet known, but archaeologists suspect they will find foundations of a number of smaller buildings, probably shrines. These could have been shrines to subcult and/or subject peoples' deities, again pointing up the issues of inclusion and exclusion. A cache of twelve identical gold and turquoise diadems, buried in the Kalasasaya, strongly suggests that ritual dramas of the highest order took place here.

The rest of the ceremonial center was filled with numerous plazas and palaces, of which only the foundations survive and ongoing excavations

106 The Sun Gate at Tiwanaku, the city's foremost decorated portal showing the Portal God surrounded by winged attendant figures with bird and human heads (see ill. 107). This imagery was spread throughout the Tiwanaku and Wari empires, primarily via textiles during the Middle Horizon. Early Intermediate Period.

107 Drawing of the Portal God (center, also known occasionally as Viracocha) and the first flanking columns of attendants. The god holds a spearthrower (left) and staff (right), while the attendants hold staffs. Early Intermediate Period.

have now begun to map. Throughout the metropolis huge stone water and sewage drains and vast numbers of adobe structures betray a well-organized, dense urban settlement. Concentrations of ceramics, bone, stone and metal objects, and tool remains indicate diverse specialized art workshops. Individual households seem to have woven their own and tribute textiles. Thus, the society was at least stratified into three classes: elites (royalty, warriors, priests), artists, and commoners (farmers, traders, and herders whose surplus from the highly productive fields, long-distance llama caravan trade routes, and vast *altiplano* herds provided the basis for the heartland's great wealth and power).

The secondary center of the city, Puma Punku, survives as a frustrating *98, 103* jumble of beautifully carved architectural fragments, especially gateways. They once presumably led to the 16-ft-high (5-m), 490-ft-square (150-m) platform, its center marked by another sunken court. Because of the proliferation of fine carvings, Puma Punku may well have been the original location of the most famous and central monument of Tiwanaku, the veritable key to the new iconography spread over much of the Central Andes, the so-called Sun Gate (incongruously found in a corner of the Kalasasaya, leading nowhere). The largest of the city's portals, the Sun Gate bears the quintessential Tiwanaku and Wari imagery and thus was almost certainly a, if not the, supremely important monument.

106, 107 The Sun Gate is carved from a solid piece of stone, its front penetrated by a double-jambed door (another feature adopted wholesale by the Incas) surmounted by an intricate frieze in relief. Boldly projecting from the top center is a frontal deity holding spears and a spearthrower. He stands on a stepped triangular form, called a dais but possibly referring to a pyramid, even the Akapana itself. Some identify him as Viracocha, the Inca creator god, while others more neutrally call him the Portal God and grant him predominantly solar aspects according to his rayed headdress. His projecting face, centrality, relative size, body position, and accoutrements signal his supernatural status. In attendance on either side are shallow-relief, bent-legged composite figures, all winged, and in the center rows bird-headed. Whether kneeling or flying, they certainly pay homage to the paramount deity. Each carries one staff, to the god's two, and being smaller, flatter, more numerous, and shown in profile they fit the criteria of lower-status beings. Presumably because most people are supplicants to the god, most of the small-scale imperial arts feature these winged staffbearers with bird, human, or feline heads. They may repre-
108, 111 sent ritually-attired bird and human priests that passed through the Gate and/or may stand for lesser supernaturals in the pantheon. In either case, humans wore the images of staffbearers and are immortalized carrying staffs of office and therefore seem to have taken on aspects of the Sun Gate attendants. Lines between natural and supernatural roles may have been deliberately blurred in an expansionistic imperial religion.

Beyond the ceremonial center, Tiwanaku directly controlled the plains around for 100,000 ha, establishing a hierarchy of medium- and small-sized centers in imitation of itself. On a smaller scale these outposts, such as Lukurmata, share Tiwanaku's long canals connecting them to the lake, moats circumscribing ceremonial cores, drained terraced mounds, monolithic slab architecture, gateways, and columnar statuary. Each supervised its portion of the vast network of raised fields. Further from the heartland, Tiwanaku sent enormous llama caravans far and wide to export the religion and import foreign products and materials. Evidence of Tiwanaku objects and representatives is found as far away as San Pedro de Atacama in northern Chile,

a 500-mile (800-km) trip, six weeks walk each way. But the principal Tiwanaku colony is Omo in the coastal Moquegua Valley, housing around 500 people stationed there no doubt to procure the rare minerals, volcanic glass, and metal for Tiwanaku luxury goods in turquoise, lapis lazuli, obsidian, gold, and copper, such as the Kalasasaya diadems. An undefended outpost, Omo had houses, a space especially set aside for beer-making, caches of portrait head *qeros* for ceremonial drinking, and many imported 109
and local copies of Tiwanaku arts. If the Inca pattern applies, colonizers encouraged local participation in a far-off state's labor plans by exchanging work and products for beer and food in large quantities. Omo's longlived presence indicates a powerful but seemingly peaceful colonization; the Wari attempt to share the wealth was neither as successful nor as pacific.

TIWANAKU PORTABLE ARTS

As in architecture and monumental sculpture, the portable Tiwanaku-style arts tend to feature versions of the staffbearer both whole and shorthand. The range of subjects nevertheless also includes images of jaguars, raptorial birds, 104
and human heads. The technical level tends to be high, as the exquisite

108 Wooden *qero* with carved attendant staffbearer (see ills. 106, 111, 119, 120). The staff is held to the left of center, the figure's head is upturned, his legs are bent, and his wings are to the right. The *qero*, or drinking cup, form was taken up by the Incas and continued into Colonial times (see ill. 183).

109 (*Left*) Drawing of a provincial effigy head *qero* found at Omo, the Tiwanaku colony in the South Coastal Moquegua Valley. Comparing this vessel with the one found at the capital (ill. 110), the range of portraiture styles at this time becomes obvious. Middle Horizon.

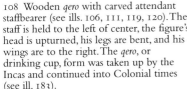

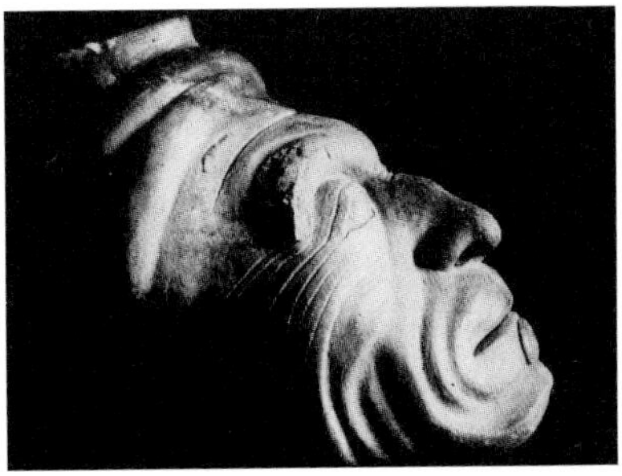

110 (*Below*) Portrait head ceramic vessel found in the Kalasasaya at Tiwanaku. With its inset eyes, deeply furrowed cheeks, and prominent nose, this image captures the idiosyncracies of a specific person, as did the Moche portrait vessels (see ills. 89, 95). Middle Horizon.

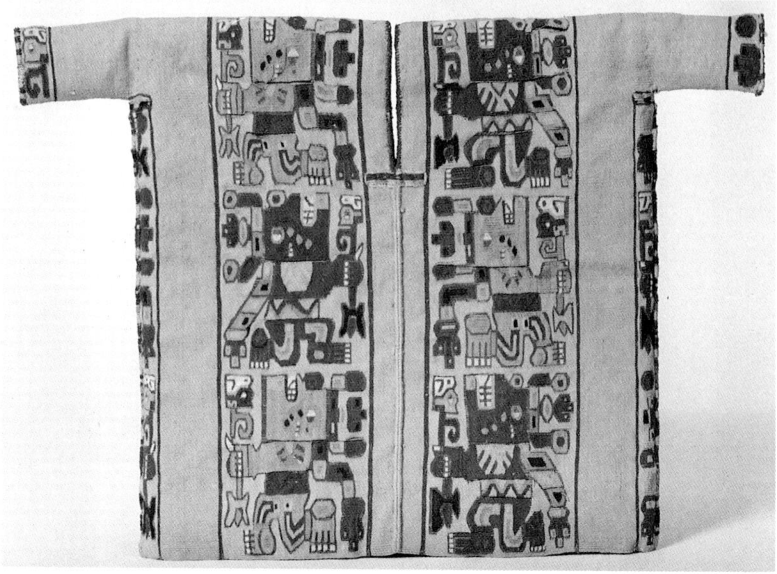

111 Miniature Tiwanaku-style tunic with human-headed attendant figures (see ill. 107). Only 12 inches (30 cm) wide, this tunic would not even fit a baby, but represents a virtuoso offering (with over 80 threads per cm). Middle Horizon.

108 carving of a wooden *qero* attests, although local variants are less carefully
109 worked, such as the Moquegua portrait vessel. In fact, the contrast between
110 the colonial versions and the singular physiognomic portrait head cup found in the Kalasasaya shows the imperial broad stylistic range, virtuosic execution, and memorialization of actual individuals. Like the Moche portraits, although not at all as widespread, the Kalasasaya image sets eyeballs within a skull, emphasizes a very idiosyncratic nose, facial lines, and gives an uncanny sense of interior presence. An interesting feature, characteristic of more abstracted Tiwanaku and Wari figures, is the incised eyepiece decoration.

Besides the eyepieces, other recurring features that make the Middle Horizon styles so recognizable include: the rayed headdress, staff, bisected round eye (half dark and half light), blunt-ended appendages ending in white squares to represent nails or claws, contrastive outlining, multicolors, the stepped fret and 'Greek' key meander patterns, bent-beak birds, and other animal heads with upturned snouts. These elements are multiplied and elaborated in many intriguing ways; for instance, the eyepiece is often also the outline of a bird, and animal heads, keys, and even lone eyes (especially in Wari versions) may be added to a headdress, staff end, torso, etc. Though the components are quite standardized, the combinations show a lot of creative variation and generate visual movement, while the color variety adds further dynamism. A set iconography does not necessarily lead to monotonous repetition.

Tiwanaku objects, in keeping with the long-distance trade network, are almost all small-scale, portable ritual pieces for religious practice and perhaps proselytizing far from the imperial center. Items include the wood and clay *qeros*, drug-taking paraphernalia, specially carved snuff tablets, as well as fine all-camelid-fiber textiles. Miniatures, such as the diminutive tunic, lightweight sheet-gold ornaments, and tiny carvings in other materials, round out the possessions of the Tiwanaku colonizer, priest, or merchant. Technical virtuosity – the tunic has 80 threads per cm – characterizes the objects deemed important enough to use at the capital and represent it abroad. Perhaps because of the need to travel light, each object was charged with extra power and complex information. *111*

WARI CITY PLANNING AND ARCHITECTURE

In contrast to the Tiwanaku sensibility, the Wari approach is more partitioned, irregular, and bold, and at the same time less accessible, personalizing, and three-dimensional. Partitioning denotes the tendencies both to subdivide, often within a grid, and to disassemble a figure until its compo-

112 A typical Wari-style wall at Pikillacta. These multi-story, rough stone walls were built by Wari subjects in sections (a seam is visible to the left of the scale marker). Originally they were plastered and painted. Middle Horizon.

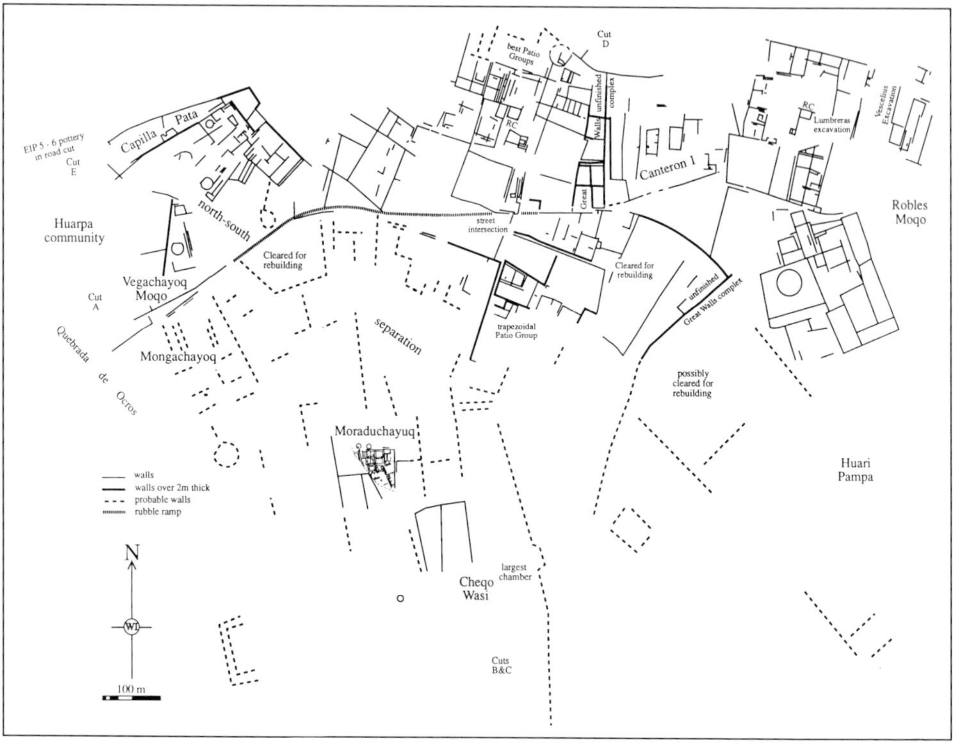

113 Plan of the architecture in central Wari, the capital city of the northern Middle Horizon empire. Its freeform arrangement contrasts strongly with the axial plan of Tiwanaku (see ill. 97), as does the stonework. Middle Horizon.

nents become independent figures. This geometric apportioning ranges
118, 119, 121 from the motif blocks within double-outlined columns in a tunic, to the
115 doorless, high-walled settlements that defy the reconstruction of human movement through them. Self-contained geometric patterns mirror
112 formidable walls (Pikillacta's measure 5 ft (1.5 m) thick and over 39 ft (12 m) high in their ruined state) to create inaccessibility, actual or visual. Irregularity occurs within the grids; how each individual staffbearer or each room is configured tends to vary, from a little to a lot. Different, even idiosyncratic parts are not particularly individualized, for example, people might have any number of geometric face paint patterns but their features will not be recorded in themselves. Wari style is imposed, not only onto state subjects, but also the body and the landscape itself, as part of its bold predilection for the brilliantly colored and the assertively shaped. Overwhelming

interest in patterning lends Wari art less three-dimensionality than its 122,110
Tiwanaku counterpart. The strong ties of Wari to Nasca may have set up this stylistic trajectory; however, those connections might not have been made had not the predilection already existed. In any case, these Wari choices pervade all media, establishing a recognizable yet exclusive imperial style in which artists directed the flow to a surprising degree.

The imperial capital of Wari, located on a spur of land in the Ayacucho 113
Valley, remains incompletely known due to civil unrest during the major recent excavations. From present knowledge, the plan appears fairly irregular and distinct from that of Tiwanaku, reflecting cosmopolitanism and opportunism in its diversity and change through time. It was established over a Huarpa town, adobe walls giving way to stone ones. Then an influx of Tiwanaku influence, even possibly stonemasons themselves, added temples, cists, and rooms in dressed-stone slabs. Gradually increasing standardization, and an approximate grid, mark the city's apogee, when patio groups with more consistent orientations were constructed over the temples. Masonry at this phase consisted of plastered rough stonework in multistory walls; as in other arts, Wari diverged from its southern counterpart. At its height the city covered approximately 6 square miles (15 square km) and population estimates vary from 10,000 to 70,000. In a final phase, high walls were erected across the city, probably as the beginnings of huge compounds left unfinished when the metropolis was abandoned around AD 800.

Since different sections vary and few are well understood, the 114
Moraduchayuq Compound in the southern center of town will serve to represent current understanding of the imperial capital's architecture. This compound began early in the city's history as a semi-subterranean temple

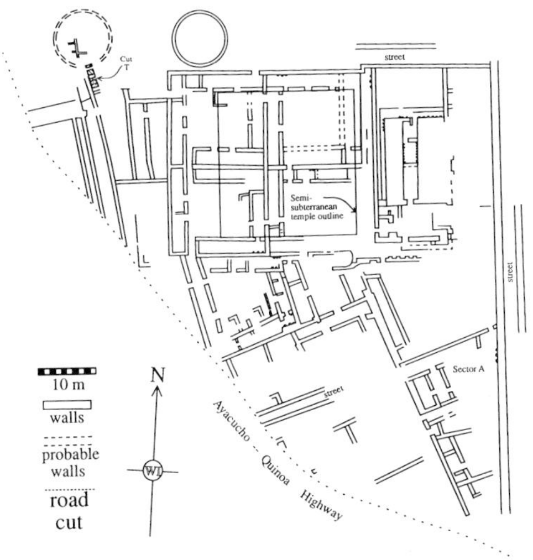

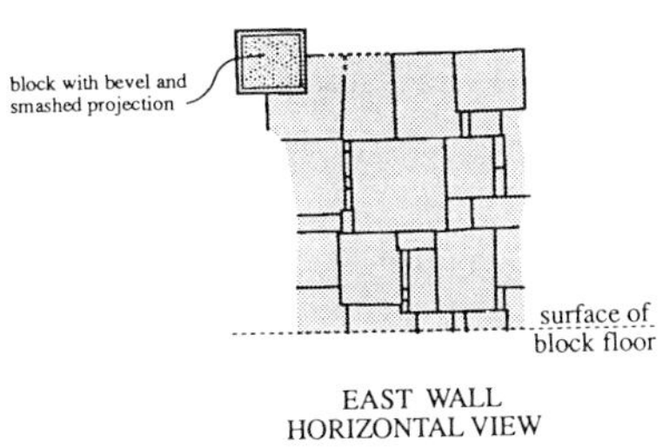

114 Plan of the Moraduchayuq Compound at Wari and detail drawing of a polygonal stonework wall (*above*) that underlies the courtyard level. Changes from ritual to administrative concerns are documented in the evolution of this compound. Middle Horizon.

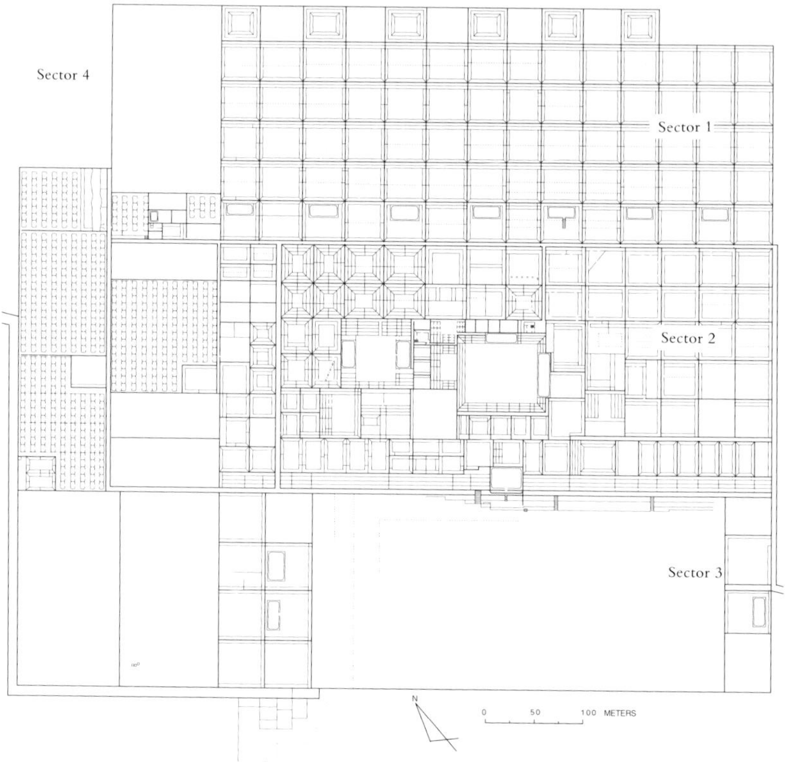

115 Plan of Pikillacta, the Wari provincial center between the capitals Wari and Tiwanaku. A single entrance near the southeastern corner pierces this enormous, high-walled complex. Middle Horizon.

built into a 16-ft-deep (5-m) natural hole in the bedrock, probably considered a *huaca.* Scientific dating places this structure in use from the sixth through to the eighth centuries, during which time floors were superimposed in a series of renovations. Fitted into the irregular hole was a perfectly square sunken room oriented to astronomical north, 79 ft (24 m) on a side. The paved floor was plastered and the walls were mortarless, polygonal fitted stonework (that interestingly almost exactly matches that of the later Incas, albeit with smaller stones). A broken-off tenon may originally have had a head, placed high on the wall, more like Chavín examples than those of Tiwanaku. After generations of small-scale ritual use, it was ritually interred with layers of gravel and colored clays (as in the ancient highland tradition first seen at Kotosh). Then a patio group was erected over it, with secular administrative buildings in which feasting predominated (according to the preponderance of serving rather than cooking ceramics). The long halls around central courtyards, all within rectangular but not identical walled compounds, also became the hallmark of the later Incas. In various rooms, subterranean cists seem to have held ritually smashed pottery and human body parts, the sanctifying remnants of ceremonial drinking, eating, and sacrificing, the socially cohesive and competitive actions of a successful expansive empire. At this point the high, thick walls incorporated an innovative feature: a single corbel, a row of projecting stones that supported wooden beams for the second story floor. This type of wall is found throughout the Wari hinterland, reflecting the broad reach of the standardizing state at its height.

While the city of Wari remains unfathomed, the southern provincial capital of Pikillacta has been more fully investigated – although its grand scale makes complete excavation nearly impossible. Highland Wari administrative nodes are spread nearly one to a valley, with Pikillacta being the *115, 116*

116 Aerial view of Pikillacta showing its geometry imposed on the landscape. The terrain actually slopes 262 ft (80 m) from one side to the other. In a similar way, Wari tunics imposed their rectilinear format over the human body (see ills. 118, 119, 121). Middle Horizon.

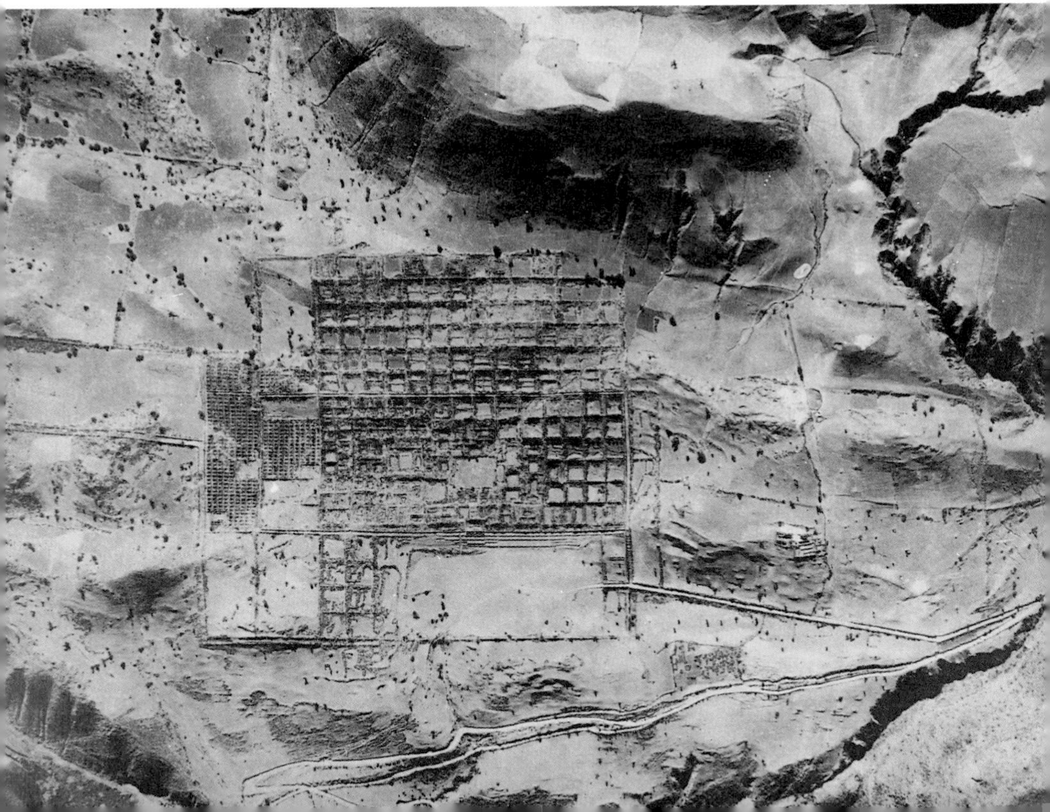

largest and most southerly, strategically located between Wari and Tiwanaku territory. Its enormous rectangular center, 2445 by 2067 ft (745 by 630 m), was built at 10,660 ft (3250 m) in the Lucre Basin at the southern end of
116 the Cuzco Valley. Seen from above – a vantage not possible in ancient times, like the Nasca Lines – its right angles belie the fact that the undulating ground slopes nearly 262 ft (80 m) from end to end. Geometric imposition rather than an organic relationship to the terrain is obvious. Yet absolute regularity is not paramount: note the 'missing' three units on the northeast and the adjunct section to the west. These are intentional deviations rather than the result of additive building. The settlement was planned and erected in one episode, according to the construction evidence elucidated by archaeologist Gordon McEwan. Such preplanned irregularities equally characterize other Wari media.

115 Pikillacta is subdivided into four main parts, separated by a very few interior passageways. There is but one exterior entrance into the main compound, along the eastern wall, leading through an extremely long, easily policed corridor and finally piercing the compound between Sectors 1 and 2. This circuitous entryway in itself speaks eloquently about control of access. Northernmost Sector 1, like the others, is made up of many very large enclosures (averaging 115–130 ft (35–40 m) on a side). McEwan has devised a typology of the many ways in which a grid section can be configured, combining the basic elements of empty walled enclosure, peripheral gallery, and rectangular building. In most, the central part of an enormous room is a patio, while long halls line the edges. Although five main schemes can be defined, there is great variety in individual spaces, betraying a flexible approach ensuring a recognizable overall arrangement without specifying particulars. This is noticeably less regimented than many imperial architectures, implying that the participants in the state could determine their own ways to accomplish a given task, from living space to more sacred duties.

Even the three sectors have their own distinctive patterns: Sector 2 has many more irregular elements than the others, from an anomalous diagonal wall to a special large central patio probably for mass celebrations and even two caches of forty greenstone figurines. Sector 2 seems obviously to be higher prestige with different, special-purpose spaces rather than repeated units. Below, Sector 3 has units either side of a huge open terrace, perhaps for colossal gatherings. Adjunct Sector 4 has 501 repeated units, possibly for storage but more probably for the garrisoning of troops. Together the four sectors allow for living, administration, ritual, and storage/defense,

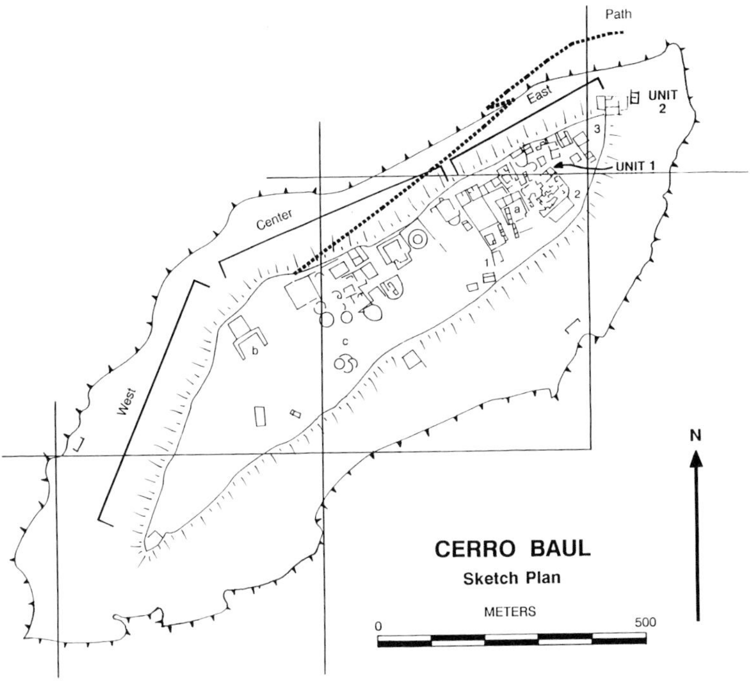

117 Plan of the Wari fortress of Cerro Baul in the Moquegua Valley. Atop a high spur of land, intrusive colonists were protected from Tiwanaku settlers at Omo; however, the Wari group soon left the area. Both groups apparently sought the rich mineral resources found there. Middle Horizon.

fulfilling the many functions of a provincial capital. The countless people, products, riches, and events that took place here are lost, but the gargantuan structure and the values it embodies remain. A series of smaller Wari settlements filled the rest of the Lucre Basin, showing an administrative hierarchy. Likewise, large Wari cities to the north, such as Viracochapampa, Jincamocco, and Azángaro, had their own local networks. All Wari outposts are similar architecturally, yet different in arrangement, reinforcing this pattern of standardization with individual variations.

Specifically defensive Wari architecture has been found, such as large walls guarding the entrances to the Lucre Basin. Most significantly, only a few miles from Tiwanaku's Omo colony in the Moquegua Valley is the Wari fort of Cerro Baúl and a typical hierarchy of local Wari settlements. It was built *117*
on the half-mile-long (1-km) summit of a sheer-sided mesa some 1970 ft

(600 m) in height, with the terraces, walls, and switchback paths below created to prevent access. The walled fort was filled with rectangular courtyards and large deep pits (probably cisterns, since the nearest water source is an hour's walk away). The same type of building techniques, typical multistory constructions, and the overall irregular arrangement rather closely follow that of the capital of Wari itself. Ceramics found there seem to be either imports from Wari or local copies. But, as an intrusion into Tiwanaku territory, this fort was occupied only briefly; apparently a confrontation caused the Wari colonists to leave while the Tiwanaku people remained.

WARI FIBER ARTS

Because the Wari expanded their operations from highlands to coast and buried some of their dead (probably state representatives) in the dry desert sands, hundreds of their spectacular textiles have survived – as against comparatively few Tiwanaku ones, kept in less preservative highland contexts. Textile primacy characterizes the Middle Horizon as much or more than any other period, considering the close ties of the Tiwanaku reliefs to textile canons, the dissemination of styles via portable fiber arts, the state-wide dedication to the production of these labor-intensive objects, and their illustration in other media. It is also possible to see that the fiber artists had a special driving role in establishing state style, another way in which textiles were favored. An interesting aspect of the imperial aesthetic is that the approach toward administrative architecture – a rectilinear geometric structure filled with repeated but consciously varied elements and deliberate anomalies – also applies to textiles. Variations in individual sectors and enclosures of the architecture parallel those in the columns and motifs of the official Wari tapestry tunic. It is no accident that two distinct media share a common orientation, especially when the powerful controlling hand of an empire commissioned both.

Tapestry, the highest prestige technique, dominates the corpus. Some tapestries feature images of camelids, even in the act of giving birth, which betray the concerns of herders who depended on camelid fiber. However,
118, 119, 121 most are tunics, probably woven for imperial officials commemorated
122 wearing them in ceramic effigies. Creating many hundreds of these large, two-piece garments entailed enormous expenditure of materials, time, and artistry; there is 6–9 miles (10–14 km) of thread in each tunic and the various colors of thread were interlocked up to a million-and-a-half times per tunic. Their colorful, nearly illegible patterns make Wari tunics among the most

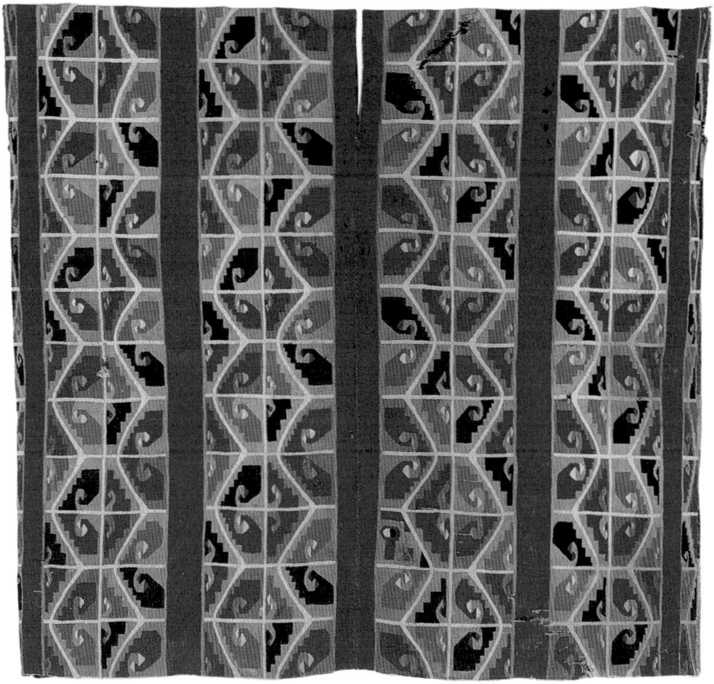

118 (*Above*) Wari tapestry tunic with 479 stepped frets and a single profile face motif (lower right, center). Such intentional anomalies appear in different but analogous ways in most Wari tunics, and may signal the contribution of individual weavers to the set design. Middle Horizon.

119 (*Left*) The so-called Lima Tapestry, a masterfully abstract interpretation of the staffbearing attendant figure (see the Sun Gate ills. 106, 107, 111). Middle Horizon.

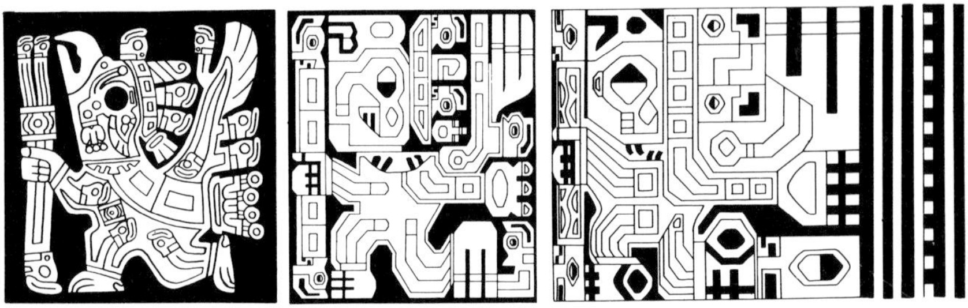

120 (*Above*) Drawings of the Sun Gate bird-headed attendant staffbearer showing how it became rectilinearized, abstracted, and distorted in woven versions. Middle Horizon.

121 (*Below*) Wari tapestry tunic with profile face and stepped fret motifs. Such tunics include an average of 6 miles (10 km) of dyed camelid fiber and cotton thread. Middle Horizon.

striking, abstract works of Andean art. They served to aggrandize their wearers, express the idiosyncratic creativity of specific weavers, and even potentially communicate imperial messages about order and chaos itself.

Tunics bore the rather circumscribed iconography seen on the Sun Gate, almost always the profile attendant figure rather than the frontal diety, and
120 its formal offshoots generated by the artistic process of abstraction. First the grid of warp and weft lends its straight lines to the curvilinear staffbearers'

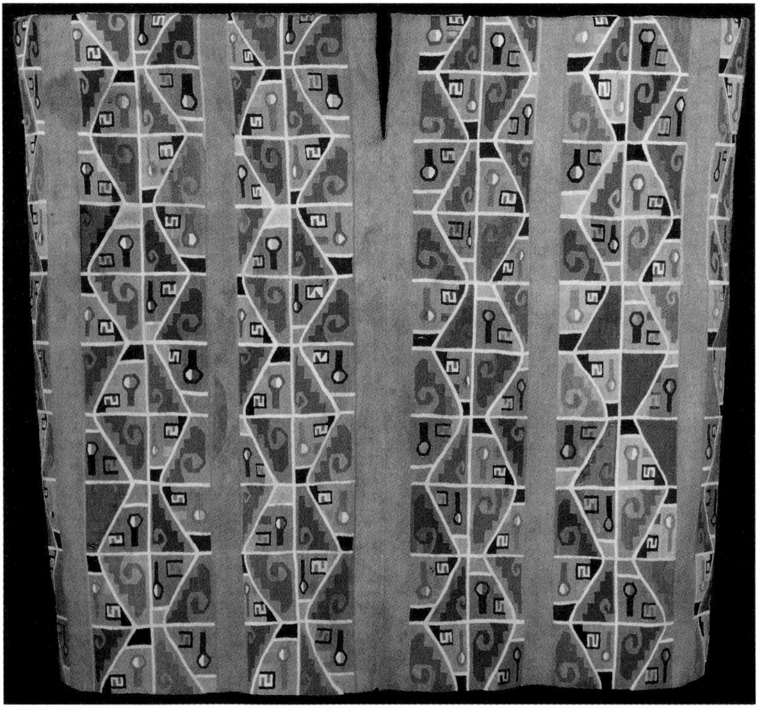

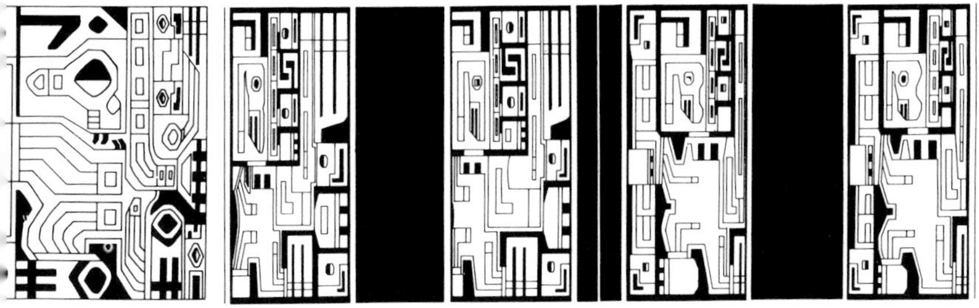

wings, legs, elaborate headdresses, and staffs. Wari textile versions tend to be bird-headed or puma-headed, not human-headed as at Tiwanaku, another divergence that may be cult-related. Weavers took this standard figure and not only rectilinearized it, but systematically distorted it: the portions of figures that were toward the tunic's central vertical seam were expanded laterally while those toward the side seams were contracted. For instance, in a row of bird-headed staffbearers facing left, on the viewers' right the staffs would be wide and the wings narrow, while on the left the staffs would be narrow and the wings wide. This makes identical repetitions appear distinct, a practice that follows the letter of the law (all figures are the 'same') but not its spirit (all figures actually look different). It is a quintessentially artistic act and an interesting visual twist that adds dynamism to a set iconography.

In fact, weavers followed the lead of colors and shapes away from the strict communication of the repeated figures, until sometimes only color and shape remain (except to the initiated). The so-called Lima Tapestry shows *119*
an extreme manipulation of the staffbearer, each so truncated as to be the separated front half and back half, with a good portion of the center head and body missing from both. A glimpse of a wing, a staff, split eye, or bent leg may be caught from the bold, repeated shapes but easily disappears back into the shifting morass. Only great familiarity allows viewers to recognize a hand as a bar or two of color. It can be argued that the subject has lost priority to the artistic process itself.

Further deconstruction of the staffbearer takes place as well. A very popular pattern repeats hundreds of times the combination of a triangular simplified profile face with another inverted triangle containing a stepped *121*
fret. The face has the typical split eye, 'N' or reverse-'N' indication of crossed fangs, a hat or headband, and sometimes a nose. Any number of shape and color variations are played on the features, which can be almost entirely deleted in some tunics. Again, set iconography is only the beginning point for creative artistic exploration. Geometric and animal motifs seem related

118 to the figures but veer off into abstraction. For instance, stepped frets occur
103 alone, and stepped diamonds, reminiscent of the carving at Puma Punku, combine with double-headed U-shaped interlocked animals. Since we do not know where the vast majority of tunics were buried and, even if we did, their portability makes their place of origin unclear, it is nearly impossible to pinpoint substyles with accuracy. However, there is enough standardization in tunic size, thread count, palette, and motifs to show the hand of the state in regulating the art form. Interestingly, it seems as if artistic license and imperial control dovetail in the official Wari style.

Theories to reconcile this apparent paradox highlight exclusivity; in other words, the illegibility allowed in the state style acted as a mysterious esoteric code to keep out the uninitiated. Tunic-wearers, seen as walking geometric billboards, withheld the visual recognition of the religious subjects. Representatives were easily seen, the colors and columns of their garments making them appear larger than life, and so impressive to the subjects. Second, and perhaps more subconsciously, the compositions may hide within their riot of colors and shapes a message about the ordering of chaos itself.

Besides esoteric abstraction, there is a pattern of very obvious, unprecedented formal choices that appear in almost every complete tunic known. These anomalies are fully intentional (tapestry is too slow and laborious a technique to allow these elements to be undetected mistakes). In a composition dominated by one motif, another suddenly materializes. For example,
118 one tunic sports 479 stepped frets and, abruptly, one profile face motif. This anomaly is 'hidden in plain view' and almost takes on the humorous quality of a surprise symphony. Several motifs are also assigned a completely unprecedented bright green color, the hue most typical for color anomalies.
121 Most anomalies are in the blue to green range, probably because indigo dyeing was a supremely difficult process and therefore this color was highly prized. Other tunics may have one red shape, five blue-green stripes, or some type of reversed shape, as ways to vary the formal regularity. There are no two tunics that vary in the same way; each has its own deviations from the norm. Signatures of individual artists are a primary way to interpret these anomalies. It is possible to claim with confidence that one of the Wari artistic rules was to break the rules. Even aberrant walls and greenstone figurines at Pikillacta can be seen as architectural anomalies.

It is possible to suggest that the state allowed such variability as part of its official message – that it was an ordering system containing and controlling chaos. In the Andes chaos can be environmental: unpredictable floods, frosts, earthquakes, droughts and the like. It is the imperial organization that mitigates the effects of natural disaster by building safe centers, storing and giving out food, mobilizing work forces, in short moving people and goods around this rugged world. Thus, the Wari may have consciously or unconsciously embraced a statement of orderliness – ranks of repeated, grid-contained sacred images – that was enlivened but not unbalanced by chaotic colors, shapes, and interpretations. This proposal assumes that the structures in art mirror those in thought, that all artistic statements are meaningful and intentional, and that individual creativity and imperial propaganda are not mutually exclusive. If nothing else, it fits with Andean traditions of corporate thinking, dualism, and reciprocity. At base, the abstraction that pervades the style, the recurrent anomalies, and the widespread standardization of the tunic form, together point to artistically-driven but state-regulated communication.

WARI CERAMICS AND GOLDWORK

Other Wari portable arts never reached the abstract level of textiles; although
influenced by them, ceramics and goldwork stayed more conservative and
receptive to outside influences. In both media, many depictions feature
tunic-wearers, quote tunic motifs in bands, and generally adopt much of the *122*
rectilinearity of the loom unnecessarily (painting on a three-dimensional
surface encourages curvilinearity). Wari ceramic painting style blended with
the various coastal styles within its sphere, maintaining its closest visual relationship to Nasca, but responding to local techniques, palettes, and variant
interpretations of the sacred iconography as part of the state's characteristic
flexible imposition. Wari metalwork, comparatively not very widespread,
stayed much like that of Tiwanaku.

Ceramic vessel forms feature pre-existing traditional shapes, particularly
the South Coastal double-spout-and-bridge, the Tiwanaku beaker (without *123*
sculptural additions), and the face neck or effigy jar. Yet, always innovative, they added a new giant urn and a flask-shaped jar to the repertoire. Like those of the Nasca, Wari pots are entirely slipped in multiple colors, distinctly outlined – mostly in black but occasionally in white if necessary for contrast – and then burnished. Well made, they often survive in pristine condition. The imagery again relates directly to the sculpture at Tiwanaku, especially on the large urn surfaces (among the largest ever made in the Andes they stand over 3 ft (1 m) tall), but the Portal God carries more references to corn and vegetation in general. Isolated figural parts, spinoff

122 (*Left*) Wari ceramic effigy of an official wearing a square pile hat, asymmetrical geometric face paint and a tunic, bearing a repeated face pattern. Like a signboard, the individual has been obscured by the high-prestige patterns which represent the Wari state to its subjects. Middle Horizon.

123 (*Above*) Wari-style polychrome ceramic double-spout-and-bridge vessel with a winged, bird-headed figure seen in various versions during the Middle Horizon (ills. 106–108, 119, 120). Wari ceramics were heavily influenced by Nasca forms and slip painting, as well as the imagery of Tiwanaku. Middle Horizon.

animals, and human heads show similar, though less extreme, abstraction to that of the other arts. Bold colors and graphic shapes, glossy surfaces and highly recognizable iconography, lent Wari vessels a distinctive look that helped the empire maintain a high profile in conquered areas. In less strictly controlled areas, such as the North Coast, Moche versions of Wari vessels continued press-molding and a more limited color scheme, melding their distinctive traditions with that of the new dominant peoples.

Wari metalwork, exclusively created in sheet technology, pares down the vocabulary into elegant simplicity. Not a great deal of it has been found, so perhaps it was not a high-priority medium, sufficiently restricted as to be kept purposefully scarce, or looted by later peoples. During the subsequent Late Intermediate Period and Late Horizon, we know from ethnohistoric records that precious metals were exclusive to the nobility; such a tradition may have started here.

Late Intermediate Period Styles

The 500 years between the fall of the Tiwanaku and Wari empires and the rise of the Incas feature distinctive regional styles along the desert coast. By the end of the Late Intermediate Period, the Chimú held sway over the North and Central Coasts, subsuming the more localized Sicán (Lambayeque) and Chancay. Further south the Ica went their own artistic way. This was also a highpoint of an independent pilgrimage center, Pachacamac on the Central Coast, whose offerings included all four groups' artistic products and so preserved them for posterity. The various Late Intermediate Period peoples shared certain political characteristics (an increased emphasis on secular hierarchy and the accumulation of wealth), artistic approaches (additive construction, mass-production, and increased standardization), general formal choices (particularly repetitive patterning and openwork), and subject matter (related to the sea and a particular frontal figure). Yet their individual styles nevertheless vary in important and recognizable ways. It was indeed a time of regionalism. All were eventually conquered by the Incas around 1460–70, yet maintained a measure of their strong traditional identities through this and the Spanish colonizations.

The Late Intermediate Period peoples, while not uniting the numbers that the Incas did, certainly operated on a grand scale. Vast quantities of art objects from this time dominate museum collections, mainly because art production became one, if not the, focus of the expansive kingdom of Chimor, and because of mass-production and elite appetites in general. William Conklin has even called the immense princely palaces/offices/mausolea of the Chimú capital of Chan Chan 'museums' for their dedication to amassing, displaying, and preserving objects, assumed to include luxury art works. Late Intermediate Period architectural complexes, from cities to cemeteries, are among the largest in the Americas. While most have been looted (the Spanish set up a commercial mining company to extract the burial offerings from Chan Chan), many have also been excavated recently. So a great deal of information is now available.

The general Late Intermediate Period artistic approach can be termed piecemeal or additive, non-individualized, and reiterative. Parts seem to take

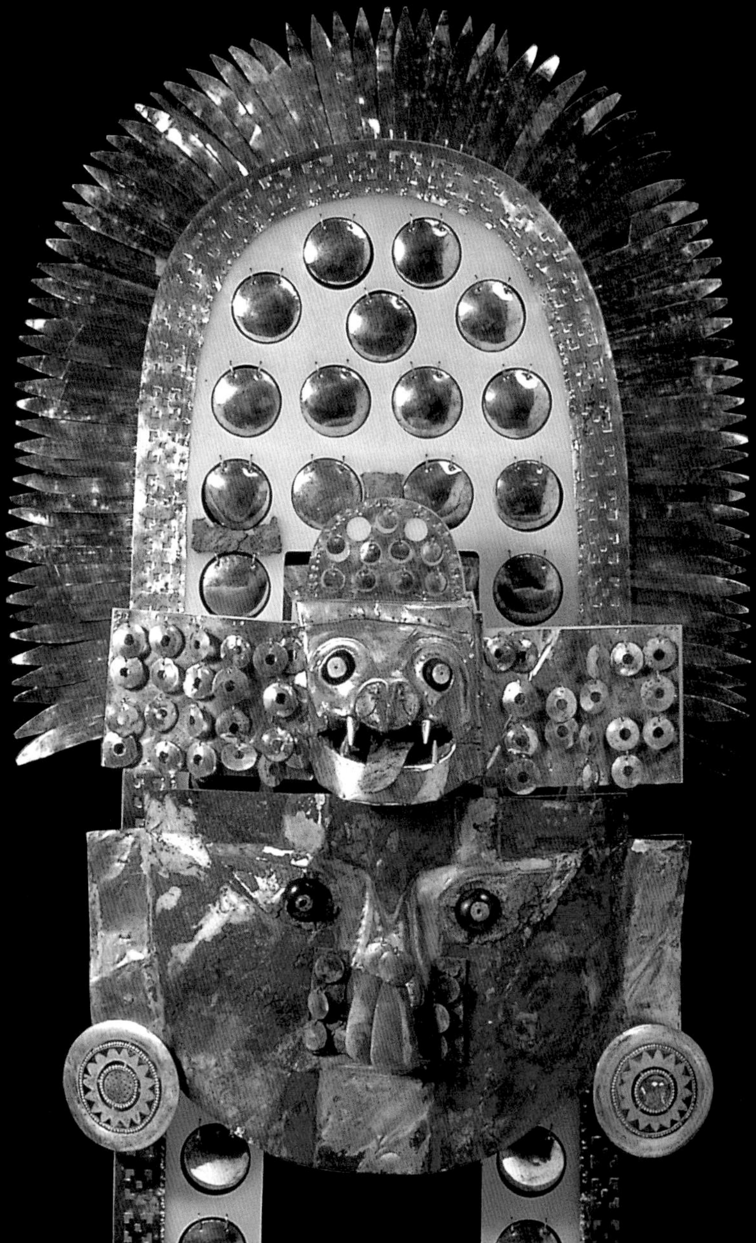

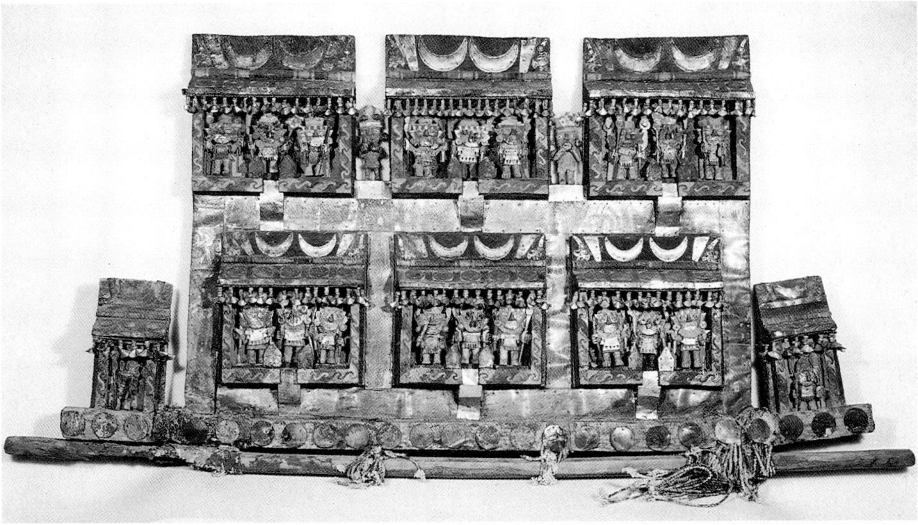

125 The so-called Chimú litter, actually Sicán, built of wood sheathed in gold and studded with feathers. Figures of the Sicán Lord stand inside six portals or temples. This litter may well have been used to transport a ruler. Middle Horizon-Late Intermediate Period.

precedence over wholes from production process to aesthetic results. Specialists probably each worked on one aspect of a complex piece, for instance compiling a litter from a wooden base, sheet-metal sheathing, paint, 125
and feathers. Portions of complex assemblages came from all different zones: importation of high-status materials was even more widespread than in earlier times. Literally tons of spondylus shells were procured from Ecuador by the Lambayeque Valley peoples and then the Chimú, as well as emeralds from Colombia and even amber from as far away as Central America. With increasingly extreme social stratification the elites pushed their artists to create more and more lavish items, without the premium on individuality seen before. Mold-made items dominate the corpus and portraits no longer appear. Patterns reiterate small motifs often arrayed in continuous all-over designs or bands, the same ones repeated almost exactly in the various media. Though made up of diminutive units, overall scale is even grander than before, also showing elite values: palaces enclose areas the size of several football fields, tunics sport thousands of metal appliqués, and ceramic molds produced huge quantities of identical vessels. In the service of enhancing elite power, exclusivity was enforced: only royalty and nobility had the right to precious metals; royal compounds had only one entrance and were filled

124 Gold Sicán mask assemblage excavated in its original, elaborate configuration from a tomb at Huaca Loro in northern Peru. With its dangles, earspools, and tall headdress representing feathers in gold, this burial mask rivals the Moche metalwork found in the royal graves at Sipán. Middle Horizon-Late Intermediate Period.

126 Chimú ceramic vessel in the shape of a lobster. An identical silver version of this lobster stirrup-spout vessel has also been found. Strict social hierarchy restricted precious metals to the elite, yet mass-production yielded many identical ceramic works of art used by the commoners. Late Intermediate Period.

with maze-like labyrinths to deter free movement; most wells were controlled by the upper class; and so on. Even the scale relationships of earlier times could be reversed: at Chan Chan the sacred mound became 'furniture' inside exaggeratedly high security walls. Power statements seem to take precedence even over practicality. Such inordinately tall or long walls, labor-intensive canals, or graves with over 200 metal beakers, cannot be justified from a solely pragmatic point of view.

Because of the value placed on both exclusivity and quantity, these artistic objects often combine – almost paradoxically – extremely precious materials and arduous processes manipulated by many skilled specialists with a hurried assemblage and lack of attention to finishing, unusual in Andean art as a whole. Lambayeque weavers broke the longstanding rules by cutting cloth and leaving tangles of threads on the reverse face. Chimú metallurgists constructed complex objects by adding sheathings of metal over baser materials. Some Chancay painters allowed the slip to drip down their clay effigies. This seeming carelessness can be attributed in large part to haste induced by high demand, perhaps coercive mass-production, and propagandistic goals in which appearance almost overcomes essence. The delineation of a hierarchy according to quality of objects means that lesser objects created for the larger lower class outnumber better ones made for the elite. However, there are always a few superb examples in any medium. Southern products are more finely made than northern ones; Chancay textiles and Ica ceramics are almost universally technically superb, implying that the hand of the expanding Chimú empire rested more heavily on the artists' shoulders. Social stratification also dictated that the exact same objects and images
126 be made in clay for the commoner, and in metal for the elite. Besides the

materials being jealously guarded, clear symbols of power were commissioned to be easily read, so styles avoid esoteric elaboration.

To help reconstruct the period, a few fragmentary ethnohistoric documents, Spanish Colonial administrative and judicial records, remain from the North Coast. These name historical figures and deeds, map out certain indigenous traditional social groupings and leadership roles, and one even describes a Chimú royal entourage. Such sources are nevertheless limited, being written down from 150 to 500 years after the fact by the Spanish who did not particularly understand their subjects. They are propagandized, often ambiguous and contradictory, and may revise events to favor certain factions. Scholars, therefore, use the documents very gingerly, if at all, in trying to correlate word with image; the imposing and complex artistic evidence must still take precedence here. Interwoven in text and image are references to the past, competing peoples capturing neighboring artists and trade routes, changes in strategy and imagery over time, and pervasive regionalism. The cross-currents are not yet all clear, but the outlines of this multi-faceted time are as provocative to us as they were to the Inca conquerors. Our discussion will proceed from north to south, with emphasis on the dominant Chimú.

THE NORTH COAST

After the Moche demise continuing reverberations of this defunct tradition were felt on the North Coast. In later North Coast architecture the Moche components of adobe pyramids, platform mounds, and walls were variously chosen and recombined. In the Moche Valley itself, where Chan Chan would eventually share in the locale's prestige and practical advantages, the small, short-lived settlement at Galindo was built *c.* AD 550–700. Its rectan- *127*

127 Reconstruction drawing of the enclosure at Galindo, which was built in the Moche Valley after the fall of the Moche and before the rise of the Chimú. Middle Horizon.

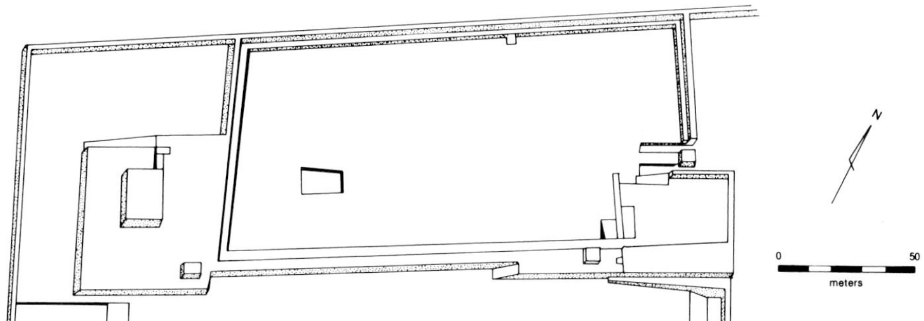

gular compounds with interior courts may have set much of the subsequent pattern for constructions in the Moche and surrounding valleys.

Farther north, the Moche pyramid was more influential, with such sites as Batan Grande featuring these over rectangular compounds. Religious and funerary architecture seems to have continued to favor uplifting masses, referring to mountains, while secular administrative buildings emphasized enclosures to an unprecedented degree, focussing on controlled spaces and thus containment. Now walls began to rival pyramids in height, suggesting an imperial sacralizing of the secular. At places like Pacatnamú, where earlier people oriented their mounds to the mountains and the Chimú imposed a Chan Chan-style administrative compound, the two schema overlapped.

THE SICÁN STYLE

Previously subsumed under a misleadingly general use of the term Chimú, scholars now use the more narrow term Sicán to denote the major pre-Chimú style centered in the Lambayeque and surrounding far north valleys. Sicán covers the period approximately AD 700–1400, with its high point Middle Sicán (also called Classic Lambayeque) taking place between 900 and 1100. The Chimú then conquered the valley under the leadership of General Pacatnamú, according to the documents and verified by descriptions of the imposed settlements. The Chimú seem to have absorbed the Sicán style, technologies, iconography, and trade networks, probably even capturing the renowned Lambayeque metallurgists and ceramicists for Chan Chan.

Although several important Sicán sites were built, the extensive Batan Grande ('Great Anvil') in the La Leche Valley was dominant. Its different sectors served various functions. The Sicán Precinct was a religious/funerary center, with over a dozen huge pyramids filled with sumptuous shaft
124, 128, 129 tombs overflowing with metal offerings. One grave contained over 220 pounds (100 kg) of copper alloy objects, while even higher-status ones held hundreds of precious silver and gold ornamented beakers among other luxury goods. All this metalwork came from Cerro Huaringa, a huge copper alloy industrial center. Izumi Shimada estimates that at least two closely-spaced workshops with many smelting furnaces were built there. Sicán produced one of the only probable currencies or standardized medium of exchange in the ancient Americas, based on non-functional copper axes of standardized sizes.

128 Gold, silver, and turquoise *tumi* knife in the Sicán style (previously thought to be of the later Chimú). A bust of the Sicán Lord (see ill. 129) with elaborate headdress surmounts the bi-metal blade of this ceremonial knife. Middle Horizon-Late Intermediate Period

Sicán Metalwork

Many of the most famous Late Intermediate Period types of art objects are
128, 124 now known to be Sicán rather than Chimú: *tumi* knives, huge burial masks,
129, 131 beakers, and large sheet-metal earspools. Other items include those usually
130 made in clay, especially impressive double-spout-and-bridge vessels with
pedestal bases and bowls, expressly and exclusively for the nobility. Gold and
silver were the most prestigious and tightly controlled, while one rung
down bronze (arsenical copper), a very hard metal alloy, was made into tools
such as digging-stick tips, hoes, chisels, and lance points. Previous peoples
did not pursue bronze nor so formally restrict gold and silver. This again
exemplifies the specialized, large-scale, mass-produced, yet elitist values of
the time.

Technically, Sicán metalwork is typically Andean, but introduces or modifies certain traditional methods. It emphasizes repoussé and cut-out sheet-
metal techniques, but beakers were produced by hammering a circular sheet
129 over a harder metal form. This approach achieves identical pieces, yet it is
nevertheless extremely difficult to create a one-piece, three-dimensional,
tall cup in this manner. Another modification of a past practice, specifically
Moche, is turquoise and spondylus shell inlay, rather than mosaic (large
round turquoise chunks nestle into cavities in the sheets). Silver and gold
also occur in the same piece, but in addition to Moche metallurgical techniques, silver sections are applied as sheathing to the gold structure below.
In general, during this and later periods, precious metal sheets are overlaid
on the human body, on textiles, ceramics, wood, and even architecture,
including metal sheets lining the interiors of tombs. (The Spanish also
melted down almost half a ton of gold from a doorway sheathing at Chan
Chan.) Some Sicán metalwork consciously revives Moche precedents, such
131 as figures with almond eyes and even spiders very like those from Sipán.

128 However, Sicán metalwork is nothing if not distinctive. *Tumi* knives have
long shafts ending in semi-circular, non-functional blades and topped with
images of the Sicán Deity, a standing figure with eyes like sideways commas,
a beak-like nose, and no mouth. These avian characteristics are explicit in
his flanking attendants. His mask can be worn by the Sicán Lord, a human
129 impersonator seen on the litter and other objects such as beakers, although
those in which the cup itself is a large three-dimensional face differ and may
represent lesser individuals. While the Sicán style is usually quite busy, there
are also elegantly simple tiered beakers that may have had a different func-
124 tion. The huge burial masks also seem to have Sicán Lord features, perhaps
to transform the deceased into the deity in the otherworld. Some masks are

129 (*Left*) Sicán-style beaten metal beaker with Sicán Lord repoussé figure. These were formed by beating metal around a three-dimensional form. Graves at Batan Grande contained as many as 200 of these stunning beakers. Middle Horizon-Late Intermediate Period.

130 (*Above*) Silver version of a Sicán double-spout-and-bridge vessel. Sicán style calls for a flaring base and an intricate, often cut-out bridge. Middle Horizon-Late Intermediate Period.

over 23 inches (60 cm) wide, and most appear to us now as glittering expanses of gold, without their accompanying additions of high, multi-partite headdresses, including projecting feathers, as well as earspools and dangles. Originally the faces were very colorful, painted in red (cinnabar), white, and green, adorned with precious jewels (masks may have stones or circular emerald beads projecting from the irises). It is a measure of the conspicuous consumption of gold that it serves mostly as a vehicle here. Dangling metal pieces added movement and acoustic effects. As many as five of these have been found on a high-status body, only one of which was reportedly over the face. Finally, there are a few preserved Sicán litters, *125*
highly elaborate assemblages of luxury materials with repeated Sicán Lord figures. These carriers epitomize the opulence of the privileged nobility at this time.

131 Silver earspool with a repoussé scene of a boat and divers gathering spondylus shells (spiny oysters prized for their brilliant orange interior). Late Intermediate Period.

132 Sicán blackware vessel of the Sicán Lord (right) and a typical double-spout-and-bridge vessel (left). Influential to the later Chimú pottery (ills. 143, 144), Sicán-style ceramics are more intricately detailed.

Other Sicán Arts

In addition to Sicán Lord iconography, metalwork and other media include waves and geometric key patterns, repeated sea birds and fish, as well as elaborate scenes of fishing, spondylus shell diving, and other as yet largely undecoded land and sea rituals. These appear primarily in wood inlaid with stone, shell, and bone, in weaving, on walls, and in clay. Fishing, the sea, and boating figured prominently in North Coast life. One of the most interesting series, recently discussed by Alana Cordy-Collins, illustrates spondy- *131*
lus-shell procurement that took place further north off the coast of Ecuador. Scenes show a boat on which sailors hold sinuous ropes tied to the divers below, who wear stone weights to gather the shells (which in shorthand form resemble tulips). To pry the spiny oysters off rocks up to 180 ft (50 m) underwater was an arduous job for specialists. Centuries later, the importance of these shells was still recorded by the Spanish who noted that, among the conquering Chimú, there was a top-level official known as the Fonga Sigde, responsible for casting a 'red carpet' of ground spondylus-shell powder before the ruler as he walked. Huge amounts of these shells are found in Sicán and later North Coast burials; certainly to pulverize them constituted equally conspicuous consumption. For burial masks, and shells,

as well as some textiles, red was a preferred color that may have signaled death or vital force (blood).

Sicán ceramics, again following but diverging from the Moche, employed complex, two-part molds to create the entire vessel at once. Press-molded reliefs often adorned the surfaces. These mass-production techniques were shared by the Chimú and Chancay ceramicists as well. More carefully made than the latter, and more varied with both blackware and polychromes, Sicán ceramics nevertheless placed little premium on variety, so the corpus appears rigidly repetitive. Distinguishing characteristics include: flaring pedestal-based, double-spout-and-bridge vessels with elaborately cut-out and modeled bridges; the head of the Sicán Lord in front of the spout, flanked by humans or animals lying on the chamber as if prostrate before him; and some strikingly Moche-like figures in red and white. Like the other arts, Sicán ceramic style is noticeably more intricate than the Chimú, its closest relative. *132*

Textiles from the Lambayeque and neighboring valleys are scantily preserved, but very impressive. Found at Pacatnamú and Pachacamac, they combine Moche, Wari, and local aspects to create a unique synthesis. Moche holdovers include an emphasis on complex narratives, like the earlier

painted ceramics and murals, now in painted and tapestry textiles. One from Pacatnamú features architectural forms with projecting thatch roofs and numerous figures offering llamas. Reminiscent of Moche murals, other textiles display a white background and a varied color scheme of red-orange, olive green, gold, brown, white, and sometimes cochineal scarlet. Wari influence can be seen in images of staffbearers wearing fancy tunics, surrounded by bird heads, and abstracted with nested rectangles. Yet, as in other media, local style is strong, with the telltale eyes and crescent headdresses, sea motifs
133 such as birds and fish, and use of the typically coastal slit tapestry (long slits sometimes sewn up for strength). Miniatures also play an important role during this time. As before, the attention to detail is striking.

THE KINGDOM OF CHIMOR

Chimú is the name used for the general style of the kingdom of Chimor, the most successful of the Late Intermediate Period regional organizations. Its capital city of Chan Chan, intrusive administrative centers in the North Coast valleys, canal system, and farflung portable arts document its spread from the Moche Valley outward for 800 miles (1300 km). The ethnohistoric record supports such physical evidence for expansion. Because the North Coast is wider and better watered than elsewhere, the Chimú eventually controlled two-thirds of *all* the coastal land ever irrigated in the Central Andes. A king (or a composite figure) known as Taycanamo founded the dynasty just north of Cerro Blanco. Archaeologists differ in their absolute dating of this and subsequent events in Chimú history, but agree on the general sequence. Beginning the first phase of their expansion under Guacricaur, they subsumed the Moche Valley and went on to take over river valleys from the Santa to the Zaña. A major El Niño flood struck, but rather than being destroyed like the Moche before them, the Chimú apparently changed their strategy from one of canalization and incorporation to one of military conquest and tribute exaction. They conquered the rich 'bread-basket' valleys of Lambayeque and La Leche under the ruler Ñancinpinco and General Pacatnamú. Chimor reached its height around AD 1400, controlling from Tumbez to Chillón (including the Chancay), under the final monarch Minchançaman, who was captured by the Incas. There must have been more rulers than these four recorded ones: some scholars believe two ruled simultaneously, as happened later, and most agree that names were left out of the documents. However, the general chronology and outlines of a two-stage expansion, including a strategy change from direct, intensive

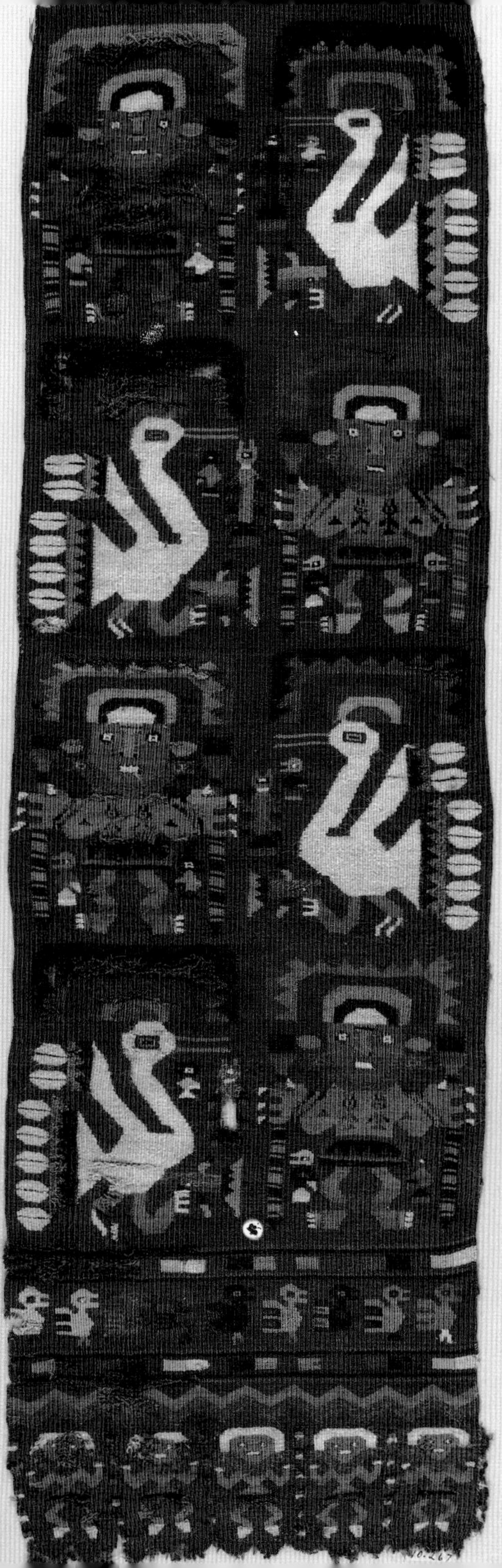

133 Lambayeque tapestry with crescent-headdressed figures and birds. The tapestry's brilliant scarlet color comes from cochineal, the most permanent natural red dye, made from a parasitic insect infesting the prickly pear cactus. Late Intermediate Period.

control to indirect extensive management, can be independently traced from the architectural record of the mighty Chimú city.

CHAN CHAN

134, 135 The vast metropolis of Chan Chan is a monument to the building potential of adobe, to status and craft specialization, to royal prerogative and succession, as well as to change over time. Its immense, high-walled *ciudadelas* ('citadels,' or combination royal palaces, administrative and storage spaces, and mausolea) encode the Chimú state image in their labyrinthine passages. As in the other arts of this time, the architectural approach was additive and surprisingly non-centralized. Chan Chan covers 8 square miles (20 square km) in a series of nodes and filled spaces, but has no true center. Unlike earlier coastal centers, the city was begun very near the sea. To direct fresh water coastward long, stone-lined inland canals connecting the nearby valleys were built over the Moche unlined ones. According to Thomas Pozorski, the general lack of water, the great lengths it had to travel on a perfectly calculated incline, plus the tendency for windblown sand repeatedly to clog the canals, made the Chimú multi-valley canalization a difficult, labor-intensive enterprise that was soon dropped in favor of easier, extortative approaches.

Nevertheless, the canals provided for an estimated 30,000 people to live in a grand, irregular grouping of royal compounds, interspersed with elite residences and commoner housing/artistic workshops. Archaeologists have postulated several possible chronologies for the compounds using a combination of adobe brick type seriation, ceramic associations (though few objects remain in Chan Chan as the clearing out began with the Inca takeover), absence or presence of damage from the major flood, and ethnohistoric reconstruction. While the royal compounds may have been built in pairs, and the exact sequence of *ciudadelas* varies from one interpretation to another, the following reconstruction introduces some of the major characteristics of the different ones.

What seems to have been the earliest of the high-walled adobe-brick enclosures, named Chayhuac by archaeologists, established many of the principal components: massive high walls in a rectangular format, a single northern entrance, and a burial platform in the southern sector. The later rectangular mounds with a T-shaped principal tomb and numerous offering/lesser burial spaces, are interpreted as the royal interments. All are heavily looted (it was these that the Spanish 'mined'), which in itself betrays

134 Aerial view of Chan Chan, the Chimú imperial capital city. Periodic El Niño rains and flooding over the centuries have eroded the tall adobe brick walls around the royal compounds and elite residences. Commoners, who were mostly artists, lived in the outskirts. Late Intermediate Period.

the riches placed within. Around the burial platform are small, restricted storage spaces, presumably to hold the offerings that were amassed before and at the ruler's death. There is relatively less storage space in Chayhuac than in later *ciudadelas*, reflecting the nascent stage of the empire. If the documents are correct, Chayhuac was Taycanamo's palace.

The next compounds, Uhle and Tello, seem contemporaneous but fulfilled different functions. A new element was added, the U-shaped structure called *audiencia* ('audience room') probably an administrator's office. In the labyrinthine passages *audiencias* must be passed to gain access to the storerooms. In Uhle some storerooms are near the royal burial area, while others are in courts near *audiencias*; this can be interpreted as a new, expanded storage of goods, such as food and art objects, for state as well as kingly uses. Redistribution figures prominently in successful Andean state strategies and

139

135 Plan of Chan Chan at its height, showing the royal compounds that were administrative centers, residences, storage depots, and mausolea. The Chimú controlled most of the North Coast from this capital city. Late Intermediate Period.

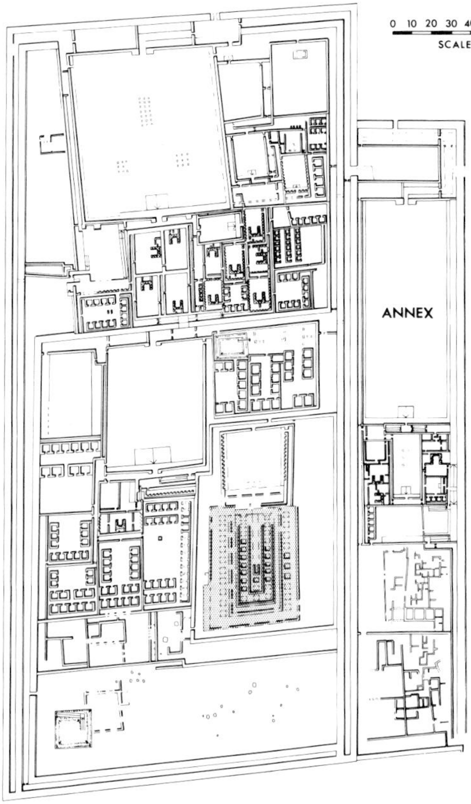

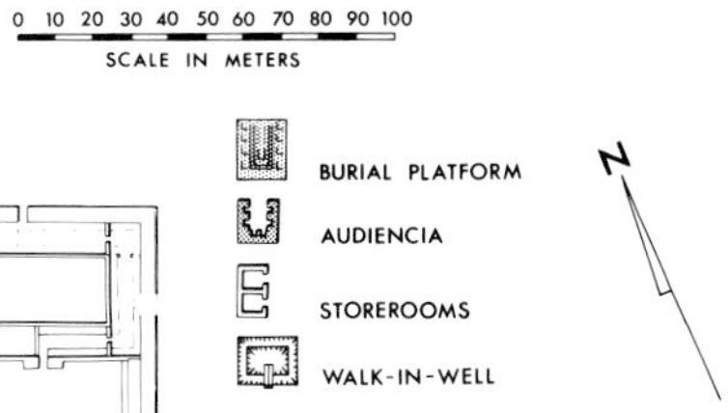

136 (*Left*) The *ciudadela* Rivero, one of the latest royal compounds at Chan Chan built at the time of the greatest standardization. The main entrance to the north restricts access and labyrinthine passageways control human movement, expressing the bureaucratic character of the late kingdom of Chimor. Late Intermediate Period.

137 (*Below, left*) Drawing of an elite residence at Chan Chan with smaller, less formalized elements such as *audiencias* (ill. 139) found in the royal compounds (ill. 136).

138 (*Below*) A typical commoner's house in Chan Chan made of cane. Thousands of artists lived and worked in such small spaces in and around the royal and elite residences. Late Intermediate Period.

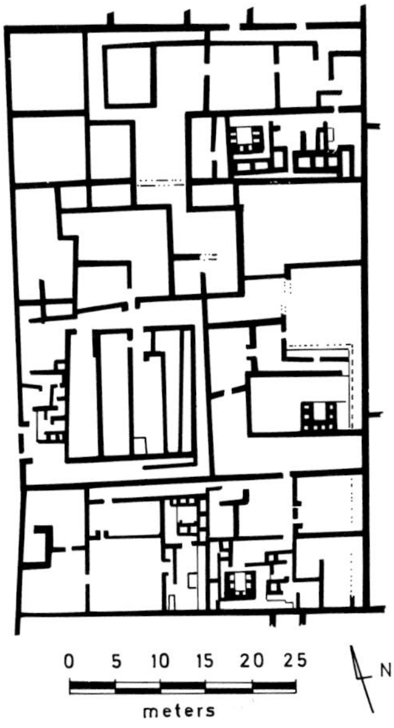

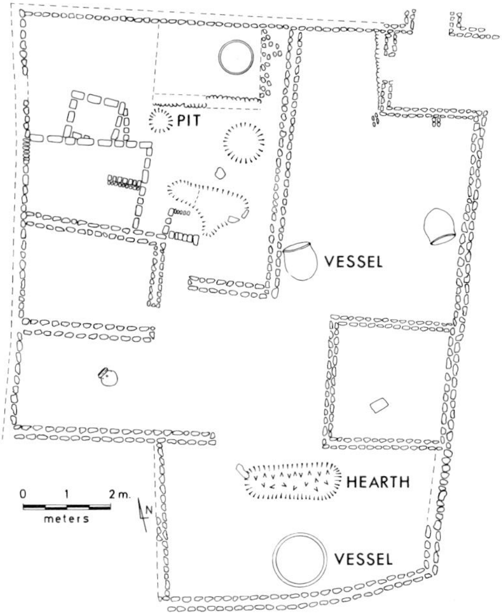

architectural choices suggest that storage expanded beyond the ruler's direct control to a wider administrative network operating outside the palace. Tello, as further demonstration of this pattern, has a great number of storerooms and no burial platform. It was most likely built expressly for administration and continued as a storage depot in later times, while the other palace/mausolea were sealed at the ruler's death. With the Moche and neighboring valleys now incorporated by Guacricaur, new ways of organizing space and processing tribute seem to have prevailed. In this first phase a small amount of elite housing clustered near the commoners' housing, presumably to oversee art production. High-ranking administrators were allowed to construct more modest versions of *ciudadelas* with formidable walls, single entrances, and *audiencias* but no burial platforms.

Laberinto is also without a burial platform (a space set aside for it was never used, perhaps because the great flood interrupted). This compound may reflect another spurt of sudden wealth, corresponding to the second phase of expansion, as it contains the highest percentage of storage space of all the *ciudadelas*. Atypically, it has two entrances, perhaps to subdivide goods by type and give somewhat more efficient access to them. Its mate, Gran Chimú, the largest of all the compounds (measuring an awesome 1310 by 1970 ft (400 by 600 m)), seems to be a kingly palace, possibly Ñancinpinco's. Gran Chimú has proportionately less royal and more administrative storage, but less total storage than other *ciudadelas* because of that in Tello and Laberinto. It is an extraordinary monument to kingly might, a veritable city in its own right.

137 Beginning at this point, four times more elite houses were built than in the first phase, showing the explosive growth of administrators to manage the incoming wealth. The houses were increasingly constructed close to the royal compounds: overseeing by the elite was apparently now needed more for goods from afar than for those produced at home. Commoners contin-
138 ued to live in small, irregularly arranged home workshops, the remains of their hearths found near evidence of woodworking, metalworking, and weaving activity. Chan Chan was a city of state-supported artists, at least several thousand creating the fabulous objects for the burial platforms and for royal exchange. Imported from all over the kingdom, especially from Lambayeque, the last generation of artists were deported to Cuzco by the Incas – so rapidly that they left pots on the fire and ingots on the ground. The premium placed on elite art objects in the late Andean empires is obvious. Wealth in difficult-to-reproduce forms drove, funded, and organized the state system. It rewarded and lured subjects, reinforced power, and

139 The surviving portion of a typical late Chimú *audiencia* in *ciudadela* Tschudi at Chan Chan. These U-shaped offices of the nobility are usually found controlling access to storerooms for foodstuffs and royal luxury goods. Remnants of spectacular adobe reliefs, here birds, and latticework can be seen. Late Intermediate Period.

occupied peoples' time peacefully. Art effectively communicated sacred and secular meanings, as well as providing a recognizable presence in a foreign territory and allowing a measure of self-expression and upward mobility in an otherwise rigid social framework. It was all these things to the Chimú.

Late-phase *ciudadelas* at Chan Chan, known as Bandolier, Velarde, Rivero, *136*
Tschudi, and the unfinished Squier, were built in rapid succession in increasingly standardized layout. This seems to indicate that the kingdom of Chimor at its height had a large and bureaucratic hierarchy. Tschudi is the likeliest candidate for Minchançaman's headquarters. These final *ciudadelas*, veritable mazes, show how important it was to keep others out and run them through a gauntlet of administrators. The compounds point to an extreme, almost paranoid, royal hoarding of wealth, bearing out the records which claim that stealing was a capital offense to the Chimú. The *ciudadelas* may even be likened to museums, as mentioned above, since *audiencias* have niches for object display, storerooms protect them while in transit, and burial platforms or other elites' 'collections' are their final destinations. Royal compounds were also works of art themselves, the courtyard and *audiencia* walls being covered with adobe reliefs in geometric and animal motifs. *139*
Openwork walls and diagonal patterns are deeply reminiscent of textiles; in *146*
a sense the friezes may be permanent wall-hangings for the highest-status people.

135 The personal, acquisitory attitude betrayed by the *ciudadelas* is played out in the city plan of Chan Chan; each compound simply takes up its own space with no easily determined relationship to the others. Geoffrey Conrad proposes that a documented rule for royal succession, known as split inheritance, relates to this format of independent kingly domains. Split inheritance is a system in which the heir to the throne receives the right to rule but none of his predecessor's wealth or land, which are kept as a royal corporation administered by the other offspring. This ingenious arrangement ensures that the disgruntled children are materially satisfied and that the heir must conquer new areas and tribute sources, guaranteeing imperial expansion. Thus at Chan Chan each *ciudadela* with a royal burial platform was sealed at the king's death, yet additions to the outside walls and limited occupancy suggest the activities of a royal corporation for a number of generations. This strategy was taken up by the Incas as well. Its 'everyone for himself' attitude can be seen played out in the unique non-unified form of Chan Chan.

BEYOND CHAN CHAN

The Chimú were concerned not only with adding to their metropolis, but with establishing centers throughout their empire to proclaim their presence. Archaeological investigation has revealed three main levels of administrative Chimú architecture beyond Chan Chan: large provincial centers (earlier Farfán in the Jequetepeque Valley and later Manchan in the Casma Valley), smaller storage depots (such as El Milagro in the Moche Valley), and tiny compounds for the overseeing of agricultural land (for example, Quebrado Katuay also near Chan Chan). Other pre-existing centers taken
140 over by the Chimú, such as Pacatnamú near Farfán, have recognizable, intrusive walled compounds to announce Chimú control.

The walled compound with interior *audiencias* and patios, as well as storage capacity for higher-level centers, define Chimú presence and level of authority outside the capital. Six compounds were built at Farfán, one of which has a burial platform that scholars interpret as a special favor to General Pacatnamú for his important conquest. Over forty storage facilities were located there in order to act as depots in the transport of goods from this northern kingdom to Chan Chan. Nine compounds at Manchan and separate, local-style elite burial structures show the even larger scale of second-phase Chimú expansion with its indirect control strategy. Nearly fifty large storage facilities served as shipment warehouses for tribute from

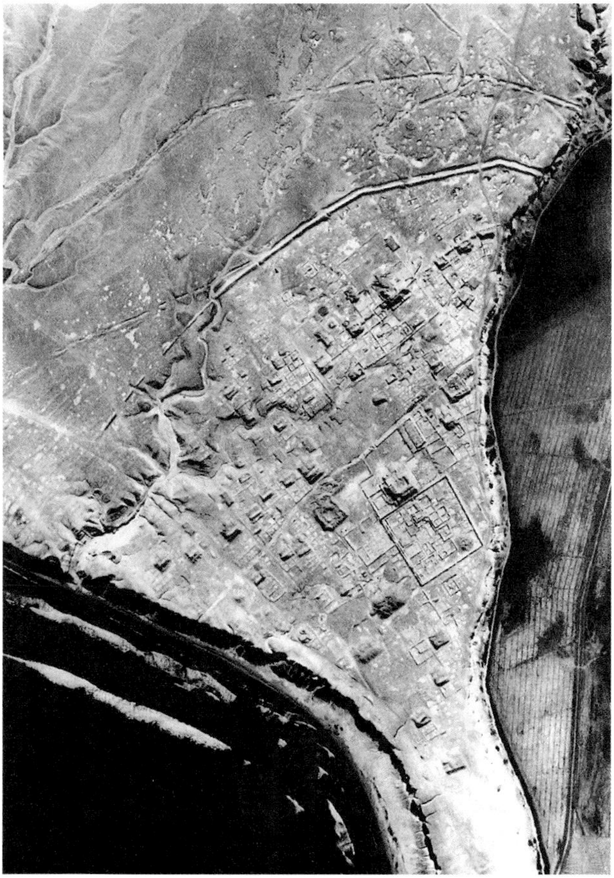

140 Aerial view of Pacatnamú in the Lambayeque Valley, showing the pre-existing pyramids and the intrusive Chimú compound (the large rectangle along the right center). Late Intermediate Period.

the southern valleys. A large permanent population of artists at Manchan shows that art was high on the administrative agenda. Lower-level settlements administered agricultural products, with little storage or permanent housing capacity, but kept key Chimú features. El Milagro, located near fields and canals, had one main structure only 180 by 148 ft (55 by 45 m) with five *audiencias* near storerooms.

Pre-existing centers with Chimú intrusions include Pacatnamú and Chotuna. Pacatnamú, named for the General but not his administrative center, was a sacred Sicán city of pyramids oriented respectfully toward the mountains. During their northern expansion the Chimú introduced one huge and easily distinguishable walled compound abutting the most prominent pyramid, as if usurping its glory.

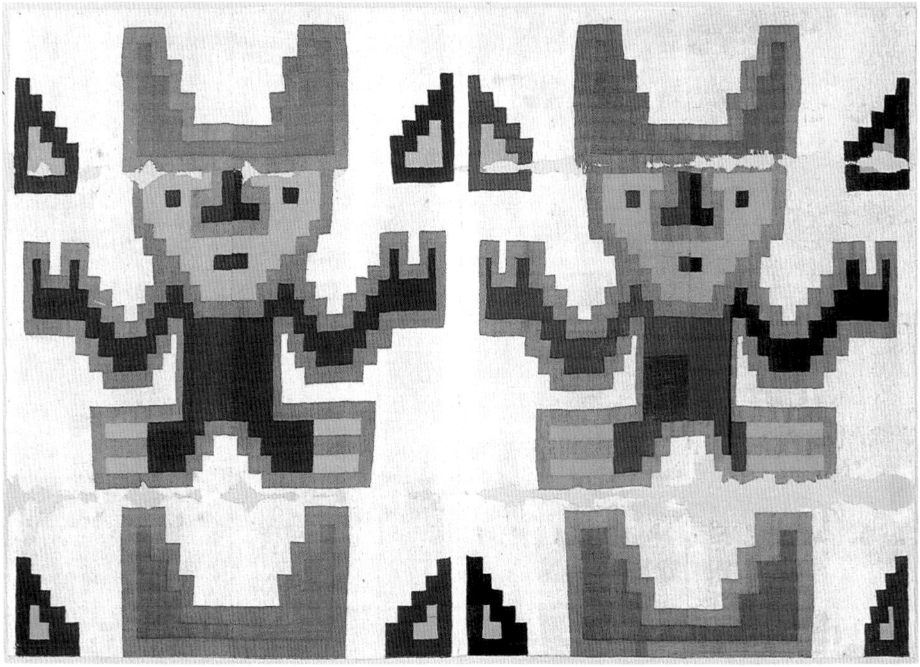

141 Chimú cotton textile in the discontinuous warp and weft technique depicting two large figures. The blue color is obtained from indigo, a notoriously difficult dye to use, especially with cotton. Late Intermediate Period.

CHIMÚ TEXTILES AND METALWORK

Architecture was the greatest achievement of the Chimú and the most clearly defined in the imperial melting pot. Chimú textiles, on the other hand – of which not very many survive – are sometimes only distinguishable from those of conquered people, especially the Chancay, by technical details. In turn, Inca and Chimú characteristics blended when the Incas took over, so there are many enigmatic 'Chimú-related' pieces. However, some found in situ give us a sense of Chimú textile offerings. Apparently these often consist of matched sets of brocaded lightweight garments. Most Chimú textiles feature white cotton; camelid fiber was used sparingly in super-structural techniques. Openwork, in which spaces are deliberately left
146 between worked areas, is characteristic here and for the Chancay. Textiles share certain qualities with the other Chimú arts: they are often woven on a large scale, some over 6 by 4 ft (2 by 1.3 m), and betray piecemeal construc-

142 Detail of Chimú featherwork tunic with pelicans borne on litters (see ill. 125). Feathers, laboriously obtained from the distant jungles, are sewn in rows to cotton backing, and represent perhaps the most prestigious medium in the Andean aesthetic system. Late Intermediate Period.

tion. The figural representations are also relatively simple versions of profile and frontal crescent headdressed figures. Textile patterns and those of wall reliefs are especially similar; the fiber arts again may have served as the influencing medium. *141*

Even more prestigious than woven textiles to Chimú elites were feather-covered and appliqué gold garments. Brilliant tropical feathers acquired via the extensive trade network were sewn in rows to plain-weave cloth backings. These are difficult to date and locate as to place of manufacture because of their simple techniques. Even more shimmering are the plain-weave tunics covered entirely in tiny gold squares, as many as 7000 on a single garment. Imagine the blinding effect of a wearer reflecting the sun at every step. Sheathing the nobility in precious metal extended to appliquéd bags and even shoes. The ethnohistoric records claim that when Chimú nobles were created they received the divine right to precious metals, what the Incas later called 'sweat of the sun' (gold) and 'tears of the moon' (silver). *142*

143 Typical Chimú blackware vessel with a bird design and a monkey appliqué at the spout junctures. A final revival of the stirrup-spout form, these mold-made examples were created by the thousand. Late Intermediate Period.

144 A Chimú double-chambered whistling vessel with a human effigy. Water levels in the two connected parts change the whistle tone which escapes from a hole behind the figure. Whistling pots and doubling of all kinds are time-honored Andean artistic choices. Late Intermediate Period.

CHIMÚ CERAMICS

Although very like those of the influential far North Coast, Chimú ceramics demonstrate that efficiency was valued over excellence to a greater degree in the empire. Forms are even more repetitively mold-made and the style is noticeably simpler than that of Sicán. Although almost entirely greyware (fired in a reducing, or low oxygen atmosphere, but not to the degree of blackware), there is nevertheless another Moche revival in the renewed preference for the stirrup-spout vessel. Chimú molds also feature two parts (for the chamber, the spout, or for the entire vessel), so the technology is more elaborate and piecemeal than before. Seams on the sides of vessels are hastily smoothed and often left visible, in an extreme version of Late Intermediate Period dispatch. Some vessels, probably those made in the Lambayeque area or by potters from there transplanted southward, appear dark, evenly black, and glossy, while most are more greyish and mottled. For commoners' consumption, Chimú ceramics rarely received detailed artistic attention.

Chimú characteristics also include small modeled elements (monkeys, birds, or simple lugs) appliquéd at the junctures of spout with vessel and arched with upright spout. Whistling vessels are very common, with two connected chambers, typically shaped like flattened spheres, the front one of which is usually an effigy. Chambers often have smooth, burnished areas contrasting with those of raised dots. The Chimú almond-shaped eye is also emphatically outlined, more like the Moche but without the sense of an actual eyeball in a socket. Individual physiognomy is not a concern in the expanded imperial aesthetic, especially in images made in baser materials.

143

144

THE CENTRAL COAST: THE CHANCAY STYLE

Before being subsumed by the Chimú, a style known generally as Chancay was spread across four Central Coast valleys – Chillón, Huaura, Rimac, and the Chancay itself – but without a centralized state organization. Aboveground architecture is scarce and undistinguished, except for its being mass-produced in tapia (clay poured into wooden forms like concrete). As seen

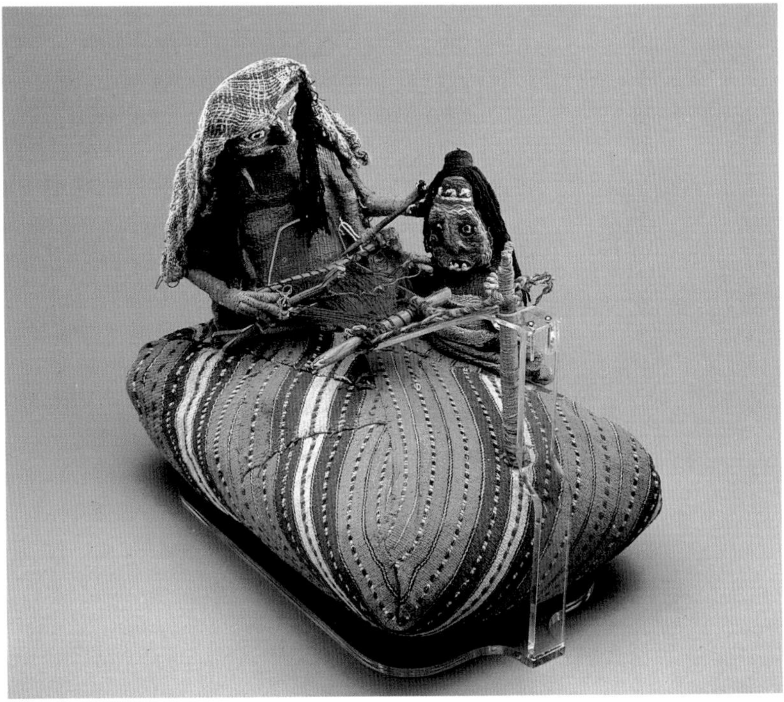

145 A fiber sculpture of a mother teaching her daughter the art of weaving. Notice the headcloth that is similar to ill. 146. This is one of the very few Andean images of the weaving process (see ill. 96).

elsewhere in the Late Intermediate Period, the finishing of buildings is casual, with unbonded corners often separating. Ceramics are quite distinct from other coastal styles and have a strong graphic appeal, but are often quite rough in execution. Elite burials, on the other hand, can be well constructed and filled with lavish art offerings, especially fine textiles and sculptures in fiber. Whereas the Chimú arts were quite uniform from one medium to the next, Chancay artists seem to have pursued their specialities into markedly different stylistic trajectories and levels of skill.

Chancay Ceramics

The boldest of the coastal clay sculpture, Chancay Black-on-White ceramics, shared two-part mold technology with their neighbors to the north. The vessels were often quite large and several unusual shapes were preferred, especially tall ovoid jars and large female effigies with short, outstretched arms. The high-contrast pairing of black and white (sometimes with added red touches) was painted over terracotta clay in thin coats. Chancay ceramicists must have painted quickly with the watery slips, as obvious drips and colors showing through each other are common. Matt, unburnished surfaces appear dull and gritty due to the sand temper in the clay paste leaching out. Poor firing is often apparent in the warping of vessel shapes, fire-clouding, surface blisters, and glassy patches where the temper has overheated.

Despite the careless approach, there are well-painted examples and all are graphically powerful. Females have elaborate body painting on their frankly sexual nude bodies; in the illustration here we know that the dark painting on her upper body does not represent a garment because the imprint of an *frontispiece* actual textile remains on her chest. Outfitting effigies in real clothing represents another way in which Andean images were granted reality and vital energy. Double-chambered whistling pots with tall, thin spouts, appliqué animals, and strong geometric designs plus bulbous-bodied animals (perhaps representing camelids, whose hair was precious to the Chancay weavers) are typical. It is striking how very different the ceramic style is from that of the textiles, although both may be white and feature geometric elements.

Chancay Textiles

Chancay techniques in fiber are extraordinarily varied and are almost without exception executed in a virtuoso manner. From gauzes and openwork embroideries to painted plain weave and tapestry, as well as fully three-dimensional figural sculptures, the most challenging avenues were explored. Openwork, ultimately derived from the ancient coastal fishing tradition of netmaking, reached new heights of lacy intricacy. Women wore headcloths *146* with complex patterns, such as snakes (that can be read inverted as felines) and interlocked birds. Significantly, the motifs could not be seen except by the weaver during their creation because the overspun threads pull together when not under tension. This again exemplifies the Andean value placed on the essence over the perceptible appearance and soundly displaces the viewer in favor of the weaver. Images of weaving, as in the tiny but accurate fiber model, suggest the importance of passing weaving knowledge *145* from mother to daughter. Literally thousands of Chancay textiles are preserved in museums all over the world, so the artistic output was staggering, in this case with no loss in quality. One is reminded of the Paracas dedica-

146 (*Left*) A Chancay openwork woman's headcloth similar to that worn by the fiber effigy of a weaver (ill. 145). Although the weaver could see the complex design of interlocking birds and felines that can also be read as snakes, when worn the threads contracted. Andean art often favors the intrinsic over the visually accessible. Late Intermediate Period.

147 (*Below*) A Chancay loincloth end in tapestry. In the central band birds carry fish in their beaks, while in the flanking bands a fret pattern reveals abstracted birds in more shorthand form. Late Intermediate Period.

tion to massive burial offerings laboriously woven and stitched. The Chancay palette features a softly harmonious combination of golds, browns, scarlet, white, and even lavender and olive green. Outlined, repeated figures, such as birds carrying fish, assign color with little regularity and thus accomplish a lively, yet subtle effect. Painted textiles follow the geometric lead of the woven techniques with all-over designs, such as the familiar crescent headdress figures slightly modified. These are among the most pleasing of the many incarnations of Andean fiber arts.

THE SOUTH COAST: PACHACAMAC

Chimú control waned at a certain point beyond the Chancay area. Neither they, nor any other group until the Spanish, had ever claimed authority over the sacred city of Pachacamac, located some 19 miles (30 km) south of Lima. For many centuries it had been a pre-eminent pilgrimage center and still in the sixteenth century boasted the most revered oracle in the land. Objects in all styles were brought here as offerings to earth deities, primarily Pachamama (Mother Earth), as well as myriad lesser figures of the broad Andean pantheon. Two later Inca constructions remain in good condition, while the earlier shrines and courts remain largely submerged in the sands. The principal terraced adobe mound, the Temple of Pachacamac, was originally covered in bright murals depicting plants and animals, a fitting claim to natural abundance. Repainted as many as sixteen times, with reed and human hair brushes found near one of the terraces, these murals were of supreme importance. This spectacular temple pyramid and a unique colonnaded esplanade below, presumably to shelter masses of supplicants, form the ceremonial core of the city. Atop the Temple was the enclosure for the oracle, a carved wooden sculpture with superimposed figures rather like a totem pole. According to the Spanish accounts, only the select priesthood was allowed in its chamber and a high priest spoke for it from another room. Tragically, the shocking arrival of aliens in the form of the Spanish caused the oracle to fall silent, which was interpreted as abandonment by the earth itself and contributed to the success of the invasion (see Epilog).

ICA

Also beyond the reach of the Chimú, the southern valleys of Ica, Chincha, Cañete, and Mala shared a degree of stylistic unity. Like the Chancay, this corporate style loosely termed Ica did not betray great political power –

148 (*Right*) The wooden oracle sculpture at Pachacamac, a long-revered independent cult center on the Central Coast. Tragically when the Spanish arrived the oracle 'fell silent.' This inauspicious occurrence probably contributed to the European takeover.

149 The characteristic style of the South Coastal Ica (not to be confused with the later conquering Incas) featured textile-like repeated geometric patterns on well-made flaring vessels. Late Intermediate Period.

there are no large cities at all – but rather denoted high prestige and a shared aesthetic. Indeed, Ica-style pottery is the only major Late Intermediate Period type to be handbuilt and uniformly well painted, so its relative status
149 is understandable. Ica ceramic vessels are mostly flaring or globular, with everted rims and narrow necks. Polychromatic, featuring orange, red, black, white, maroon, purple, and a sparkly purple-black made from specular hematite, the patterns are almost entirely geometric, often interlocking in bands, or all-over arrangements. Determinedly rectilinear, they have the look of textiles. The approach is meticulous, with thin, even walls and elegantly symmetrical elemental shapes, precise painting and burnishing; though repetitive in its own way, Ica vessels avoid the mass-produced look to the north. When conquered by the Incas, this aesthetic was applied to the new prescribed vessel shapes, but after the Spanish takeover the South Coast reverted to its own strong earlier aesthetic traditions. In fact, all the Andean cultures had a tenacious sense of identity not extinguished through the political upheavals of the final era.

With the late fifteenth-century advent of the last native conquerors, the Incas, coastal artistic and ethnic diversity prevalent during the Late Intermediate Period was minimized, although it was never completely suppressed. The art and architecture of the coastal peoples also served to inspire their overlords with its beauty, ingenuity, and variety.

CHAPTER SEVEN

Inca Art and Architecture

On the heels of Late Intermediate Period diversity, the conquering Incas enforced a new level of uniformity, albeit not absolute, on the entire Central Andes. Their meteoric rise to power in less than a century spread their style
from Quito in Ecuador to below Santiago in Chile, a span of *c.* 3400 miles *150*
(5500 km). They controlled the largest territory of the Renaissance world and developed one of the most elegant, subtle, and recognizable art styles in history. The Inca genius was mainly in stonework, from a network of roads
more than 20,000 miles (33,000 km) long, to cities perched high in moun- *164*
tain saddles, to walls of perfectly fitted monoliths. For the Incas art was not *160*
directed principally toward the dissemination of a new or complex iconography, as with the Moche or Wari and Tiwanaku. Instead, the presence and look of stonework itself formed the imperial message. Secondary arts, textiles and ceramics, were more regularly geometric, while metalwork and sculpture, almost all of which was destroyed by the invading Spanish, seem to have been quite representational. Thus, the surviving Inca art and architecture, abstract and seemingly minimalistic, must be carefully observed to understand its communicative richness.

The Incas approached politics and art by standardized units and yet avoided rigidity, an extremely successful balancing act in both practical and aesthetic arenas. Standardization, though powerfully unifying, did not necessarily lower the quality of art; technically Inca tapestry thread count, large-scale ceramic vessel production, mortarless masonry, and miniature sheet-metal sculpting are unsurpassed. To an unexpected degree subject peoples continued or blended their religious and artistic traditions with the new lords so that while Inca standard shapes and patterns were imposed, aspects such as color scheme were locally interpreted. As long as the Incas received tribute in food, art, and labor (for building and conquest) they were satisfied. State control was typically Andean: based on tribute, a network of centers, and syncretism rather than blanket domination. In an empire of this size, absolute control would have been impossible anyway. It was the Incas' unique ability to organize and standardize that made their ruling presence palpable, especially through impressive and ubiquitous masonry reminders.

Generally speaking, they also made their presence palatable by paying back the workers in redistributed food, support during labor tax projects, and improved lifestyle. At least in the ideal, the state performed these services; imperial reciprocity is, however, rarely completely symmetrical.

The Incas called their empire Tawantinsuyo, 'Land of the Four Quarters.' They capitalized on longheld Andean traditions – verticality, reciprocity, dualism – to integrate their six to ten million subject peoples into a larger system. They were neither, as sometimes portrayed, dull bureaucrats nor fascistic dictators. It is important to recognize their unique qualities, their complexity and aesthetically sensitive side. And despite the greater role of Spanish documentation in our understanding, the artistic remains continue to take precedence if we are interested in the vast, unadulterated messages the Incas left about themselves.

ORIGINS AND HISTORY

Like the Mexica (Aztecs) of Mesoamerica, the Incas were a relatively lowly, unimportant group that nevertheless propelled themselves into political prominence during the fifteenth and early sixteenth centuries. As a result of both their humble beginnings and impressive accomplishments, they developed an elaborate, but rarely accurate, version of their origins. Scholars are still disentangling myth from reality; embedded in the myths, however, are values and beliefs held by actual personages linked to real events.

In brief, Inca propaganda claimed that they were born of Inti, the Sun God, at Tiwanaku, where the gods themselves had originated in the distant past. Miraculously traveling underground, the first eight Incas, four brother-sister pairs under Manco Capac and Mama Ocllo, emerged from Pacaritambo, a cave near the Cuzco Valley. Led by prophecy to a place where Mama Ocllo's golden staff would easily penetrate the rich earth, the group journeyed, losing some members. Along the way one of the brothers was turned to stone, becoming a particular outcrop on Huaynacauri, a Cuzco Valley peak. Finally they drove the staff into the ground, entered the valley, fought off the inhabitants, and took over easily. When they defeated the Chanca, a neighboring power to the west, the Incas claimed the rocks in the fields rose up and fought as humans to help. The rest, as they say, is history: conquests, success, power, wealth.

In fact, the small band that later formed the core of Inca nobility seems to have been a peripheral highland group long eking out a marginal existence in the vicinity of the rich and sought-after Cuzco Valley. Pacaritambo

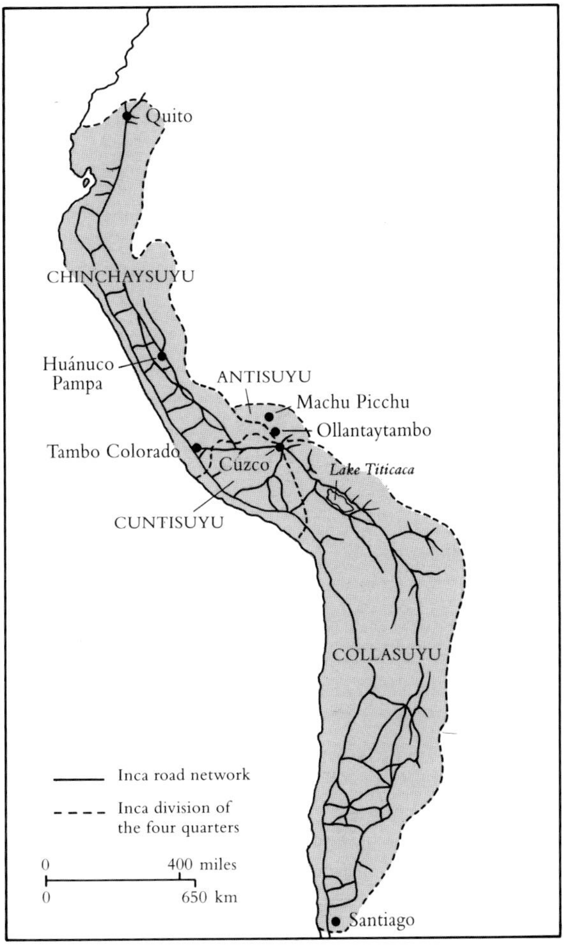

150 Map of the principal Inca roads and the four parts of Tawantinsuyo, The Land of the Four Quarters, showing the extent of the Inca empire (shaded area). Well over 15,000 miles (25,000 km) of roads connected the coast and highlands like a giant ladder. The four quarters emanated from the capital city of Cuzco. Late Horizon.

is most likely Maukallaqta, according to Brian Bauer, a village the Incas later marked with special architecture to commemorate their rise. While they did eventually settle in Cuzco and gain prominence there, it was a long, gradual, and perhaps serendipitous process. Their first major skirmish with neighbors in 1438 succeeded against all odds, engendering a nascent imperialist attitude, and conquests followed in quick succession. However, the Incas had to keep conquering and reconquering people throughout their rise. With their sudden prominence and the concomitant need for loyal administrators, the Incas expanded their noble class to include Quechua speakers in the heartland.

The king list contains eleven names, of which scholars agree that the first eight were local leaders. Beginning with Pachakuti (Earthquake), in the early fifteenth century, the Cuzco Valley and adjacent areas were brought under Inca sway. He is attributed with the designing of the imperial capital – the Incas characteristically allying rulers with architecture – but in reality Cuzco seems to have been transformed over a longer period. While Pachakuti is recorded as being the king, in fact there was dual rule: principal and secondary leaders to represent respectively the *hanan*, or dominant moiety, and the *hurin*, subdominant moiety. The next ruler was Topa Inca, Pachakuti's son, who has been called South America's Alexander the Great. He expanded the kingdom an astonishing 2500 miles (4000 km). The final monarch was Huayna Capac, a consolidator who established a second capital in Quito since the extended empire had grown so unwieldly. He was residing there when European diseases preceded the invaders into South America and he died of smallpox in 1526 without naming an heir. The plague together with the ensuing civil war between two of Huayna Capac's sons, Huascar and Atahualpa, paved the way for the Spanish takeover (see Epilog).

EMPIRE AND ART

Conquests and battles cannot fully explain the ideas and institutions of an empire, nor do they account for the art style chosen to represent the conquerors to their subjects. Yet the Inca political realm had almost universal expression in art, architecture, and ritual life. An understanding of the organizational and religious aspects of the imperial vision form the necessary background to an appreciation of Inca stonework and the other arts.

150 The Incas divided up their world into interlocking parts, from the four quarters of Tawantinsuyo, to taxpaying units, to the walls they built. Units were the key to constructing such a complex hierarchy out of enormous ethnic diversity, ecological challenge, and sheer size. The ruler oversaw governors of the quarters, who in turn controlled regional and local administrators (who usually had been leaders before the Inca conquest). The population was divided into multiples of ten taxpayers (10, 100, 1000, 10,000, etc.); in fact, the Incas probably had a more accurate census than in modern times. This information, among many other types of data, was
151 recorded on a unique writing device, the knotted string *quipu*. Taxes (*mit'a*) were owed in goods and labor, especially in textiles, food, and construction of roads, waystations, and centers throughout the realm. *Mit'a* (taxpaying)

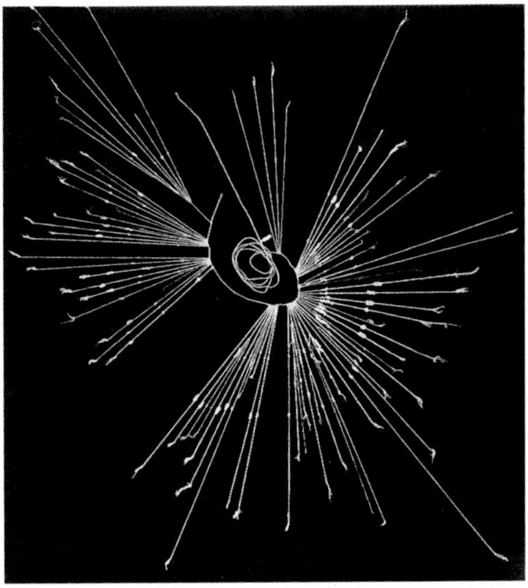

151 The unique Inca fiber recording device, the *quipu*. Through knot type and position, cord color and placement the Incas could encode incredible amounts of information from the census to astronomy, and even history and poetry. Their mathematical system was virtually identical to our own. Late Horizon.

laborers often had to travel long distances to reach their worksites and were supported for the duration of the project. Subjects also received corn beer, redistributed food from other vertical zones (especially during times of hardship), and generalized state assistance. Thus, reciprocity, verticality, and nomadism – time-honored Andean survival strategies – were employed by the Incas on a new global scale and taken to extremes for political purposes. Certain groups of people (*mitimae*) were even forcibly relocated far from their homes as a means of preventing rebellion. *Mitimae* were required to maintain their native dress so as *not* to be integrated into the new area. Loyal subjects were also moved so as to promote cooperation in a newly-added region.

Conquest by the Incas brought with it gifts of sumptuous, imperial-style art, especially textiles. These large-scale movements of people and products served to create identification with the conquerors, manifested by the use of standardized Inca artistic style by people all over the Central Andes. This style emphasized units, recognizability, and universality. It could not afford to rely on specific or detailed past associations, such as another Chavín or Moche revival, because these would have had a limited reception. As an exception, Tiwanaku was a favored, if generalized referent, familiar to more subjects than any other because the Wari and Tiwanaku states had spread over most of the same territory previously. Yet the staffbearer and other complex earlier imagery was not specifically revived; instead, the Incas constructed an elemental geometric vocabulary that drew on basic patterns from all regions but matched none. Without acknowledging the debt, they absorbed many elements from the Chimú, from split inheritance to bronze technology. In the recombination of pre-existing political and artistic elements and reduction to new essential forms, the Incas were quite innovative. They were also highly practical. Reiterated across architecture, textiles, and ceramics, their layouts and motifs were simple enough to be faithfully reproduced in any part of the kingdom and recognizable enough to announce Inca presence at every turn. Standardization thus achieved the twin goals of unity and distinctiveness, yet was not absolute; local materials, techniques, color schemes, and figures coexisted with the Inca long-necked jar, checkerboard pattern arrangement, and trapezoidal city block.

Control was never far, however; the Incas captured foreign leaders, artists, and religious icons (*huacas*) and held them hostage in Cuzco. King Minchançaman and his artists at Chan Chan were removed to the capital, along with all the best female weavers in the realm. State-supported, protected, and revered, they nonetheless cast and wove for the ruler and the Sun as prisoners. As with the Chimú, precious metals were reserved for Inca nobility, as were the finest silky vicuña textiles (the ruler or Sapa Inca owned all vicuña herds). Atahualpa even commissioned a mantle woven from bat hair! Royalty ate and drank only from gold and silver, wore silver-soled sandals and feather garments, walked on the finest tapestries during wedding celebrations, in short, lived a stupendously opulent life. Upon death, the ruler was treated as if still alive, his mummy ritually fed, consulted, dressed, paraded, and all his wealth preserved in his palace, as with the Chimú. His non-ruling heirs maintained his estate intact and lived off its proceeds. These mummies existed into Colonial times when the Spanish destroyed them as heretical. The cyclical view of life and death reached an extreme in immortal kings as reminders of Inca power.

Ritualism of all sorts was fundamental to the state, from the daily sacrificing of a llama and periodic burning of the finest textiles as offerings to the Sun, to limited child sacrifices to ensure the king's health (known as *capac hucha*), to calendric, agricultural, and cleansing rituals of all sorts. Complementary to the permanent forms of Inca cities and roads, the daily observances also solidified state control. Naturally much of this ceremonialism took place in Cuzco, the *axis mundi* or world center into which only the elite were allowed. Its visible, and even invisible, parameters proclaimed the close Inca relationship to the natural world. Forty-one radiating invisible lines, known as *ceques*, subdivided space and ritual time from Cuzco outward. A fascinating abstract conceptualization and manipulation of the landscape, this system of imaginary lines tells us much about the Incas' grandiose yet respectful sense of themselves in nature, spelled out in every working of stone from natural outcropping, to terrace, to town, to wall.

Inca religion was an important guiding force of the empire and combined Andean traditions with new twists. Royal mummies were an extension of a broader ancestor cult, with roots in Andean consciousness long before the Incas. The mummies helped to fabricate a long past for the Incas and connect them to the supernatural realm. Sacrifices propitiated the dead and the divine to help the living. Another mythical connection was made to the creator god Viracocha and the Sun God Inti through the belief that both these gods and the Inca people emerged from the impressive ruins at Tiwanaku, and/or from the Island of the Sun in Lake Titicaca. The Incas imported their stonemasons from this area and built a shrine on the island itself. Thus, ancester veneration, an expanded pantheon that stressed the sun, direct connections to the gods, and a vague link to an impressive past, were the basis of Inca politicized religion.

The Incas deified natural forces and made their greatest politico-religious statements in sculpting nature – terracing the mountains, modifying stone outcrops, nestling cities into peaks and one stone into another. According to Spanish descriptions of the high altar in Cuzco's main temple, the sun, constellations, water, rainbows, and thunder were represented. In keeping with the Andean embeddedness in a hostile environment, they sought to control the uncontrollable flood, earthquake, drought, and frost by ritual and by redistribution. They held processions on important astronomical days, performed elaborate ceremonies for planting and harvesting the all-important maize, and tended 328 natural springs, special rock formations, and other landmarks in Cuzco and beyond. This constant round of attention to their surroundings filled a calendar mapped out on the earth itself. The Incas utilized sightlines to the mountains and other landmarks to locate key celestial movements and literally tell time by space. In a deeply Amerindian way, they coordinated their sacred duties to the rhythms of the cosmos itself.

STONEWORK

The profound Inca sense of identity with the earth, especially their rocky highland homeland, took to a new level the Andean embeddedness in nature. The Incas felt a special interchangeability with stones, believing them to be alive and able to transform into people and vice versa. Thus their stonework defers to organic forms, placement, surfaces, and the play of light

152 (*Right*) The triple zigzag walls of the fort-ritual center of Sacsahuaman, partially dismantled since Inca times. Characteristically, the shadows cast by the walls echo the shape of the peaks beyond. Late Horizon.

153 (*Below*) One of the many rock outcroppings that the Incas carved in their evocative, understated dual statement of embeddedness in nature and domination over the landscape. This one echoes the terraced fields in the valley near Chinchero. Late Horizon.

154 (*Below, right*) The Inca 'throne' carved into the living rock of Rodadero Hill across from the zigzag walls of Sacsahuaman. The sharp edges and precise planes of Inca landscape carving catch the high-altitude sun to create a bold play of light and shadow. Late Horizon.

155 The Sacred Rock at the northern end of Machu Picchu, designed by the Incas to echo the form of the peak beyond. The subtle focussing of attention onto natural and manipulated shapes characterizes the Inca approach to architectural landscaping of their mountain homeland. Late Horizon.

and shadow that occurs in nature. Yet, at the same time, this identity encouraged them to manipulate stones, mountains, and streams toward imperial expressive ends. Being one with the earth, they proclaimed themselves able to construct cultural statements with its materials and pre-existing forms.
155 To geometricize, enhance, frame, and move people through the environment they subtly changed natural outlines. Theirs was a 'prepositional' atti-
156 tude toward the landscape: vision and movement were directed over, under, through, around, between, and among stones, walls, fountains, waterways, rooms, and clefts. The world was primarily to be experienced, rather than just viewed, as one would expect from a people for whom nomadism formed a worldview.

The fascinating interplay of the organic and geometric achieved in Inca stonework does, however, alter one's perception of the world. The lines between untouched and altered natural forms are blurred and the Inca hand
153 can be seen or imagined everywhere. This was a conscious, and extremely effective, way to convey dominant power without a specific set of motifs or

a complex pantheon, by controlling the elemental: vertical and horizontal, light and dark, scale, distance, similarity, interlockedness. We can follow a progression from the less- to the more-manipulated stonework by reviewing the treatment of rock outcroppings, terraces and waterways, roads, walls, and finally cities.

Previously we have seen rock drawings, artificial mountains in the form of pyramids, and all manner of natural subjects in Andean art and architecture. However, the Incas were the only ones to concentrate so much creative energy on modeling the ubiquitous rock outcrops of the Andes themselves. *153, 154, 163*
Outcroppings range from small boulders to those large enough to contain interior space in their clefts, from caves to hillsides. Especially in the heartland around the capital, but even as far away as Bolivia, outcrops were sculpted, some minimally others more extensively. Rather than carving a stone into an image of something, such as animal (although there are a few rather rudimentary felines), steps or stepped forms, rectangular shelves and *162*
niches, zigzag channels, and the occasional semi-circle were the preferred abstract forms. In the harsh high-altitude sun the lighter horizontal planes contrast with the darker vertical cuts. The play of light and shade unerringly draws attention to the freeform geometries that are at once like the hills and terraces around the outcrops and, upon closer inspection, significantly differ-

156 This dramatic cascade of agricultural terraces at the Inca site of Pisac epitomizes their vast geometric vision, equally practical and aesthetic. Terracing enabled maize to flourish above its normal altitude and also marked areas as under Inca dominance by its visual power. Late Horizon.

ent. Thus, without a sense of artificiality or imposition, the Incas managed to suggest an elusive human hand at work modifying the living rock. As with all Inca stonework, each one is different, reflecting the characters of the stones themselves and the contributions of the carvers.

154 One supremely important rock carving was the Inca 'throne' at Sacsahuaman, a series of sharp steps sliced into the curve of the stone hillside. From here the Sapa Inca likely reviewed his troops and watched ceremonies. It is typical of the Inca aesthetic to extend to the highest monarch the same forms as elsewhere and to set him into the living hill rather than above or apart from the base of his power, nature itself. Yet one only has to think of the appearance of thrones in almost any other society to see how singular is this choice. On other carved outcrops food offerings were left on the flat planes, where standing, drinking, animal sacrifices, even weddings also took place.

156 As practical people as well as aesthetes and dominators, the Incas developed the most extensive network of terraces that the highlands have ever known. On the Wari model yet on a scale infinitely more vast, they converted mountainsides into stepped fields and sometimes even ornamental gardens. Terraces allowed the Incas to grow maize at much higher altitudes than previously possible, because they were essentially huge windowboxes: retaining walls were built of fieldstone, the packed earth scooped out, a layer of stones laid at the bottom for water drainage, and the earth loosely repacked. With canals supplying water, these terraces could withstand frost and drought, and produce several crops per growing season. (Maize, even more than before, was crucial as a portable protein source in a redistributive imperial economy.) Yet other terraces were decorative; according to the
166, 165 Spanish, those at Ollantaytambo displayed flowers, and at Moray, with no apparent water sources, the circular terrace patterns may have been principally a regularization of the earth's forms. All Inca terraces followed the natural topography, but managed to stripe and step the mountains with geometries not found in nature. Like the outcroppings, the effect balances the subtle with the obvious. As a power statement, Inca terraces are unsurpassed because they announce control over the very edge of the earth itself.

The Incas also specialized in the practical and ritualistic movement of water. Canals teased the limited output of springs into snaking paths down
161 the steep terraces, and fed baths and fountains. Even at tiny sites such as Tambo Machay the architects designed water to flow in one stream, then split, go underground, and re-emerge with a dramatic flourish. Rock outcrops were often carved with channels for liquids to be poured into during

ceremonies. Watering and drinking vessels were also important portable art forms. Water, the life blood of the Andes, was considered as or more alive than stone; it vivified the earth itself.

Following the concern with movement, they also had their subjects build for them the most impressive system of roads in the pre-modern world. Like *150*
a giant ladder, over 20,000 miles (33,000 km) of roughly parallel highland and coastal roads were connected to each other across the mountain passes, according to a massive study by John Hyslop. In the highlands, the road was typically paved, edged with a low wall, and varied from a footpath to 33 ft (10 m) across depending on conditions. In particularly steep areas the road became a series of hundreds, even thousands, of steps. This underscores the fact that it was a road only for foot traffic and pack animals, the llama in particular. But with a system of runners, each sprinting a short distance, the Incas were able to send messages more swiftly than the Spanish on horseback, as an early Colonial experiment proved. Again the Incas proved themselves flexible in their approach to connecting up their vast territory, yielding to the exigencies of the terrain and relying on the many tribute-payers at their disposal.

The expenditure of labor on roads was matched by the investment of energy in wall-building. Terrace retaining walls and everyday housing were constructed from fieldstones laid in mud mortar. The Incas called this type of masonry *pirka*. But their crowning achievement was the high-status, dressed-stone, mortarless wall built for royal, elite, and sacred structures by *mit'a* laborers, usually commandeered from the Lake Titicaca region. Some monolithic stones in these walls reached over 10 ft (3 m) high and weighed many tons. The effort expended in quarrying and transporting such stones was matched by the time-consuming fitting of the stones together. River-cobble hammerstones were literally bounced on the monoliths, pecking out round-edged natural shapes. The process of fitting consisted of rough pecking, placing the stones together, moving them apart, gauging where the rock dust was not compressing (a loose fit), pecking some more, and so on. Stones in the lowest course were modified to fit the shape of their neighbors. For the next course, monoliths were lifted into place by ropes on the projecting knobs (often still visible), and the same procedure followed until the fit was perfect. It is indeed true that the thinnest coin does not fit between the stones in an Inca mortarless wall. The resulting interlocked polygonal shapes form calculatedly irregular but ultimately balanced freeform compositions. Protrusions punctuate the surface, left for aesthetic reasons and/or to demonstrate the process of building itself, referring to the time and skill appropriated by the Incas. The beveled edges where stones

meet create a pattern of shadow lines picking out each dynamic intersec-
tion. Some rocks were modified to such a great extent that they sport as
160 many as twelve angles. This extreme dovetailing not only holds walls
together without mortar but means that they can withstand the frequent
earthquakes that rock the Andes (over 1500 hit Cuzco in one year).
Their remarkable stability is also because each stone is bedded in another,
the one below concave where it meets the convex base of the one above.
Practical, beautiful, organic, geometric, standardized, individual, repro-
ducible, elitist, technologically simple, and incomparably elegant, the wall
epitomizes Inca aesthetics. It can also be seen as a social statement: divergent people were to interlock, adjust, and resettle into a dynamic whole by
pooling their varying forms, smoothing their ethnic edges, and holding
together with no visible means to face the hostile environment. And the
Incas were to engineer it.

157 The Inca capital of Cuzco was a city of the finest masonry buildings,
made exclusively to house royalty (alive and in the form of mummies),
nobility, kidnapped provincial dignitaries, deities' images, and priests. Even
the highest-ranking people could not enter the city without bearing gifts.
Cuzco had been speedily promoted to royal center and *axis mundi* from
being a relatively obscure village, located in a rich highland basin at an altitude of *c.* 10,170 ft (3100 m) and ringed with higher peaks. Its prime location was enhanced by the confluence of rivers, the Huatanay, the Tullumayo,
and the Chunchul. Recall that the laudatory Quechua term *tinkuy* conveys
the harmonious balancing of opposites where paths or rivers meet. The
Incas straightened and canalized the first two rivers – the stone lining still
visible in places today – to create an acute angle. This point and the wid-
ening space between them was envisioned and planned, perhaps by
Pachakuti himself, to represent the shape of a puma. The neighborhood near
the rivers' union is still called Pumac Chupan, 'the puma's tail.' At the other
152 end of the city, the shrine-fortress of Sacsahuaman topped a steep hill to
define the puma's head, while in the center, the plaza of Haucaypata formed
the open space beneath the belly. As far as we can tell, this is the only Inca
city, or Andean one for that matter, to be conceptualized as a mighty animal.
Its corporate message contrasts markedly with the amorphous, individualized accretions of Chan Chan, Wari, or Cerro Blanco: Cuzco palaces and
temples are wedged within the body like the stones in a wall, parts subsumed
in the unified, royal image of the supreme mountain animal.

The animal shape was not the only significant organization of space in Cuzco. Elevations, invisible radiating lines, and roads joined the capital to

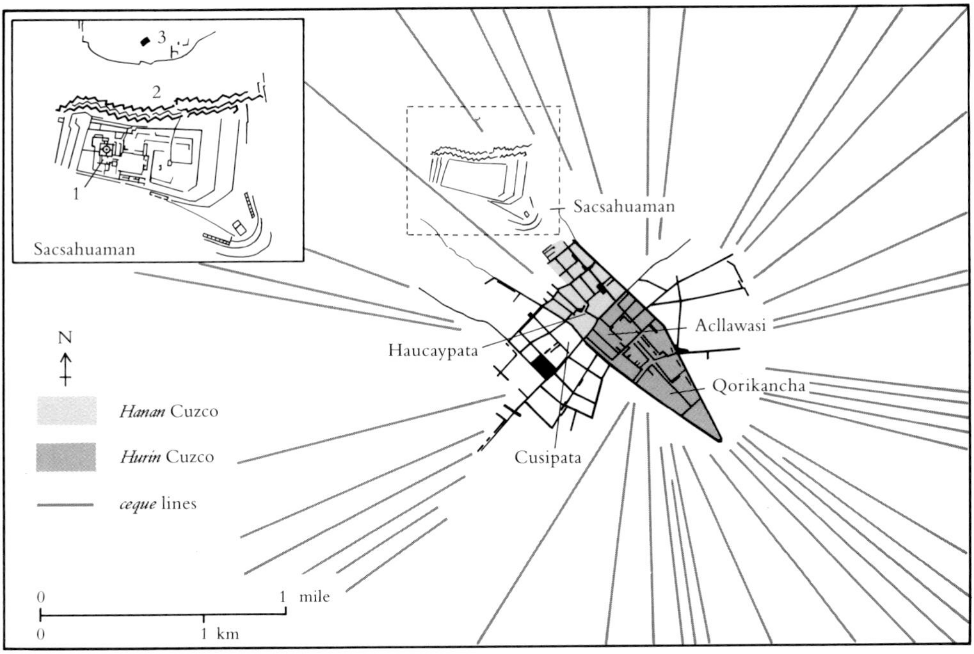

157 Plan of the Inca capital of Cuzco, which was conceived of as a puma with Sacsahuaman (ills. 152, 154) as the head and the canalized rivers' junction as the tail ('Pumac Chupan'). Two social divisions, *Hanan* and *Hurin*, as well as the roads to the four quarters of the empire, further differentiate the urban space. The *ceque* lines radiated outwards from Cuzco, the *axis mundi* of the Inca empire. Late Horizon. (Inset) Plan of Sacsahuaman, the fort–ritual center above Cuzco. Remains of a tall tower (1) and three tiers of defensive monolithic walls (2) lie across the parade ground from the Inca 'throne'(3). In its original form the tower reportedly could hold 1000 warriors, but ironically was used only by the Spanish against the Incas during the Conquest. Late Horizon.

the entire empire both literally and symbolically. Although the important buildings remained concentrated within the puma, the city outgrew its boundaries, spreading to the west and south between the Huatanay and the Chunchul Rivers. In the middle of the city a large trapezoidal plaza, called Cusipata, was joined to the smaller Haucaypata plaza so that the city center formed one great open space, indicating that enormous ritual gatherings once took place here. In the plaza was an *usnu*, a square masonry platform from which the Sapa Inca could preside over ceremonies held below. In a fascinating holistic gesture, and a striking aesthetic flourish, the plaza floor was covered in sand from the coast. The mountain's opposite, the sea, was appropriated for the *axis mundi*, thus proclaiming the full geographic extent of the empire. This dualism inevitably brings to mind the long Andean tradition encapsulated best in the Moche vessel seen in ill. 69.

157 Relative elevation within Cuzco created another important partitioning of the urban space. The front half of the puma, uphill toward Sacsahuaman, was designated *Hanan* Cuzco, for the dominant moiety, while the hind part was *Hurin* Cuzco, for the subdominant one. It is distinctly implied in ethnohistoric records that there were always two Inca rulers; apparently one from *Hanan*, the other from *Hurin*. The king list reflects the sequence of the dominant or Sapa Incas. This subdivision of space gives priority to the highlands within the highlands, as might be expected, and especially to the leading ferocious 'head.' The most sacred religious structure, however, the main temple, the Qorikancha ('Golden House') was located in *Hurin* Cuzco. The military-religious dominant half, with Sacsahuaman as its pivot, and the more religious-domestic half, with the Qorikancha as its focus, balance one another.

158, 159 The Qorikancha was in many ways the absolute center, not only as the house (*kancha*) for all the deity images and high priests, but also as the point from which radiated the 328 *ceque* lines like the spokes of a wheel. As the preeminent *huaca* in the land, this 'Golden House' invisibly subdivided all space and time. *Ceque* lines were arrayed not at arbitrary, even intervals but their placement determined by a sequence of lined up *huacas*, such as natural

158 Interior view of the Qorikancha, the 'Golden House,' the Incas' main temple in Cuzco. Its elegantly simple trapezoidal doors, windows, and niches take the hallmark Inca shape. The structure visible beyond is the Santo Domingo church built over the Qorikancha by the Spanish. Late Horizon-Colonial.

159 The curved Inca wall of the Qorikancha, the main temple, surmounted by the Colonial Santo Domingo church built over it by the Spanish. The Qorikancha got its name 'Golden House' from its sheathing in gold, 700 loads of which the Europeans removed after the fall of the Inca empire. Late Horizon-Colonial.

springs, caves and rock outcrops, strung like beads on a string or knots on a cord (see the *quipu* below). *Ceque* lines were also expressions of time, one *151, 157*
each for a segment of the ritual calendar. Different groups of people attended to the ritual needs of the *huacas* on one line, with processions, incantations, prayers, sacrifices, and offerings. Each line was tended in turn, so that by the year's end all ministrations were complete, time and space encircled. It was a landscape calendar and cosmogram, the natural cycles ordered by the geometricizing Inca vision, all the sacred places and all the days mapped out and activated. Other rituals, such as the *capac hucha* involv- *176*
ing sacrifice of children for the king's health, were organized along the imaginary extensions of the lines to the edges of the kingdom. Because they had a beginning but no ending point, *ceque* lines conceptually projected the Incas even beyond the Andean land mass itself; sacrificial burials have been found on the offshore islands of Ecuador. Yet the *ceque* lines around Cuzco, like other Inca inventions, were not only symbolic but highly practical: scholars agree that they also subdivided the water rights of the capital's res-

idents. Access to water, as we have seen, was a permanent preoccupation of
highlanders, and nowhere more so than among those living uncharacteris-
tically in a densely populated city where conflict over scanty resources
would have been destructively divisive.

Finally, Cuzco's layout reflects the segmentation of all Tawantinsuyo into
quarters. Again not a regular 90-degree division, the four *suyus* were
accessed by roads leading from the royal city across the nearest passes in their
150 general direction: Antisuyu to the northeast, Collasuyu to the east,
Cuntisuyu to the southwest, and Chinchaysuyu to the northwest. People
from or connected to each *suyu* lived in the corresponding sector of the city,
so that Cuzco structurally mapped out the empire. The roads all led to and
from the capital, thus connecting goods, troops, ideas, rulers, and subjects.
Along these roads, more tangibly than the *ceques*, the Incas strung their
settlements. In sum, the city was an all-inclusive image of authority, unity,
duality, hierarchy, cosmic confluence, and time-space itself.

All of Cuzco's monumental constructions suffered in the burning of the
city during the Conquest, and subsequent dismantling by the colonizers,
recurrent earthquakes, and modern modifications. Yet Sacsahuaman, the
Qorikancha, some walls, and the Acllawasi (House of the Chosen Women)
retain clues to their former glory. High above, on a naturally defensible jut
152 of land, Sacsahuaman presides in semi-dismantled state. Its main feature is a
157 trio of monolithic zigzag walls that barred access to the fortified temple
complex containing three towers (of which only foundations remain) and
other enclosures. Across the parade ground is the rock outcrop known as
Rodadero Hill into which the 'throne' is carved. The zigzag walls are some
of the most impressive made by the Incas, with individual stones – some
10–13 ft (3–4 m) tall – laid in asymmetrical but dynamically balanced
patterns. The undulating walls capture dark triangular shadows where
they 'zag,' not coincidentally echoing the chevron shadows in the peaks
beyond. The result is a complex orchestration of environment, sculptural
form, and surface patterning that defines the richly abstract sensibility of
its makers.

159 The Qorikancha features a different version of Inca design principles,
with more regularized stonework courses in its stunning curved wall and a
large courtyard with surrounding enclosures for the holy shrines. (The
Colonial monastery of Santo Domingo was built around and over the Inca
temple, hence the juxtaposition of conflicting architectural styles.) The
Spanish carted away 700 loads of gold sheathing from the outside, originally
probably arranged in a series of horizontal stripes. Interior walls were also

160 The famous 12-angle monolith in the wall of Cuzco's Hatun Rumiyoc Street. Its complex form resulted from being modified by all the surrounding stones. Elaborate Inca stonework does not use mortar; these interlocked stones hold together without it. Late Horizon.

sheathed and studded with precious stones. A shining Golden House (often referred to erroneously as the Temple of the Sun), the Qorikancha was also *177*
'planted' with a gold and silver garden, mimetic of nature down to the tiniest details of earthen lumps, animals, and plants. An underground channel connected the temple directly with the main plazas, so that sanctified liquids could run magically between the two points of power. Doorways were double-jambed, and these and all windows and niches were trapezoidal, the preferred Inca shape. The simple trapezoid is not only visually powerful, but *158*
also eminently practical, as the narrower lintel across the top survives well in earthquakes. Again, the elegant, repetitive Inca solution fulfills functional requirements as well as aesthetic and political goals. In fact, the Qorikancha is only a larger, plated, holy version of the basic architectural form used for housing throughout the empire. Thus, a standardized image of equality can nonetheless serve to reinforce hierarchy.

Only walls and the city blocks remain of the many royal palaces and other buildings that filled the capital. These vary from the irregular polygonal stonework type, epitomized by the twelve-angle stone on Hatun Rumiyoc *160*

Street, to the very rectilinear, bricklike courses of the Acllawasi. It is tempting to see in the choice of building method messages about levels of control – the more regimented Acllawasi perhaps reflecting the restrictions placed upon the *aclla* women weavers within, who spent their lives there in the service of the Sapa Inca. As we shall see, the provincial center of Huánuco Pampa has a better preserved Acllawasi that demonstrates architecturally the physical containment such high-status slaves endured. All the enclosures in Cuzco seemed to have had high walls, limited entrances, and interiors most probably based on the *kancha* form.

BEYOND CUZCO

The environs of Cuzco are filled with small Inca sites and carved outcrops,
161, 162 *huacas* along the *ceque* lines. Of these, Tambo Machay and Qenqo display important characteristics of Inca stonework and ritualized space. Both lie above Sacsahuaman and in close proximity. Tambo Machay is semi-dismantled but retains a picturesque quality in its elegant siting. Nestled into the hillside, it has three shallow terraces with fine dressed-stone masonry walls marked with tall trapezoidal niches. On the second terrace to the left a natural spring emerges from below a plain wall. The spring is undoubtedly the reason for the stonework, which is less a building than an architectural frame. The Incas designed the water to run in one stream, fall down the lower terrace, disappear into the ground, and reappear in two streams cas-

161 The site of Tambo Machay, above Cuzco, near Qenqo. Elaborately embracing a natural spring, its polygonal stonework juxtaposed with unworked boulders, Tambo Machay summarizes many central Inca aesthetic choices. Late Horizon.

162 View of the 'seated puma' stone at Qenqo just north of Cuzco. A semi-circular courtyard creates a ritual space around a framed, untouched tall boulder reminiscent of a seated cat, next to a huge outcrop subtly geometricized with steps and channels. Underneath the outcrop (not shown) a natural cleft has been transformed into a special room, as at Machu Picchu (see ill. 169). Late Horizon.

cading down the last terrace. Another important feature of the *tambo* (Quechua for waystation, used to denote any small outpost along the road) is how rocks from the hillside are periodically incorporated into the built structure. The dressed walls merge into the rocks and out again as one scans the walls. In particular, a doorway frames a boulder whose edges are somewhat modified to accommodate the polygonal dressed stones nestled around it but whose rough, natural surface seems unaltered. Thus, Tambo Machay uses fine masonry to draw attention to the 'untouched' pre-existing water flow and rock formation, both of which the Incas have actually geometricized and brought under their dominion.

What Tambo Machay does on a subtle level, Qenqo explores more radically. This very large outcrop is carved all over its bulbous surface with steps, shelves, indentations, and a striking zigzag channel for liquids that also branches and rejoins. It is so heavily modified that it re-approaches natural irregularity, yet the sun catching a completely flat area periodically shocks the viewer out of such an inattentive assumption. Underneath, the boulder has a large cleft which has been worked into a small room, a common Inca choice for ritual purposes. The 'heart' of such a stone must have been considered a very spiritual place, alive, isolated from the secular world, and one with the earth. On one side of the outcrop, a separate jutting triangular *162*
monolith is doubly framed by its small square wall and the enclosing courtyard defined by a curved wall. This stone has been left alone, its own evocative shape (perhaps a seated puma) suitable for veneration.

163 (*Above*) The Intihuatana Stone ('Hitching Post of the Sun') at Machu Picchu's highest point. In many Inca cities these elegant, enigmatic carved outcrops seem to connect earth and sky, and possibly were used for astronomical rituals. Late Horizon.

164 (*Right*) General view of the famous Inca city of Machu Picchu, which follows the topography of a steep mountain saddle above the Urubamba River. Probably a royal retreat, Machu Picchu lies about a three-day walk from the capital Cuzco. Late Horizon.

In the heartland, within three days walk of Cuzco, more extensive sites were built to feed and supply the capital: to the east Rumicolca, to the north Pisac and Chinchero, to the northwest Ollantaytambo and the famous Machu Picchu. Myriad mid-size *tambos*, terraces, and clusters of buildings
165 dot the countryside, among them the spectacular circles of Moray. Moray represents the quintessentially Inca geometric organicism, a topographic exercise in molding the earth according to its own essential shapes.

156 Pisac demonstrates the principles adopted in most Inca settlements: leave the rich bottomland uncovered, terrace the hills, place the elites in a well-defended outlook, and provide minimally for the *mit'a* laborers. This small outpost was built of stone high above the Vilcanota River in the saddle of a

mountain spur, with lower-status workers' housing clinging to the unusable edges.

The site of Ollantaytambo has a flight of seventeen terraces that span the dip between two promontories; according to the Spanish, these were planted exclusively in colorful flowers. Not only an extravagant gesture in this parched land, these ornamental terraces again frame and focus the natural and the constructed. One is made to walk straight up the center of this juxtaposed world, before the path meanders up the left-hand rock face set with steps. The path exemplifies the Inca 'prepositional' use of architectural space by not only calling attention to natural forms but by necessitating and controlling movement. Paths, doors, steps, clefts, passes, all are used *166*

to effect and free exploration is not allowed. On the summit of Ollantaytambo is an unfinished temple reminiscent of Tiwanaku in its alternating tall monoliths and filler stones. Its crowning illusion is a vertical series of three barely visible, carved diamond outlines that emerge via shadows only to retreat into the temple face when concentration wavers or the sun goes behind a cloud. They are, at once, the steps one has just mounted, the
103 carved diamonds at Puma Punku, and an optical trick designed to reveal and withhold geometry at the wave of the Inca hand. A final important feature of Ollantaytambo is the town, located across from the sanctuary, which is laid out in a large trapezoid shape. This standardized form was used routinely not only for stones and openings, but also for *kanchas*, plazas, and

165 (*Above*) The concentric terraces of Moray follow, yet regularize, the terrain in a typically Inca manner. Without any known canals to irrigate them, these terraces may have been primarily aesthetic statements. Late Horizon.

166 (*Left*) The seventeen terraces of Ollantaytambo. To reach the temple on top, which was never completed, one is led up the center then over to the left. Accounts claim that these terraces were planted with colorful flowers, an incredibly extravagant gesture in the dry highlands. Late Horizon.

towns themselves. It is probable that the Incas recognized how the trapezoid optically exaggerates scale (the rapidly converging sides visually telescope space into greater depth). Inca community spaces, already enormous, seem even larger.

Machu Picchu, the most famous monument of ancient South America, *164*
was rediscovered (it was known to the local peoples) in 1911 by Hiram Bingham of Yale University. Its dramatic setting, on the top of a high mountain spur overlooking the Urubamba River as it makes a hairpin turn, has made it justifiably admired over the years. Machu Picchu is both a very special Inca settlement and a typical one. Bingham wrote of the area: 'Not only has it great snow peaks looming above the clouds more than two miles overhead; gigantic precipices of many-colored granite rising sheer for thousands of feet above the foaming, glistening, roaring rapids; it has also, in striking contrast, orchids and tree ferns, the delectable beauty of luxurious vegetation, and the mysterious witchery of the jungle.' Like Pisac and other sites, it was built in an easily defensible position over an important river, set into a saddle with agricultural and living terraces hugging the steep hillside. The top was partly flattened for a main plaza. Clusters of buildings, over 200 residences in all, are arrayed in no clear format, unlike the Cuzco puma or the Ollantaytambo trapezoid. At its highest point is a carved boulder (found in other Inca settlements as well) known as the Intihuatana Stone, 'Hitching *163*
Post of the Sun.' The projecting trapezoidal portion elegantly thrusting upward may have held offerings to the sun. Again, abstract ritual forms yield elemental meaning, but defy specific interpretation.

Another important boulder is encased in the building now known as the *167, 168*
Torreón, 'the Observatory.' The building's rounded wall was almost seamlessly joined to this tall outcrop whose top inside the room has been somewhat modified. Sets of niches alternate with windows, the central one of which is oriented toward the rising sun on the June solstice. As at Qenqo, the outcrop was split below with a large cleft, recarved and set with masonry to create a small room with a stepped diagonal entrance. This is an especially *169*
diagnostic Inca treatment, combining all levels of interference and accommodation of the natural forms. The far left remains untouched mottled stone; the left side of the slanting cleft was smoothed, but not completely straightened; the right side was stepped, but not altogether regularly; and the odd-shaped interstices to the far right were filled with stonework that fits like liquid poured into a crack despite its courses and accentuated beveled edges. Stones are even inserted into the rightmost grey stone so that the vertical wall might progress more smoothly. To devote such extraordi-

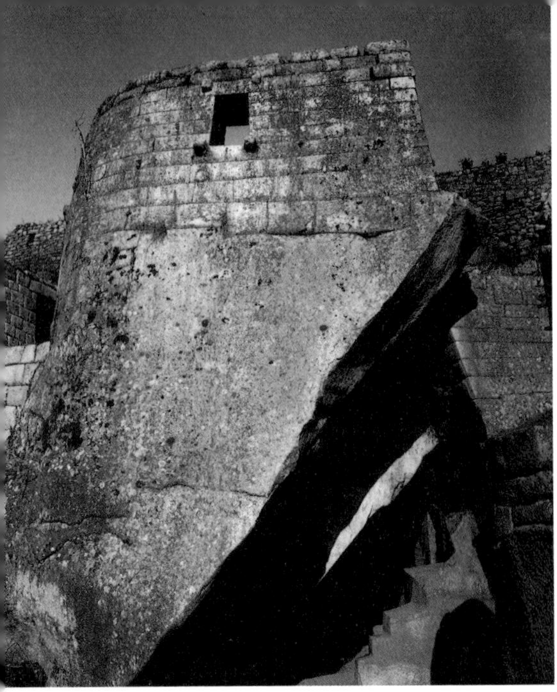

167, 168 The Observatory at Machu Picchu looking from above (*below*) and below (*left*). The curved wall, a rare form also found at the main temple in Cuzco (ill. 159), embraces the top of a two-story outcrop with an elaborate room carved into its natural cleft below (see ill. 169). On the summer solstice the sun shines directly through the central window onto the outcrop, hence the name Observatory. Late Horizon.

nary care and skill to the invisible inner space bespeaks the Incas' great refinement in the Andean notion of essence.

While the heartland is dotted with a huge variety of constructions, the Incas also lavished their organizational skills on the periphery. The best-
170 studied site of the highland hinterland is Huánuco Pampa along the northern road to Quito. This sprawling city was oriented so that the road passed through its central plaza along a southeast–northwest diagonal, the plaza

169 The cleft room beneath the Observatory at Machu Picchu. Subtle sculpting of the rock edges combined with in-filling of dressed stonework show the Inca fluency in organic geometry. Late Horizon.

enclosing an enormous area of 1800 by 1200 ft (540 by 370 m). Fanning out on the four sides of the plaza were heavily-populated sectors, over 4000 structures in all, and above the plain lay over 700 storehouses for tribute, rations for the army, and provisions for the laborers housed here temporarily. Barracks have been identified to the north, and commoners' housing made of *pirka* are found outside the city on all sides except the east, where fine gateways led through courtyards to an elite residence complete with a bath. This building was reserved for the ruler on royal visits, and perhaps also for the highest local administrator. The eastern sector was aligned with the massive *usnu* (platform) in the center of the plaza and oriented toward the sunrise. On the north side of the plaza lay the city's Acllawasi, as at Cuzco

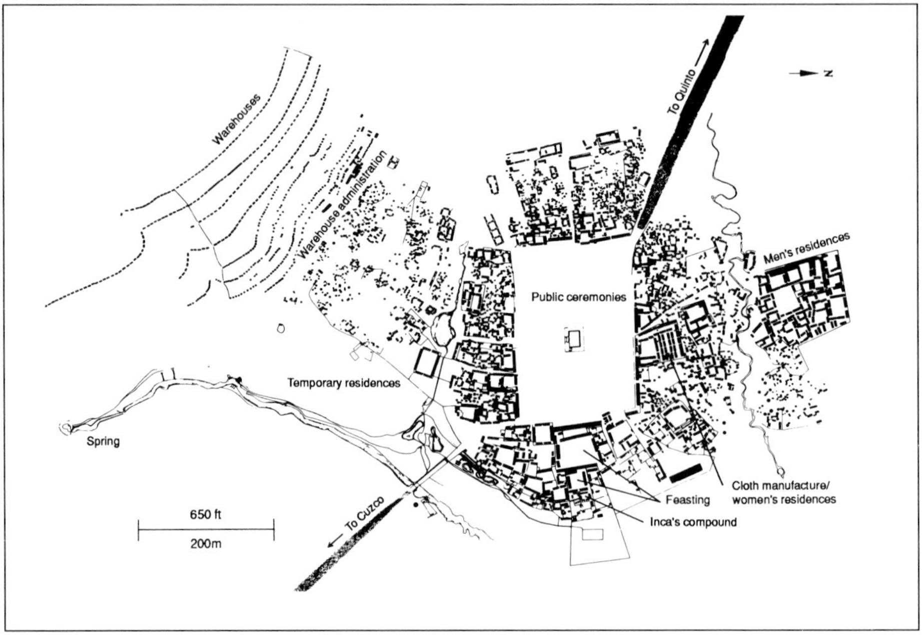

170 Plan of the provincial Inca administrative center of Huánuco Pampa, on the road from Cuzco to Quito. Over 4000 buildings and 700 storehouses were built primarily for temporary state workers' housing and food storage for redistribution. Late Horizon.

171 The coastal Inca waystation, Tambo Colorado, shows a typical combination of Inca elements, although built entirely in adobe: a large trapezoidal plaza, adjoining *kanchas* (walled enclosures of rooms around courtyards), and trapezoidal niches, windows, and doors.

an enclosed structure built to house the local chosen women (*aclla*) who wove for the elites and made corn beer to serve the workers. Their own self-contained world, emphatically walled off, had a central courtyard set with long halls for group activity and rows of identical house/workshops. Finally at Huánuco Pampa there were long halls (*kalanka*) all around the main plaza used as ritual drinking places for the *mit'a* laborers. The various architectural contexts – for royalty, male workers, and female artists – show the contrasts of control and regimentation possible within a very limited vocabulary of forms. Massive, permanent settlements such as Huánuco Pampa dedicated primarily to temporary, shifting populations, helped inculcate thousands of subjects over the years with Inca style, reciprocity, and power.

The Incas were also concerned with their coastal conquests and could
adapt their designs to wholly different environments and materials. Tambo 171
Colorado in the Pisco Valley is a much more modest waystation, but evinces values similar to the highland centers. Set so that the coastal road travels through the plaza diagonally, it has an *usnu* for rituals, and surrounding buildings with trapezoidal niches. All are made in adobe, but retain the characteristic Inca proportions, shapes, and simplicity.

OTHER ARTS

The Incas may have been consummate architects, but their artistic imprint extended into other media as well, notably textiles, metalwork, and ceramics. The same general approach can be traced – technical excellence, standardization, geometric organicism – although the three media had noticeably different roles to play and imperial styles to project. Textiles were the most highly valued (they were the first gifts offered to the Spanish, not goldwork) as well as the most colorful and abstract, metalwork the most restricted and mimetic, and ceramics the most standardized and practical. Portability was a key issue in this farflung kingdom, and textiles were used extensively as gifts to cement political relationships, reward, indoctrinate, and brand subjects as ethnically identified with their conquerors. The textile
record, the *quipu*, also played a special role in the administration of the 151
empire. Metalwork was highly exclusive and not terribly plentiful, and so features less prominently in the exportation of the Inca style, although it remains significant in understanding elite and sacred art. Unfortunately, very few pieces have survived the Colonial era (only those that were buried escaped being melted down); however, some descriptions of lost works survive as well. Ceramics were used, among other things, to transport maize

over long distances, despite their often impressive size. Thus, they served to spread a secular vocabulary of forms. Given the large-scale necessity for feeding *mit'a* laborers, huge numbers of serving dishes and other mundane objects were produced. A few higher-status ritual items were also made in
179 clay, especially *qeros* (beakers) and *pacchas* (watering devices).

Weaving, an occupation of all Andeans, was organized and regulated by the Incas at several levels. All subjects owed something in tax – even the most aged and infirmed had to give the tax collector the lice off their head! Therefore, children, the sick, and the elderly were all required to spin fiber into thread, if not weave to the best of their ability. Everyday cloth was called *awaska* and sufficed for household use. The Incas cared most about the fine
173 cloth they called *qompi*, of which there were two levels, good cloth woven by male *qompicamayocs* (keepers of the fine cloth) as tribute, and the best cloth made by female *aclla* for royal and religious use. Control over the finest textiles was an obvious priority as they served to adorn the ruler, grease the most important political wheels, and even to propitiate the sun (*qompi* were burned as sacrificial offerings). One offers only the most prized possessions to the highest spiritual powers. At its best, Inca weaving is unsurpassed technically in the pre-industrial era, with thread counts reaching several hundred per centimeter.

The highest-status Inca textile that survives today is a royal tapestry tunic
172 we know was made for a king because of the sixteenth-century illustrations
175 by Guaman Poma de Ayala of Inca rulers. In addition, the tunic bears as its motifs the images and patterns of other tunics. Notice the tiny black-and-white checkerboard with red stepped yoke that is the Inca army uniform in
174 miniature. The square geometric designs known as *tocapus*, reserved for elites and usually only seen in small bands, broadcast the message that the king controls more diversity, more ethnicity, almost the totality of possible patterns in his clothing. (By contrast, lower-status tunics are limited to a single motif.) And the king is above the rule of regularity, as well, since these motifs and their coloration do not repeat in any order, while those of lesser tunics follow strict checkerboard and stripe patterns. Standardization applies to lower status textiles even in the number of squares per row. Clothing was an instrument of conformity, unmistakably signaling imperial power. Imagine 10,000 warriors in checkerboard tunics advancing over the hill! The graphic boldness of simple, high-contrast geometry is thus both aesthetically pleasing and politically effective. Motifs make only rare, tangential reference to pre-Inca styles (stepped diamonds come the closest to a Wari model) and so proclaim the universal, elemental quality of Inca rule.

172 An Inca royal tunic now held at Dumbarton Oaks in Washington D.C. Drawings by Guaman Poma of Inca rulers (ill. 175) show that they wore tunics with all-over designs of geometric patterns called *tocapus.* Notice that one such *tocapu* is the checkerboard tunic (ill. 174), probably worn by the army; the ruler thus signals his control over others by the motifs he wears. Late Horizon.

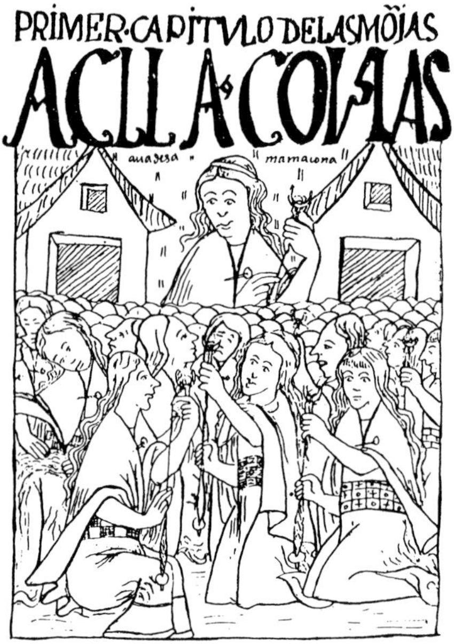

173 (*Left*) Early Colonial drawing by Guaman Poma de Ayala of the *acclawasi*, the house of the 'chosen women' who wove the finest cloth in the Inca empire (ill. 172). These weavers were carefully overseen, and virtually imprisoned, showing how important control over textile production was to the Incas. Early Colonial.

174 (*Right*) The standardized Inca checkerboard tunic, in black and white with a red yoke, apparently was some sort of army uniform epitomizing the Inca graphic, bold, and often minimalistic style and the technological prowess of the artists (here over 120 wefts per inch (50 per cm) were achieved). Late Horizon.

175 (*Far right*) Drawing by Guaman Poma de Ayala of the ruler Topa Inca Yupanqui, now called the 'Alexander the Great' of the Inca empire for his prodigious conquest record. He is shown as an old man and wears a *tocapu* tunic, like that in ill. 172.

151 Special note must be taken of the unique Inca recording device, the *quipu*. Over 400 of these are preserved, giving a good, if tantalizing, sense of Inca mathematics and thought; they were mnemonic devices and the oral referents are unreconstructable, although their basic principles are understandable. Long *quipus* reach over 10 ft (3 m) and contain more than 2000 strings. Perfectly portable when rolled up, they represent an ideal adaptive device for the Andean world. According to the Spanish, *quipus* kept information as diverse as the population census, storage, taxation, astronomy, even history and poetry. Being a coded method using numbers, positions, string colors, and knot types for different aspects of complex data, it was remarkably flexible. Certainly the Incas managed to organize a complex empire within its parameters. Intense study by Marcia and Robert Ascher has revealed the elegance and intricacy of this fiber 'computer' that proves that the Incas independently devised the same base-10 mathematical system as the Arabic world, complete with zero, the four operations, and fractions. It is also revealing that they sought to reduce reality to units and relative positions, just as they maneuvered people, stones, and motifs.

Late Horizon metalwork was largely appropriated from the Chimú, but with changes in scale and quality of execution. Metal was worked both on a grander scale (for instance the enormous sheathing of the Qorikancha)

and on a more minute one (some figures only a few centimeters in height were painstakingly constructed from as many as eighteen sheets). Large-scale sculptures of the gods are mentioned in Spanish documentary sources, as is the remarkable golden garden in the main temple. Garcilaso de la Vega gives a description of these gardens, of which there were many in the kingdom: 'they made fields of maize, with their leaves, cobs, canes, roots and flowers all exactly imitated. The beard of the cob was of gold, and all the rest of silver. . . . They did the same thing with other plants, making the flowers, or any other part that became yellow, of gold and the rest of silver. In addition to all this, there were all kinds of gold and silver animals in these gardens, such as rabbits, mice, lizards, snakes, butterflies, foxes, and wildcats. . . . Then there were birds set in the trees, as though they were about to sing, and others bent over the flowers, breathing in their nectar.' Because of the Spanish extirpation of idolatry and appetite for gold, almost all of these
wonders are forever lost to us, except for a partial corn stalk, small animals, *177*
especially camelids, human figures that were originally elaborately dressed, *176*
and ceremonial bronze knives. Charmingly and straightforwardly mimetic, *178*
these sculptures demonstrate a less-abstracting side to the Inca stylistic vocabulary. Details such as kernels of corn or genitalia did not escape recording even on such a scale.

176 (*Above*) A cast silver figure dressed in a miniature feather headdress and woven mantle, found with a child sacrifice at Cerro del Plomo in Chile. In the *capac hucha* ritual, a few special children gave their life force in the belief that it would strengthen that of the ruler. Other nude silver and gold figures were originally dressed in this way, as were Andean effigies from other eras (see frontispiece).

177 (*Above, right*) This fragmentary silver and gold corn stalk shows the degree to which Inca sculpture could be mimetic. Gardens of precious metal plants, animals, and even lumps of earth were created for the nobility. Late Horizon.

178 (*Right*) A gilded bronze (arsenical copper) ceremonial knife with the handle as the neck and head of a camelid. Visible on the left side of the blade are the remains of the wrapping textile, converted into metal. This Andean tradition of encasing precious objects in fiber goes back at least 10,000 years, as shown by the ancient fiberwork remains found at Guitarrero Cave. Late Horizon.

Ceramic vessels were mass-produced with the characteristically Inca
concern for shape and surface geometry. The *urpu* (a long-necked jar with 180
low-set handles and pointed tip for insertion into holes in the ground, previously called an *aryballo*) and a single-handled plate were new forms, while
the *qero* was a simpler version of earlier beakers. *Urpus* were made in gradu-
ated sizes from miniatures to as tall as 4 ft (1.3 m). Their internal volumes
were standardized, so that at a glance the Incas could know how much corn
was stored (and record it on a *quipu*). The patterns slip-painted on them in
bands include repeated diamonds, zigzags, and stylized corn. Not mass-produced was an elaborate watering device called a *paccha*, fewer than thirty of 179
which may still exist. Completely hollow, water or corn beer was poured
through representations of all the stages of growing maize: the digging stick
used for planting (the curved element joined to the pointed one), the half
grown corncob, and the *urpu* for storage. When activated in ritual and the
tip driven into the ground, the *paccha* resembles a corn stalk itself.

179 (*Far left*) An Inca *paccha* or watering device, that encapsulates the entire cycle of growing maize. Wear on its pointed tip shows it was 'planted' in the earth so that water or corn beer could ritually water the field. Late Horizon.

180 (*Left*) An Inca *urpu* (a long-necked jar with low handles previously called an *aryballo* for its resemblance to a Greek vessel type). Although *urpus* were sometimes massive, Inca subjects transported corn in them on a tump line that ran across their foreheads, through the handles, and over the protrusion at the base of the vessel's neck. Late Horizon.

181 (*Right*) North Coast Inca-influenced blackware vessel, showing the characteristic mix of an Inca *urpu* shape and local Chimú technique and surface design. Late Horizon.

LOCAL STYLES

Despite standardization, control, and politicization, art in the Central Andes under Inca rule was not totally uniform nor was it intended to be. Just as local peoples maintained some of their previous power structures and religious practices, and provided for their own food and clothing needs, the Incas allowed, or could not suppress, a measure of leeway in artistic interpretation. What seems to have mattered was obeisance to the recognizable Inca shapes or design structures, but not the particular technology, color patterning, or even iconography. For example, Chimú-Inca works of art take on the dominant outline, but interpret all else in a traditional North Coast
181 way. An *urpu* assumes the correct form of long neck, low handles, and pointed base, but was made in blackware and features familiar birds and dotted background. Tunics may adopt the stepped yoke format but add the traditional bent-armed frontal figure or cover an otherwise Inca tunic with appliqué metal squares. In this manner, a multitude of fascinating hybrid objects were created during the last 100 years before the Spanish, and stylistic amalgamation continued to a degree under Colonial rule as well.

EPILOG

In the early sixteenth century a turn of world events shook the Americas and brought entirely foreign elements into the Andean artistic milieu. The Inca empire was destroyed by the European-introduced plague and the active civil war that followed Huayna Capac's premature demise, as well as by the military sabotage and invasion of the Spanish. It was not, as is so often portrayed, the simple or miraculous dominance of a few hundred Europeans swiftly toppling the Incas. The Conquest in South America took at least a generation, if not nearly fifty years before the new order was truly established. Disease played a central role in devastating the population and undermining their religious faith. Certainly many reluctant Inca subjects were eager to believe Spanish promises that they were liberators rather than the next dominators. And, with no clear ruler, the army divided, two capitals, and a ritualized version of warfare that did not involve ambush and deceit, the Incas were not in a position to unify against the invaders. Finally, rupturing the delicate balance of reciprocity meant that sustenance, communication, and overall organization broke down rapidly. Given the challenges of the Andean environment, the traditional system could not be altered substantially, as the Spanish swiftly found out for themselves.

The early Colonial era was one of upheaval, depopulation, resistance, and

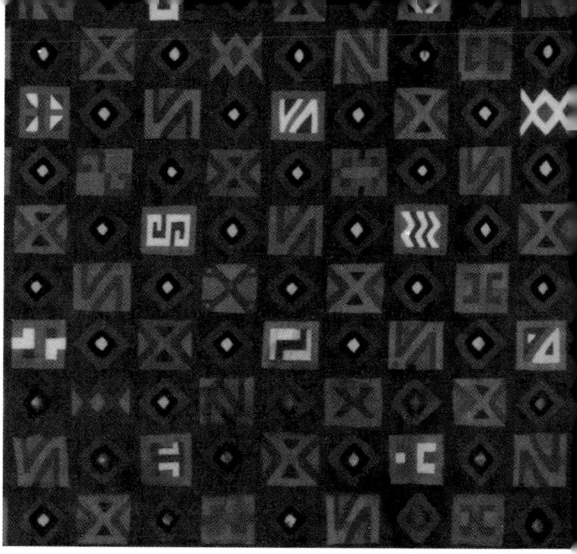

182 Detail of a neo-Inca prince's mantle and burial shroud. This unique tapestry seems to date from just after the Spanish invasion, its Inca affinities signaling a rebellious political statement. Early Colonial.

tragedy. In the Americas overall, during the sixteenth century an estimated *ninety million* indigenous people died, making this the greatest holocaust in world history. When the coastal Andean populations declined precipitously the Spanish then began the further holocaust of African slavery. Highland peoples fared a little better than their more accessible coastal neighbors, being able to fade into the mountains and return to herding and farming to survive. A neo-Inca state was formed near Cuzco and continued to defy the Europeans for a generation.

There are some politically-charged works of art that seem to document *182* this conflicting time. In particular a spectacular child's mantle and burial shroud combines Inca technology (with over 78 threads per cm) and overall *tocapus* (geometric designs) with a Colonial flavor: neither the square motifs, which no longer encapsulate the patterns of other mantles, nor the diamonds are anchored in a grid. It is hypothesized that a boy who would have been an Inca prince wore this special garment in life and death during the first generation of the Colonial era. Other Inca-Colonial objects are more ubiquitous, such as hybrid painted wooden *qeros*. Full-scale paintings on *183* canvas were introduced as a new art form and artists learned the new conventions for three-dimensional illusionistic figures and landscapes. However, the Andean mentality shows through; for instance, in an interpretation of the Christian Trinity, the faces of the three figures overlap in order to share four eyes. As in Chavín religious images of multiplicity in unity, the mimetic is less persuasive than the supernatural paradox.

The most informative Colonial works for the reconstruction of the ancient past are a few manuscripts composed and illustrated in the late sixteenth and early seventeenth centuries. Most notably the 1000-some page letter from Guaman Poma de Ayala to the Spanish monarch, with hundreds
173, 175 of line drawings, gives insight into the history, rituals, practices, and values of the pre-Hispanic and Colonial eras. Incisive analysis by such scholars as Rolena Adorno has shown the many layers of political messages embedded in its text and illustrations. Cautious use of this information, keeping in mind the Colonial context of the work, can help us determine such things as the
172 overall geometric designs or *tocapus* that were reserved for royalty (and the
182 fact that the child's shroud mentioned above was Colonial, as the patterns in ill. 175 more exactly match it than they do the royal tunic in ill. 172).

Despite the profound changes of the last 500 years, the Andean people have maintained a strong and vital continuity with their independent past.
4 Herds of camelids still constitute wealth and walk the Inca roads, the Humboldt Current still yields fish by the billions to the coastal fisherfolk in reed boats (and to large companies), textiles are still woven and exchanged (albeit to tourists too). Without overemphasizing continuity or seeking to prevent 'picturesque' cultures from inevitable and rightful change, one can recognize that the deeply-held values of duality, reciprocity, hierarchy, and embeddedness in nature are still fundamentally Andean today. And art, both ruined and continually recreated, still holds a pre-eminent place in the expression of a unique world and worldview.

183 An Early Colonial wooden *qero* (drinking cup), typically Inca in its shape and incised geometric patterns, but painted with figures and flowers in a Spanish-influenced manner. Such hybrids show how indigenous forms and the values they embody (ritual communal celebration) survived, with some alterations, the upheavals of European conquest. Early Colonial.

Select Bibliography

1 Introduction

George Kubler's *Art and Architecture of Ancient America*, 3rd edition, (Penguin, Harmondsworth & New York, 1984) remains the most comprehensive survey of ancient American art (not only of the Andes, but of Mesoamerica and Central America as well). The *Handbook of South American Indians*, ed. J. Steward, (Smithsonian Institution, Bulletin 143, Bureau of American Ethnology, Washington D. C., 1946) covers a vast array of information on many aspects of Andean culture, environment, linguistics, and so on. Several recent archaeological treatments are extremely useful resources, especially Michael E. Moseley, *The Incas and their Ancestors* (Thames and Hudson, London & New York, 1992), Karen Olsen Bruhn, *Ancient South America* (Cambridge UP, Cambridge & New York, 1994), Craig Morris and Adriana Von Hagen, *The Inka Empire and its Andean Origins* (Abbeville Press, New York, 1993), and Luis Lumbreras *The Peoples and Cultures of Ancient Peru* (Smithsonian Institution Press, Washington D. C., 1989). The section on the Andes in *The Ancient Americas: Art from Sacred Landscapes*, ed. Richard F. Townsend, (The Art Institute of Chicago & Prestel, 1992) is relevant as well. For specific media see Christopher Donnan, *Ceramics of Ancient Peru* (Fowler Museum of Cultural History, UCLA, 1992), Rebecca Stone-Miller, *To Weave for the Sun: Ancient Andean Textiles* (Thames and Hudson, London & New York, 1994), Duccio Bonavia, *Mural Painting in Ancient Peru* (University of Indiana Press, Bloomington, 1985), *Pre-Columbian Metallurgy of South America*, ed. E. Boone, (Dumbarton Oaks, Washington D. C., 1979), and portions of *The Art of Pre-Columbian Gold: the Jan Mitchell Collection*, ed. Julie Jones, (The Metropolitan Museum of Art, New York, 1985).

Colonial chroniclers such as Pedro Cieza de León, *La Crónica del Peru* (Calpe, Madrid, 1922 [1550]), and Felipe Guaman Poma de Ayala, *El Primer Nueva Corónica y Buen Gobierno*, eds. J. Murra and R. Adorno, (Siglo Veintiuno, Mexico, 1980 [1614]) add greatly to our understanding of the pre-Hispanic past (see also R. Adorno, *Guaman Poma: Writing and Resistance in Colonial Peru*, Latin American Monographs no. 68, University of Texas Press, Austin, 1986).

2 Early and Chavín Art

The single most important source on the Initial Period precursors and Early Horizon Chavín style is Richard Burger, *Chavín and the Origins of Andean Civilization* (Thames and Hudson, London & New York, 1995). John Rowe's classic, *Chavín Art: an Inquiry into its Form and Meaning* (The Museum of Primitive Art, New York, 1962) introduced the important idea of kennings (visual metaphoric substitutions). On textiles see Alana Cordy-Collins, 'Cotton and the Staff God: Analysis of an Ancient Chavín Textile,' in *Junius B. Bird Pre-Columbian Textile Conference*, ed. Ann P. Rowe, (Washington D. C., 1973) and Rebecca Stone, 'Possible Uses, Roles and Meanings of Chavín-style Painted Textiles of South Coast Peru,' in *Investigations of the Andean Past*, ed. D. Sandweiss, (Ithaca, New York, 1983). For articles on individual sites of interest, see the bibliography in Burger and *Early Ceremonial Architecture in the Andes*, ed. C. Donnan, (Dumbarton Oaks, Washington D. C., 1985).

3 Paracas and Nasca

Anne Paul is the foremost art historian of Paracas art. See her *Paracas Ritual Attire: Symbols of Authority in Ancient Peru* (University of Oklahoma Press, Norman, 1990); ed. *Paracas Art and Architecture: Object and Context in South Coastal Peru* (University of Iowa Press, Iowa City, 1991); 'Procedures, Patterns and Deviations in Paracas Embroidered Textiles,' in R. Stone-Miller, *To Weave for the Sun: Ancient Andean Textiles* (Thames and Hudson, London & New York, 1994); and Paul and S. Niles, 'Identifying Hands at Work on a Paracas Mantle,' *The Textile Museum Journal* 23 (1985).

On Nasca art, *The Lines of Nazca*, ed. A. Aveni, (The American Philosophical Society, Philadelphia, 1990) has many valuable articles, such as Helaine Silverman, 'The Early Nasca Pilgrimage Center of Cahuachi and the Nazca Lines: Anthropological and Archaeological Perspectives.' See also Johan Reinhard, 'Interpreting the Nazca Lines,' in *The Ancient Americas*, ed. R. Townsend, (The Art Institute of Chicago & Prestel, 1992).

4 Moche Art

The pre-eminent scholar of this subject is an archaeologist, Christopher Donnan. See his *Moche Art of Peru* (Museum of Culture History, University of California, Los Angeles, 1978); with W. Alva, *The Royal Tombs of Sipán* (Fowler Museum of Cultural History, UCLA, 1993); with D. McClelland, 'The Burial Theme in Moche Iconography,' *Studies in Pre-Columbian Art and Archaeology*, No. 21 (Dumbarton Oaks, Washington D. C., 1979); with L. J. Castillo, 'Finding the Tomb of a Moche Priestess,' *Archaeology* 45, 6 (1992). See also Elizabeth Benson, *The Mochica :A Culture of Peru* (Thames and Hudson, London, 1972) and her article 'The World of Moche,' in *The Ancient Americas*, ed. R. Townsend, (The Art Institute of Chicago and Prestel, 1992).

5 Wari and Tiwanaku

On the new work at the city of Tiwanaku, see Alan Kolata and Carlos Ponce Sangines, 'Tiwanaku: the City at the Center,' in *The Ancient Americas*, ed. R. Townsend, (The Art Institute of Chicago & Prestel, Chicago, 1992) and D. Browman, 'New Light on Andean Tiwanaku,' *American Scientist* 69, 4 (1981).

On textiles see R. Stone-Miller, 'Camelids and Chaos in Huari and Tiwanaku Textiles,' in *The Ancient Americas*, ed. R. Townsend, (The Art Institute of Chicago & Prestel, 1992); R. Stone, 'Color Patterning and the Huari Artist: the 'Lima Tapestry' Revisited,' in *Junius B. Bird Pre-Columbian Textile Conference*, ed. Ann P. Rowe, (Washington D. C., 1986). For cross-media comparisons see R. Stone-Miller and G. McEwan, 'The Representation of the Wari State in Stone and Thread: A Comparison of Architecture and Tapestry Tunics' *RES: Anthropology and Aesthetics* 19 (1990). On architecture see *Huari Administrative Structure: Prehistoric Monumental Architecture and State Government*, eds. W. Isbell and G. McEwan, (Dumbarton Oaks, Washington D. C., 1991).

6 Late Intermediate Period

Most research has been conducted on the North Coast in general and on the Chimú in particular. On the Sicán culture, see Izumi Shimada, 'Behind the Golden Mask: Sicán Gold Artifacts from Batán Grande, Peru,' in *The Art of Pre-Columbian Gold: the Jan Mitchell Collection*, ed. Julie Jones, (The Metropolitan Museum of Art, New York, 1985), and I. Shimada and J. A. Griffin, 'Precious Metal Objects of the Middle Sicán,' *Scientific American* 270, 4 (1994), 62–68. An important comprehensive work is *The Northern Dynasties: Kingship and Statecraft in Chimor*, eds. M. Moseley and A. Cordy-Collins, (Dumbarton Oaks, Washington D. C., 1990). *Chan Chan: Andean Desert*

City, eds. Moseley and K. Day, (University of New Mexico Press, Albuquerque, 1982) remains seminal. On Chimú textiles see Ann P. Rowe, *Costumes and Featherwork of the Lords of Chimor: Textiles from Peru's North Coast* (The Textile Museum, Washington D. C., 1984) and on the period more generally see Margaret Young-Sanchez, 'Textile Traditions of the Late Intermediate Period,' in R. Stone-Miller, *To Weave for the Sun: Ancient Andean Textiles* (Thames and Hudson, London & New York, 1994).

7 Inca Art and Architecture

Relatively speaking, the most work in the Andes has been done on the Inca empire, although the majority remains from an archaeological point of view. Julie Jones, *Art of Empire: the Inca of Peru* (The Museum of Primitive Art, New York Graphic Society, Greenwich, 1964), although spare, is still a good resource, as is John Rowe, 'Inca Culture at the Time of the Spanish Conquest,' in the *Handbook of South American Indians,* ed. J. Steward, (Smithsonian Institution, Bureau of American Ethnology, Bulletin no. 143, vol. 2, Washington D. C., 1946).

Architecture can be best appreciated by the art photographs of Edward Ranney in John Hemming, *Monuments of the Incas* (Boston, 1982; University of New Mexico Press, Albuquerque, 1990) and by an overview, Graziano Gasparini and Luise Margolis, *Inca Architecture* (Indiana University Press, Bloomington, 1980). Reconstruction of Inca methods of working stone is found in Jean-Pierre Protzen, 'Inca Stonemasonry,' *Scientific American* 254, 2 (1986), and *Inca Architecture and Construction at Ollantaytambo* (Oxford UP, Oxford & New York, 1993). John Hyslop has contributed greatly to our understanding of *Inka Settlement Planning* (University of Texas Press, Austin, 1990) and *The Inka Road System* (Academic Press, New York, 1984). A comprehensive study of the best-known provincial Inca center is Craig Morris and Donald Thompson, *Huánuco Pampa: An Inca City and its Hinterland* (Thames and Hudson, London & New York, 1985). On the *quipu* see Marcia and Robert Ascher, *The Code of the Quipu: A Study in Media, Mathematics, and Culture* (University of Michigan Press, Ann Arbor, 1981). On Inca textiles see Ann P. Rowe, 'Technical Features of Inca Tapestry Tunics,' *The Textile Museum Journal* 17 (1978) and John Rowe, 'Standardization in Inca Tapestry Tunics,' in *Junius B. Bird Pre-Columbian Textile Conference*, ed. Ann P. Rowe et.al., (Washington D. C., 1979). For a consideration of Inca and post-Inca Peruvian textiles see Susan Niles, 'Artist and Empire in Inca and Colonial Textiles,' in R. Stone-Miller, *To Weave for the Sun: Ancient Andean Textiles* (Thames and Hudson, London & New York, 1994).

Sources of Illustrations

Unless otherwise stated, measurements are given in inches followed by centimeters, height before width; a third measurement indicates depth.

Abbreviations

AMNH – courtesy Department Library Services, American Museum of Natural History, New York; AMUT – Archaeological Mission of the University of Tokyo; FMCH – © UCLA Fowler Museum of Cultural History; MCCM – Michael C. Carlos Museum, Emory University, photo Jamie Squire; MFA – Museum of Fine Arts, Boston; MNAA – Museo Nacional de Arqueología, Antropología e Historia del Perú, Lima; NMAI – Photo courtesy National Museum of the American Indian, Smithsonian Institution; RSM – Rebecca Stone-Miller; SAN – Servicio Aereofotográfico Nacional de Peru; UMAE – University Museum of Archaeology and Ethnology, Cambridge.

Frontispiece 13½ x 11¾ (34.3 x 29.9), MCCM; **1** Philip Winton; **2** David Drew; **3** © Edward Ranney; **4** David Drew; **5** length 8½ (21.5), AMNH, neg. #328612; **6** Ferdinand Anton, *Ancient Peruvian Textiles*, Thames and Hudson, London, 1987; **7, 8** Yoshio Onuki, AMUT; **9** After T.C. Patterson, The Huaca La Florida, Rimac Valley, Peru, in *Early Ceremonial Architecture in the Andes*, ed. C. Donnan, pp. 59–69, Dumbarton Oaks Research Library and Collections, Washington D.C., 1985; **10** Redrawn after J.C. Tello, *Arqueología del Valle de Casma: Cultural Chavín, Santa o Huaylas, Yunga y Sub-Chimu*, Publicación Antropológica del Archivo 'Julio C. Tello' de la Universidad Nacional Mayor de San Marcos, I. UNMSM, Lima, 1956; **11** George Kubler, *The Art and Architecture of Ancient America*, Penguin, Harmondsworth and New York, 1962 (drawing by K.F. Rowland); **12** Chan Chan-Moche Valley Project; **13** Redrawn from S. Pozorski and T. Pozorski, *Early Settlement and Subsistence in the Casma Valley, Peru*, University of Iowa Press, Iowa City, 1987; **14** Kubler, *op.cit.*; **15** Michael E. Moseley; **16** G. H. S. Bushnell, *Peru*, Thames and Hudson, London, 1956; **17** After Richard L. Burger; **18** Richard L. Burger; **19** Pauline Stringfellow; **20** Richard L. Burger; **21** Richard L. Burger and Luis Caballero; **22** John Rowe; **23** Cornelius Roosevelt; **24, 25** Wilfredo Loayza; **26** Redrawn from J.C. Tello, *Chavín: Cultura Matriz de la Civilización Andina*, 1960, Publicación Antropológica del Archivo 'Julio C. Tello' de la UNMSM, II. Lima; **27** Annick Peterson; **28** Richard L. Burger; **29** John Rowe; **30** Ferdinand Anton, *Ancient Peruvian Textiles*, Thames and Hudson, London, 1987; **31** 4¾ (12.2), former Bliss Collection, Dumbarton Oaks Research Library and Collections, Washington, D.C.; **32** 9¼ x 5½ (23.3 x 14), NMAI; **33** RSM after A. Cordy Collins; **34** Ferdinand Anton *Ancient Peruvian Textiles*, Thames and Hudson, London, 1987; **35** height 9⅛ (23.2), FMCH, photo Denis J. Nervig; **36** height 9¾ (24.8) x depth 5¼ (13.2), MCCM; **37** Georges Bankes, *Peru before Pizarro*, Phaidon, Oxford, 1977 (drawing by Michael Jones); **38** height 7⅜ (18.8), FMCH, photo Denis J. Nervig; **39** height 11¼ (28.4), width 10¼ (25.9), depth 7¾ (19.5), The Brooklyn Museum (64.94) Frank L. Babbott Fund and Dick S. Ramsay Fund; **40** Michael E. Moseley; **41–44** Anne Paul, *Paracas Ritual Attire: Symbols of Authority in Ancient Peru*, University of Oklahoma Press, 1990; **45, 46** J.H. and E.A. Payne Fund, courtesy MFA; **47** Denman Waldo Ross Collection, courtesy MFA; **48, 49** 55⅞ x 94⅞ (142 x 241), William A. Paine Fund, courtesy MFA; **50** Edwin F. Jack Fund, courtesy MFA; **51** Museo Amano, Lima; **52** height 3¾ (9.5) x depth 5¼ (13.3), MCCM; **53, 54** height 8 (20.3) x depth 4½ (11.4), MCCM; **55** height 3⅛ (8), FMCH, photo Denis J. Nervig; **56** Heinrich Ubbelohde-Doering, *On the Royal Highways of the Inca*, Thames and Hudson, London, 1967; **57** 6⅞ x 6 (17.5 x 15.2), Art Institute of Chicago, Buckingham Fund (1955.2137), photo Colin McEwan; **58** height 7⅞ (20), UMAE; **59** 15⅞ x 7½ (40.3 x 18.9), MCCM; **60** 7⅞ x 20½ (20 x 52), The Textile Museum, Washington, D.C., 1966.46.1; **61** 35⅞ x 44⅞ (91 x 114), Private Collection, New York, photo Lyle Wachowsky; **62** The Textile Museum, Washington, D.C., 1964.31.2 detail; **63** Hans Mann; **64** Photo David Drew; **65–68** © The Field Museum, Chicago, IL., negs. #72303, 72301, 72300, 72302; **69** Linden-Museum Stuttgart; **70** Rafael Larco Hoyle; **71** 8¼ x 8 (21 x 20.3), MCCM; **72** 11¾ x 12⅝ (30 x 32), Museo de América, Madrid; **73** Chan Chan-Moche Valley Project; **74** height 9½ (24), AMNH, trans. #5053(3), photo John Bigelow Taylor; **75** Shippee-Johnson Expedition, AMNH; **76, 77** Chan Chan-Moche Valley Project; **78** Félix Caycho Q; **79** height 4⅜ (11), FMCH, photo Christopher Donnan and Donald McClelland; **80** diameter 3¼ (8.3), FMCH, photo Susan Einstein; **81** average height 2¼ (5.8), FMCH, photo Christopher Donnan; **82** length of largest 3½ (9), FMCH, photo Susan Einstein; **83** diameter 3¾ (9.4), FMCH, photo Susan Einstein; **84** diameter 3¼ (8.4), FMCH, photo Susan Einstein; **85** height 7⅜ (18.8), Staatliches Museum für Völkerkunde, Munich; **86** height 6¼ (16), Peabody Museum, Harvard University, photo Hillel Burger; **87** height 7½ (19.1), photo © 1994 The Art Institute of Chicago, All Rights Reserved, Gift of Nathan Cummings, 1957.611; **88** (above, left) 8¾ x 7½ x 13¾ (22.2 x 19.1 x 34.9), (above, right) height 7¼ (18.4) x depth 2¼ (5.7), (below, left) height 9¾ (24.8) x depth 4⅝ (11.8), (below, right) 8½ x 5½ (21.6 x 13.8), MCCM, photo Edward M. Pio Roda; **89** height 11⅝ (29.5), Staatliches Museum für Völkerkunde, Munich; **90** Staatliches Museum für Völkerkunde, Berlin; **91** From Gallardo et al., *Moche Senores de la Muerte*, Museo Chilenu de Arte Precolombino, Santiago, 1990, drawing by Donna McClelland and Christopher Donnan; **92** FMCH, drawing by Donna McClelland; **93** FMCH, drawing by P. Perlman and Donna McClelland; **94, 95** MNAA; **96** diameter 13½ (34.3), copyright British Museum, London; **97** Richard Townsend, *The Ancient Americas: Art from Sacred Landscapes*, The Art Institute of Chicago, 1992 (drawing by Carlos Fuentes Sanchez; **98** Philip Winton; **99** Abraham Guillén; **100** UMAE; **101** Nick Saunders; **102** Colin McEwan; **103** RSM; **104** 14 x 9⅞ x 6 (35.5 x 25 x 15.2), Instituto Nacional de Arqueología de Bolivia, La Paz, photo Dirk Bakker; **105** Bunny Stafford; **106** Abraham Guillén; **107** Ferdinand Anton, *The Art of Ancient Peru*, Thames and Hudson, London, 1972; **108** height 4½ (11.4), The Metropolitan Museum of Art, The Michael C. Rockefeller Memorial Collection, Purchase, Nelson A. Rockefeller, 1968 (1978.412.214); **109** William H. Isbell and Gordon F. McEwan, *Huari Administrative Structure*, Dumbarton Oaks Research Library and Collections, Washington D.C., 1991; **110** Alan Kolata; **111** 8¾ x 12¼ (22.1 x 31), The Brooklyn Museum (71.180) Gift of Mr and Mrs Alastair Bradley Martin; **112** Gordon F. McEwan; **113, 114** William H. Isbell and Gordon F. McEwan, *Huari Administrative Structure*, Dumbarton Oaks Research Library and Collections, Washington D.C., 1991; **115** Gordon F. McEwan; **116** SAN; **117** Robert Feldman; **118** 41⅞ x 77⅛ (106.5 x 196), Staatliches Museum für Völkerkunde, Munich, photo Marietta Weidner; **119** 39⅜ x 36⅜ (100 x 92.3), MNAA, photo Dirk Bakker; **120** Alan R. Sawyer, *Tiahuanaco Tapestry Design*, 1963 (drawing Milton Franklin Sonday, Jr., courtesy the Museum of Primitive Art, New York; **121** 43¼ x 47¼ (109.8 x 119.9), The Art Institute of Chicago, Kate S. Buckingham Endowment, 1955.1784, photo © 1994, The Art Institute of Chicago, All Rights Reserved, photo Nancy Finn; **122** height 11⅜ (29), Museo Amano, Lima; **123** height 6 (15.2), copyright British Museum, London; **124** approx. 41 x 26¼ (104 x 66.6), Sicán Archaeological Project, photo Y. Yoshii; **125** backrest 22⅞ x 44¾ (58 x 113.5), Fundaciòn Miguel Mujica Gallo, Lima, Peru, photo courtesy Royal Ontario Museum, Toronto; **126** MNAA; **127** Chan Chan-Moche Valley Project; **128** 10⅞ x 4 (27.7 x 10.3), Fundaciòn Miguel Mujica Gallo, Lima, photo courtesy Royal Ontario Museum, Toronto; **129, 130** height 7⅞ (20), Fundaciòn Miguel Mujica Gallo; **131** diameter 2½ (6.35), NMAI; **132** (left) 7⅞ x 5⅛ (20 x 13), (right) 7¾ x 5⅛ (18.5 x 13), MCCM; **133** 29⅞ x 9⅜ (76 x 23.7), Denman Waldo Ross Collection, courtesy MFA; **134** AMNH; **135–139** Chan Chan-Moche Valley Project; **140** SAN; **141** 57⅞ x 84¼ (147 x 214), Textile Income Purchase Fund, courtesy MFA; **142** 38⅝ x 26¾ (98 x 68), Textile Museum, Washington D.C.; **143** UMAE; **144** 9⅛ x 5⅛ (23.2 x 13), MCCM; **145** 12⅝ x 14 x 9 (32 x 35.5 x 23), AMNH, trans. #5094(2) photo John Bigelow Taylor; **146** 29 x 29 (73.7 x 73.7), MCCM; **147** 24 x 26 (61 x 66), Gift of Landon T. Clay, courtesy MFA; **148** RSM; **149** 3¼ x 6½ (8.1 x 16.5), MCCM; **150** Philip Winton; **151** Peabody Museum, Harvard University, photo Hillel Burger; **152** Patricia A. Essenpreis; **153** © Edward Ranney; **154** Susan A. Niles; **155, 156** © Edward Ranney; **157** Philip Winton; **158** Nicholas Saunders; **159** © Martín Chambi; **160** Paul Bahn; **161** Heinrich Ubbelohde-Doering; **162** © Edward Ranney; **163, 164** David Drew; **165, 166** © Edward Ranney; **167, 168** © Martín Chambi; **169** Nick Saunders; **170** After Craig Morris; **171** © Edward Ranney; **172** 35⅞ x 30⅛ (91 x 76.5), Dumbarton Oaks Research Library and Collections, Washington D.C.; **173** Felipe Guaman Poma de Ayala, *Nueva cronica y buen gobierno*; **174** 33¼ x 30¾ (84.5 x 78), William Francis Warden Fund, courtesy MFA; **175** Felipe Guaman Poma de Ayala, *Nueva cronica y buen gobierno*; **176** 5½ x 4½ (14 x 11.5), Museo Regional de Atacama, Chile, photo Johan Reinhard; **177** RSM; **178** 5¼ x 5½ (13.5 x 13.8), MCCM; **179** 12 x 5 (30.5 x 12.7), MCCM; **180, 181** UMAE; **182** 46⅞ x 67⅜ (119 x 171), Charles Potter Kling Fund, courtesy MFA; **183** UMAE.

Index